"Thought-provoking, profane, and frequently hilarious . . . getting to know Offerman through his stumbling courtship with Megan Mullally and Kabuki theater training is well worth the price of admission." —*Publishers Weekly*

"Offerman touches on everything from his days as a break-dancing, football-playing farm boy in Minooka . . . to his freewheeling, hedonistic twenties in Chicago to the inevitable Hollywood struggles that followed. But he doesn't gloss over embarrassing moments, including his two trips to jail during college at the University of Illinois—one for shoplifting Ronnie Milsap cassettes from Kmart as a joke; the other, he says, a convoluted case of mistaken identity. Between anecdotes, he delivers impassioned pleas and rants." —*Chicago*

"Ron Swanson is a mustachioed, breakfast-food-loving, woodworking red-meat connoisseur. Nick Offerman is a mustachioed, breakfast-food-loving, woodworking red-meat connoisseur but, more important, also a real person—a grateful, gracious, bemused actor in love with his wife, Megan Mullally, and the earnest simplicity of his not-so-Hollywood Hollywood existence. Not only does he recall his life, but he also offers chuckle-worthy anecdotes, diagrams, even a haiku (about—what else?—bratwurst) to help his readers find their own ways toward delicious living. Ron Swanson would be proud." —*Booklist*

"Equal parts memoir and advice for grabbing life by the gonads. It's funny, highly nostalgic, and will make you seriously contemplate taking up carpentry. It's sort of like reading Garrison Keillor if he wrote for *Playboy*. . . . It's fun, it's visceral, and I learned things. When I finished the tome I had to take a long walk to soak everything in. We should all be so lucky to one day drink with this man, or at least purchase a table from him." —Man Cave Daily

"Offerman's funny advice book offers practical tips about living more successfully, with the sort of dry and laconic delivery that comes through in his role on *Parks and Recreation*." —*Time Out*

continued . . .

"Uniquely honest and consistently hilarious. . . . Fans of Offerman may not be surprised by his candor; however, this book is not specifically written for the fans. [It] will be enjoyed by many, specifically those who have the capacity and the will to wonder and to want more out of life, while maintaining a degree of simplicity and happiness, just like Nick Offerman." —Rare

"A hilarious walkabout . . . teeming with tasteful vulgarity, self-deprecating hilarity, and a most humble wisdom bordering on [being] sagelike. It's rare to find a memoir that is all at once touching, funny as sh*t, and capable of schooling you in basic modi operandi like not being a total ass." —Newcity Lit

"Offerman is a funny man. . . . But what is special about *Paddle Your Own Canoe* is the ability it gives Offerman to reveal himself as more than just the character he plays. He believes, and has always believed, in nonconformity. He believes in humility, honesty, hard work, and loyalty—values he attributes to his parents and two favorite teachers. He believes those qualities are what truly define 'manliness,' but that any person, regardless of gender, should aspire to them. *Paddle Your Own Canoe* is a delight." —The Manual

"You don't have to be able to properly work a table saw (I can't) or be in the market for a custom-made chair (I'm not) to buy what *Parks and Recreation* star/woodshop owner Nick Offerman is selling in his memoir . . . [a] modulated and admirable concept of what it means to live well and be a man. Offerman writes hilariously and honestly about boyhood chores and collegiate shenanigans, Chicago theater dues-paying, and sobbing 'for, like, twenty minutes' when receiving the call about landing the *Parks and Rec* job. . . . [He] offers a vivid look at how he charted the course for real happiness. It's nothing if not inspiring." —RedEye (Chicago)

PADDLE YOUR OWN CANOE

One Man's Fundamentals for Delicious Living

Nick Offerman

NEW AMERICAN LIBRARY

New American Library
Published by the Penguin Group
Penguin Group (USA) LLC, 375 Hudson Street,
New York, New York 10014, USA

USA | Canada | UK | Ireland | Australia | New Zealand | India | South Africa | China
penguin.com
A Penguin Random House Company

Published by New American Library, a division of Penguin Group (USA) LLC. Previously
published in a Dutton edition.

First New American Library Printing, September 2014

Copyright © Nick Offerman, 2013
Illustrations copyright © Mike Mitchell, 2013
Penguin supports copyright. Copyright fuels creativity, encourages diverse voices, promotes free
speech, and creates a vibrant culture. Thank you for buying an authorized edition of this book
and for complying with copyright laws by not reproducing, scanning, or distributing any part of
it in any form without permission. You are supporting writers and allowing Penguin to continue
to publish books for every reader.

 REGISTERED TRADEMARK—MARCA REGISTRADA

New American Library Trade Paperback ISBN: 978-0-451-46709-6

THE LIBRARY OF CONGRESS HAS CATALOGED THE HARDCOVER EDITION OF THIS TITLE AS FOLLOWS:

Offerman, Nick, 1970–
    Paddle your own canoe: one man's fundamentals for delicious living/Nick Offerman.
        p. cm.
    ISBN 978-0-525-95421-7 (hardcover)
    1. Offerman, Nick, 1970–. 2. Actors—United States—Biography. 3. Carpenters—United
States—Biography. 4. Conduct of life. I. Title.
    PN2287.O275A3 2013
    791.4502'8092—dc23
    [B] 2013023379

Printed in the United States of America
10 9 8 7 6 5 4 3 2 1

Set in Zapatista and Dante MT Std
Designed by Alissa Amell

PUBLISHER'S NOTE
Penguin is committed to publishing works of quality and integrity. In that spirit, we are proud to
offer this book to our readers; however, the story, the experiences, and the words are the author's
alone.

To Megan, my wife, cherry blossom, and legal property, who teaches me life every day.

And to her mother, Martha, who has taught us both beauty and humor. She also taught Megan class but got to me too late.

CONTENTS

A gentleman is someone who can play the accordion, but doesn't.

—Tom Waits

Foreplay

I am a jackass living in America and living surprisingly well. Let's make that our jumping-off point. I come by it honest. I am your average meat, potatoes, and corn-fed human male, with a propensity for smart-assery, who has managed to make a rewarding vocation out of, essentially, making funny faces and falling down. I have also exhibited some tool skills and an inclination for eating delicious meatstuffs, and have then been somehow rewarded quite over-handsomely for these tendencies. I grew up literally in the middle of a cornfield in the village of Minooka, Illinois, where I spent a lot of time learning to use intoxicants, chasing girls, screwing around in the woods (mostly without the girls), and serving under Father Tony (unmolested) at our local Catholic church, St. Mary's. I learned the word *nonconformist* in fourth grade and immediately announced that I would grow up to become one.

I have a hell of a great family in Illinois and now some more in Oklahoma via my wife, Megan. I have spent the vast majority of my adult life working as an actor and also, to a lesser extent, as a woodworker. I'm going to run on at some length about the excellent people whom I have called friends, and some others whom I have had the privilege of calling teachers, and, while those parts are all well and good, there will also be some dirty parts, and I believe cunnilingus gets at least two mentions (favorable). On top of all that, and woven all throughout it, I'll describe my wife, who is just a goddamn blessing to me in a great many ways, enriching my life to such an extent that I can go nowhere anymore without passersby muttering, "There goes that lucky bastard." I can only make a dimple and solemnly nod in agreement.

Each story comes with a delicious fundamental—advice about living life that I hope you'll find useful. Of course, my fundamentals may not work for everyone. A beautiful aspect of the human race is our endless variety. Like maple leaves and snowflakes, there are no two of us alike. Therefore, while my tactics involving the cultivation of lush facial hair and the consumption of pork products, as well as those derived from beef, may not be exactly the steps of the path you might tread on your own way to "delicious living," perhaps my techniques will at least inspire you to forge your own discipline, providing you with the necessary skills to blaze your own trail.

Basically, this book boils down to how an average human dipshit like myself, relying solely on warped individuality and a little elbow grease, can actually rise from a simple life of relative poverty to one of prosperity, measured in American dollars and Italian band saws, sure, but more importantly, laughter, wood shavings, and kisses. The key lies in finding the delicious flavorings in one's life, no matter how fancy your blue jeans may or may not be. The notions herein are meant to inform, inspire, and engender mirth. Enjoy, please, and thank you.

1

Not-So-Little House on the Prairie

Jesus, Mary, and Joseph. Where do I begin chapter 1? I suppose we'll do a chronological thing and start you off with some of the early years, a taste of the vintage stuff.

I showed up on Earth, in the tri-county area of Illinois, to be more precise, in 1970. This was, reportedly, the year Tom Waits showed up in LA to start pushing his demos around town. I haven't had the chance to ask Tom if he was trying to send me a personal message of serendipity with his beautiful and haunting songs of the day like "Grapefruit Moon" and "Midnight Lullaby," but it seems too crazy-on-the-nose to just be coincidence. Right?

Somewhere in the Arizona desert, Tom Laughlin was shooting the movie *Billy Jack*, and warlock-style wax albums were dropping all about the realm with names like *Look-Ka Py Py*; *Black Sabbath*; *Sex Machine*; *Moondance*; *Bitches Brew*; *The Man Who Sold the World*; *After the Gold Rush*; *Free Your Mind . . . and Your Ass Will Follow*; *Kristofferson*, for cryin' out loud; *Let It Be*; and the most weirdly kabbalistic—Randy Newman's *12 Songs*. Potent magicks coalesced and fluctuated across the void, whilst strange nether-clouds swelled with great portent above the green crop fields, awaiting . . . what? Some child? A chosen man-cub?

Despite some loose popular misconceptions, I did NOT in fact drop from my mother's womb wielding a full moustache and a two-headed battle-axe. Nor was there sighted evidence of even the first follicle of the first hair of my chest bracken. Those laurels would come later.

The luckiest part of my very lucky life (pre-Megan) has been being raised by my family in the environment they created for the rearing of my siblings and me. My mom, Catherine Ann Offerman (née Roberts), and my dad, Frederic Dames Offerman, grew up about three miles from each other in the middle of the countryside, outside of Minooka, Illinois. Where is that? Right next to Channahon, as I like to joke. (I told you this shit was gwine to be humorous.) Southwest of Joliet. My mom grew up in a family of four kids, born to Mike and Eloise Roberts, and they raised pigs, soybeans, and corn. My dad, born to Raymond Offerman and Marilyn Dames Offerman, grew up on a dairy farm with two siblings before moving into town as a teenager. They attended all the same Minooka schools that I eventually did, and married young. Dad was twenty-four and Mom was nineteen. Which seems batshit crazy to me these days.

Minooka is, surprisingly, only about an hour from Lake Shore Drive in Chicago, if there's no traffic. But it seems like it's fifty years distant, or at least it did in my youth. It was very bucolic and idyllic, like *American Graffiti* or *Happy Days*. Saturday night you would get together and "buzz the gut" in your jalopy, which meant drive past the five businesses on Main Street. At the time I was growing up the population was 768. It's grown ridiculously—it's up near twelve thousand now. It used to be primarily a farming community, but by now, the commuting suburban population has reached it and subsumed it. There are now many inhabitants of Minooka whom I would consider "soft," and yes, that is a judgment.

My dad went to Illinois State University. I had always heard various legends of his prowess as an athlete as a young man, primarily in baseball and basketball. I wrote to him, asking for some facts on this subject for my book, because he has always been pretty humble about it to the point of being mum. Here is an excerpt of his reply:

> *Well, I don't know what you heard but remember it was a very small high school. In baseball I started every varsity game for four years except one as a freshman and in that one I pinch-hit and hit a triple, then later in that game I hit another triple (that never happened again). As a sophomore I batted second, third as a junior, and fourth as a senior and was the shortstop the last three years. . . . I hit .333 (22 for 66) and led the team in RBIs. That was second to your uncle Mark, who hit 1.000 (1 for 1). I never considered myself as a terrific player but I had one damn burning desire to play and was surprised many times when I did well.*

This might begin to give you an idea of from whence I sprung.

They have yet to make a man I like better or respect more than my dad. And he'll be the first to tell you that my mom is even better. They married young, and my mother had my older sister, Laurie, when she was twenty. Twenty! The balls on these people! They rented an old farm for one hundred dollars a month plus utilities. It was right in between the two farms they grew up on, and that's where I lived for my first five years.

Looking back on it now, I am just astonished at how little income we got by on. The older I get, the more my parents just seem like absolute heroes to me. My dad was teaching junior high geography, history, and social studies in Channahon, as well as tacking on every bit of extra income that he could squeeze in. He drove a school bus, he coached basketball, and in the summer break he would work on a local blacktop crew or earn wages on the Roberts's farm, where my mother grew up. Meanwhile, my mom was running a household with four children, making a lot of our clothes, and cooking up a storm. Not too far off from Ma and Pa Ingalls. They raised us four kids, Laurie, me, Carrie, and Matt (the baby, aka "Matt Mailman"), as solid as Illinois livestock. My sisters and brother are the cut of folk who I'd be damn glad to stand beside in a bar brawl, a square dance, or a pie-eating competition, and preferably the latter.

It was an old farmhouse, and drafty, so we nailed blankets over the doors to combat the drafts. We had our first big garden there, and I have the most wonderful memories of my parents' gardens. To this day my dad has two huge gardens, one at home and one out at the Roberts's farm. One of my earliest memories is of sitting in the garden, in the strawberry patch, in my diaper, probably fertilizing the strawberries more than I'd care to admit, ironically happy as a pig in shit, just sitting in the mud and eating strawberries.

We were right across the road from the Aux Sable Creek, which is the creek that ran through my life. No matter where my mom's family was farming or where we lived, we were always within a few miles of the creek. That's where I learned to fish and eventually canoe.

*   *   *

My first job on the farm was shoveling pig shit in the barn basement for my grandpa Mike Roberts. He probably paid me a nickel for lending him a hand in procedures of animal husbandry. One of my most distinct memories as a small boy was handing my grandfather the one-year-old pigs, which he would then sequester upside down in this clamped bracket so that he could handily cut their nuts out with a razor knife and then spray the wound with a medicinal purple spray. You may begin to understand why this memory is particularly poignant, for I promise you've never heard anyone scream like a one-year-old pig screaming for its balls.

It was never so *Little House on the Prairie* that we'd have our own pig-killing day. It was something I always loved reading about, though. The whole neighborhood would come out together, as I've read in *Little House on the Prairie* and also in the fiction of Wendell Berry (our nation's most venerated living agrarian author and far and away my personal favorite writer; he has a great short story, "Don't Send a Boy to Do a Man's Work," where somebody uninvited shows up with some whisky and it turns into a very messy hog-slaughter day).

We were eventually aware that a couple of Grandpa's pigs would come home from market and go straight into the freezer. As kids, we'd have our favorite pigs and we'd name them. There were a few gray years before we realized, "This bacon used to be old Fat Albert."

As the oldest male grandchild, I suppose the guys were trying me out at different tasks to see if I would take to farming. I remember a time when there was a pig who died of an intestinal sickness, and a vet came out and removed its intestines to determine what it had. My uncle Don Roberts and I took the pig on the end loader—which is a tractor with a bucket in the front—out into a field and buried the pig and the intestines separately. This may be revisionist history, but I recall that pile of guts being the same purple as the neuter spray. That color purple was ruined for me—I was later a big fan of Prince, but his greatest album unfortunately gave me visions less redolent of Apollonia's beauty and more suited to the abattoir. On that day in the field, I remember Uncle Don explaining that you had to bury both deep enough and cover them with rocks so the coyotes wouldn't dig them up.

Out in the hog lot there were big, round feeder bins into a top central hatch of which one would dump hog feed. The pigs would then access the feed off the chutes at the bottom, which was handy for them, but unfortunately it was also handy for the rats, which are always a big problem on a farm. So, when the rats got bad enough, Grandpa and the uncles would hoist this feeder up in the air with the same bucket loader. We would assemble a whole neighborhood of friends, who would surround the feeder. There would be twenty neighborhood men and boys armed with pitchforks, spades, and hoes. They'd have half as many dogs, standing at the ready. When the feeder took to the air, maybe a hundred rats would scatter in every direction. Many would elude the weapons, but I don't believe a rat ever escaped the dogs. Those pooches had a field day. It was really quite something.

There were lessons of life and death pretty much from the get-go on Grandpa's farm. Hilarious book, right, people?

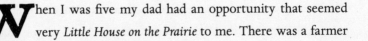hen I was five my dad had an opportunity that seemed very *Little House on the Prairie* to me. There was a farmer

named Bob Heartt who was going to tear down his old two-story farmhouse and build a newfangled, single-story ranch house. He offered my family his old house if we could simply ROLL THE HOUSE ON WHEELS to a new three-acre plot of land in one of his cornfields. In exchange, Bob Heartt would receive a new heater in his expert-machinist tractor shop, new cabinets for his wife's kitchen, the filling-in of the old basement hole, and compensation for the three acres. Still, it was a great deal. My folks borrowed $27,000 and spent most of the $10,000 they had in savings. My dad still says it's one of the best financial moves he ever made.

Until this writing, I had never put together my own penchant for moving audacious loads of scenery (or tree slabs) with my dad's Paul Bunyan–esque relocation of a gargantuan two-story farmhouse. I could write a whole book on the lessons I received from Dad, and Uncles Dan and Don, and Grandpa Mike, as well as Grandpa Ray, my dad's dad. I learned early to respect my tools and my machinery, knowing that with the proper lashing-down and utilization of simple machines—the wheel, the lever, the screw, the inclined plane—there was no job of work that could defeat us.

Over and over, for years, I would accompany them in tasks of carpentry and mechanics, and they would set me to work with a hammer and nails and patiently repeat, "Hit it! Don't make love to it, hit the gol-dang thing!" After years of attempts, I was finally able to feel the strength come into my arms and shoulders and operate a tool in a manner that they would pronounce satisfactory. For one of those impossibly proficient men to deem my work a "nice job" filled me with more satisfaction than any A-plus grade I ever received in school. In my burgeoning competence with a ratchet—and more importantly, their approbation thereof—there was a complicit understanding that I was on the right path to one day have the ability to use tools to my creative benefit, just as they did every day.

My mother has two brothers and one sister. My uncle Don is the baby of the family. Later I was astonished to realize that he is young enough to have been my older brother. He was so great with us—all my aunts and uncles were like the Super Friends to me, but Uncle Don was Aquaman (the coolest). My mom's younger sister, Michele, whom we called Aunt Micki, she was more mature and studious, as well as being fun—like when she used to name our freckles for us. She's a librarian/historian in Minooka now, and my older sister, Laurie, works with her. Aunt Micki turned me on to the Chronicles of Narnia books, the Lord of the Rings trilogy, the Madeleine L'Engle books. I can't give her enough "props," as the kids are saying, for turning me on to such great fiction. (My brother and sisters didn't like reading in the same way. They eventually caught on.) And *Little House on the Prairie*. I got so turned on by a series of books set in an alternative world. I wanted to know everything about the world— what *has* Pa got in his pockets?

Uncle Don was the tangible version of that notion. I don't know how it came to happen, but he bought this little motorcycle and left it at our house. I think it was just generosity, knowing we couldn't afford to get something like that for ourselves. My mom's oldest brother, Uncle Dan, and his wife, Dee, became the overseers of the farm as my grandparents grew older. They had a boy and a girl, Ryan and Angie. Ryan is six months younger than me, so we grew up like brothers. They had the resources of the farm at their disposal, so Ryan had a go-kart and a snowmobile. But I couldn't afford that stuff, which could have been why Uncle Don left the motorcycle at my house.

Uncle Don was just fun. He was and is really funny. He went to college and studied mechanical engineering. Motors, basically. He worked for a while in town as the bus mechanic for the school. But I think he and Uncle Dan were both destined to stick on the farm. Their knowledge is just amazing. To be a successful farmer you have to be a high-end mechanic, a botanist, and a soil engineer. You have to be a carpenter. Uncle Don was an incredible student of life but also loved to have fun. He was so freehanded—he would take us with him on snowmobiling trips and motorcycle rides, or we'd just go ride bicycles. Our family loves to fish, so we'd go boating. We've always had some version of our own boats, and now everybody's got his/her own getaway cabin in Indiana or Wisconsin or Minnesota.

Uncle Don had the most throbbing boner of a vehicle you could have in 1978—the Pontiac Firebird with the phoenix on the hood and the T-top. It was so badass. He would take us for a treat to Shorewood, the near suburb of Joliet, to the Tastee Freez to get ice cream. I'd get a vanilla cone dipped in cherry—whatever that cherry candy shit is; it's the greatest. And he'd play Frank Zappa, which was forbidden.

We had a very decent household. We weren't allowed to watch *The Three Stooges*. Our TV was governed pretty closely. There was a ban for a while on *Tom and Jerry*, but eventually that was lifted. My parents didn't want their kids to see things with violence in them, which is so hilarious and sad now. (Looking at you, video games where one can chop the heads off prostitutes. [Which is my own surmise—I don't know if that actually exists, but I'm pretty sure you can find it.]) So something like Frank Zappa singing, "Don't eat the yellow snow," and having to puzzle out the meaning of that was an early awakening of the notion "I like that use of language." My neighbor Steve Rapcan lived next door on another three-acre parcel. His parents were slightly more licentious and he was allowed to have things like KISS and Eddie Murphy records. My folks did not know that we would hole up in his bedroom and listen to Eddie Murphy over and over. We'd lie back on the floor, and as I've now damn near gotten into a stand-up career of my own, I think how astonishing it was to me that someone like Eddie Murphy could talk hilariously about eating pussy in public and get paid for it. The amazing thing is it sparked something in me that remained an ember for a couple of decades. It never occurred to me that "humor" was remotely something I could aspire to.

By the age of eight or nine it began to dawn on me that I wasn't exactly like the other kids in Minooka. I remember my fourth-grade classroom well. I had Miss Christensen, one of many top-drawer teachers in our school. She was just an admirable woman, with whom everybody was in love, of course. Fourth grade was a big reading year, and there was a contest called "Battle of the Books," for which we would read titles like *Caddie Woodlawn*, *My Side of the Mountain*, and *Island of the Blue Dolphins*, and then compete by answering questions about the subject matter. We were learning the rudiments of plot, theme, and vocabulary, and one of our vocabulary words was *nonconformist*. I just dug that word. I heard the explanation, the definition, and I felt like I had just learned about a new hero in a kick-ass Marvel comic book. I raised my hand and I said, "Nonconformist. That is what I would like to be." This was met by a bemused smile by

Miss Christensen, who was probably already aware of my status as a creative thinker but couldn't have imagined how far I'd take the execution.

It didn't take me long to discern that I had essentially announced to the world, "Excuse me, everyone? I am a weirdo." But no matter. The die had been cast.

I also recall a moment in second-grade art class. We were given a piece of wood and a little paper cutout of a clown head. (The assignment was to finish the wood with stain, then glue the clown head to the wood after coloring it in with crayons, then varnish the whole shebang.) I adorned my clown head with color and glued it on with the clown's head cocked to the right. My teacher gave me a C.

I said, "What the fuck are you talking about? This is so much better than what the rest of these squares made."

And she said, "You glued it on quite crookedly."

I replied, "He's got his head tilted at a rakish angle, asshole!"

I remember thinking, "You don't fucking get me. This is my art! This is my shit!" I recall being outraged, thinking, "I don't understand. Don't you realize mine is uniquely creative and therefore way better than these other dipshits'?"

I simply knew that I was peculiar and that I was a puzzle to those around me. I was also learning that this weirdness was a part of me that was not to be extinguished.

But for the time being, Minooka and the family farm were all that I needed. In the summers, when we would get together for family picnics, we would have enough people to field two teams of ten and play softball out in the meadow. I was charmed that half of the participants would have their beers out in the field. You'd have old people saying, "I'll go out and play right field. I can't do much." It's something that's unfathomable today. To even suggest to the teenagers, or anybody now, "Let's go play a sport." They'd say, "Are you crazy? We're watching the football game." Or, "We're playing our Wii." All we needed back then was a bat and a ball.

We would amuse ourselves with what we had on hand. After dinner, we would get on the hayrack, and everybody would ride around and look at the crops. It was a recreational ride, sitting on hay bales, singing songs. It was so heartwarming, and all it cost was the price of the fuel. We didn't have to do anything to have a good time. It's an incredible gift to be able to make your own fun.

Eat Red Meat

Unless you're an ignorant fool (creationist), you'll have noticed that a great deal of attention is being paid to humankind's evolution over the millennia, especially with regard to our diet.

According to science and smart anthropology types, our particular mammalian species evolved into sentient bipeds who learned to develop and then employ tools to further the domestic comforts of their caves. We then learned to advertise and sell these implements to one another. The progression is easy to track: the hammer—the spearhead—the flyswatter—the Clapper—the Xbox—the perfusion catheter.

As we human-folk learned to kill and eat other animals, we came into a period of social development that I would liken to the "Quickening" of *Highlander* fame. The added proteins in our diet turned us into physical specimens the likes of Sigourney Weaver, Schwarzenegger, and, at the very least, Ringo Starr.

In short order, with knives of obsidian (a brief fad) and then sharpened steel, we learned to butcher animals in such a way as to garner the tastiest portions of their musculature, or "meat," for eating. Then we learned to cook those muscle scraps over an open flame. Then we learned to apply sprigs of rosemary and thyme to the offerings. We learned to "rub" our seasonings into the flesh. Then we added garlic and butter to mashed potatoes, and then we invented barbecue sauce, and that creation, gentle reader, finally seems worthy of a restful seventh day. If there is a God, no part of the Bible or Christian doctrine will convince me of his existence half as much as the flavor of a barbecued pork rib. It is in that juicy snack that I can perhaps begin to glean a divine design, because that shit is delicious in a manner that can be accurately described as "heavenly." I have never had need of a firearm in my life, not remotely, but I'll happily sport a bumper sticker that reads, "You can have my rib eye when you pry it from my cold, dead fingers," or even write a bit of poetry.

The Bratwurst: A Haiku

Tight skin flute of pork.
Juices fly, explode in mouth.
A little mustard.

Ready for some controversy? I can actually understand the factions of people like those in the PETA organization when they raise hell about any time an animal is treated cruelly. I think mistreating animals is a shameful practice, and bad for one's karma, to boot. When I talk about the mistreatment of animals, I'm thinking of some brute kicking a dog, or beating a horse, or, say, the countless horrors enacted upon the chickens, hogs, and cattle in the meat factories that supply the bustling shit dispensaries we call fast-food chains.

And therein lies the problem. Fast food. For God's sake, and also the sake of Pete, if you don't respect your own body enough to keep it free of that garbage, at least PLEASE STOP FEEDING IT TO YOUR KIDS. Read *Fast Food Nation*. See the excellent documentary *Food, Inc.* If your excuse is a lack of time, then you need to get your priorities straight. There is no part of this country where one cannot find a source of fresh, organic meat and produce. I'm not talking about Whole Foods, I'm referring to farmers' markets and local butchers and fishermen and -women. If you can't find a source for fresh produce and eggs and/or chicken, bacon, and/or dairy products, by Christ, become the source! What more noble pursuit than supplying your community with breakfast foods?! If you want to read more about this notion, by actual smart and informed writers, pick up some Michael Pollan and some Wendell Berry.

I have no intention of ever ceasing to enjoy red meat. However, I firmly believe that we can choose how and where our meat is raised, and I'm all for a grass-fed, happy steer finding its way to my grill long before a factory-farmed, filthy, corn-fed lab creation. It's up to us to choose farm-to-table fare as much as possible until it becomes our society's norm once again.

One of the most tried-and-true methods by which we humans can collect our own protein from the land is that of fishing. My family doesn't hunt (except for Uncle Terry—Aunt Micki's hubby—who takes one or two bucks a year, usually with a bow and arrow, and keeps us all happily in venison, jerky, and sausage), but we fish like crazy. Between the family households, we have cabins in Wisconsin, Minnesota, and Indiana. Fishing is the default vacation for the entire family; if there's a break, you can find us out on the lake. I have had the opportunity over the years to take some assorted friends on these Offerman/Roberts family fishing trips, and nothing gives me more pleasure than teaching them to clean their own fish. *Of course* it's unpleasant in comparison to being served a delicious white fillet of sole in a butter sauce with capers, but every one of my students has expressed a primitive satisfaction in the knowledge that they can harvest their own meat from a lake or river, should "the shit" ever really go down. I

YES

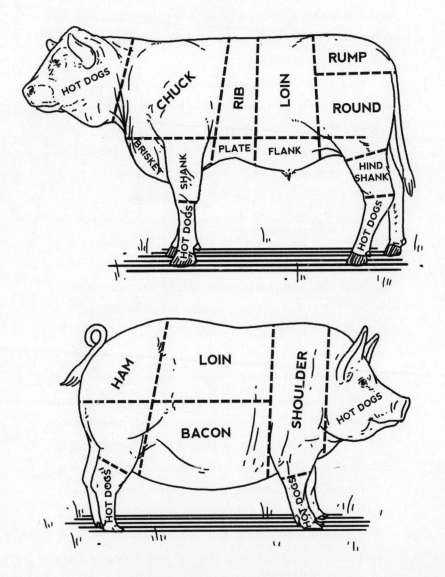

EAT RED MEAT

NOPE

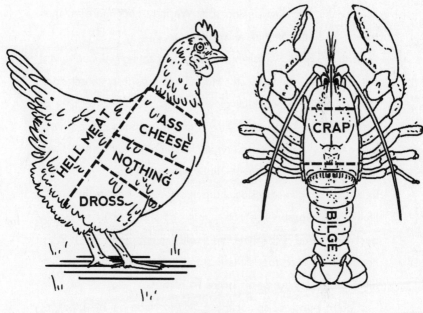

EAT RED MEAT

admire my uncle for his hunting discipline, because he doesn't do it for the fun of killing an animal, and he doesn't do it wastefully. It's simply a choice to fulfill some of his family's grocery needs in the larder of the forest rather than the Albertsons. Among the other advantages of harvesting this meat himself, Uncle Terry is keeping himself from getting soft. We may hear more on that topic a bit further into these woods.

Everybody knows, but many deny, that eating red meat gives one character. Strength, stamina, stick-to-it-iveness, constitution, not to mention a healthful, glowing pelt. But take a seat for a second. Listen. I eat salad. How's that for a punch in the nuts, ladies? What's more, as I sit typing this on a Santa Fe patio, I just now ate a bowl of oatmeal. That's right. Because I'm a real human animal, not a television character. You see, despite the beautifully Ron Swanson–like notion that one should exist solely on beef, pork, and wild game, the reality remains that our bodies need more varied foodstuffs that facilitate health and digestive functions, **but you don't have to like it.**

I eat a bunch of spinach, but only to clean out my pipes to make room for more ribs, fool! I will submit to fruit and zucchini, yes, with gusto, so that my steak-eating machine will continue to masticate delicious charred flesh at an optimal running speed. By consuming kale, I am buying myself bonus years of life, during which I can eat a shit-ton more delicious meat. You don't put oil in your truck because it tastes good. You do it so your truck can continue burning sweet gasoline and hauling a manly payload.

2

Hail Mary, Full of Beans

My family was, and still is, very involved in St. Mary's Catholic Church in Minooka. Now, let's get off on the right foot about religion, especially Christianity and the Bible. I generally think that organized religion has a lot of great attributes, and I think the Bible is largely an amazing and beautiful book of fictional stories from which we can glean the most wholesome lessons about how to treat one another decently. I'll have some rather different-seeming opinions later in the book. These opinions have to do not with Christians in general but rather with ways that I believe people misuse Christianity in modern society, or ways in which people in our democratic government try to use a religious text to influence legislation. I disagree with these specific notions, and we'll talk about that in a bit.

But for now, I'll say that growing up as a contributing cog in the clockwork of St. Mary's had many excellent benefits for me. I was an altar boy by age eight or nine, and I quickly learned that I could make the people in the congregation, or "audience," laugh into their missalettes if I were I to, say, sniff the unstopped cruet of Eucharistic wine and deliver an unpleasant review of its bouquet with a wrinkling of the nose, coupled with a raised eyebrow, a look I had been practicing tirelessly in school in emulation of my hero, John Belushi.

My dad had a differing opinion, as you might well imagine, of my first attempt at comedy (which pretty much killed—sorry, Dad). He made it quite plain that he was not interested in any further display of opinion on my part from the altar. Thus, my surreptitious cultivation of the deadpan style was born. From the Catholic proscenium I had to find a way to entertain my loyal following of cousins and friends whilst remaining undetected by those joyless adults. I mean, come on, who doesn't want a good laugh in the middle of boring old church?

My family went to church every Sunday. There was no discussion or vote. Sometimes there were tears. Our hair was cut regularly and without mercy, so as to appear presentable in church, and you can bet your fanny we wore our Sunday clothes. Little sister Carrie, our only blonde, was allowed to grow her locks long, and she is still the prettiest of us, as well as the finest at belching, beating out older sis Laurie by the merest decibel. Church was where the community would countenance and then assess one another on a weekly basis to make sure we were all well scrubbed, well clad, and well barbered.

When I began "serving mass" as an altar boy, the priest was Monsignor Seidl, an old-school (and also just plain old), venerated frog of a man. Great guy, just looked a bit amphibious. Things felt very institutional on his watch. It was easy to understand that our diocese (like a Catholic precinct, if *NYPD Blue* was about church) was directly connected through an ever-ascending chain of command to Rome and the Vatican.

There were ten of us altar boys manning a strict schedule, serving in different permutations of three altar boys at a time. We'd cover a mass on Saturday evening and three more on Sunday morning in addition to the baptisms and funerals and weddings that peppered the calendar. The manning of special occasions was a highly coveted gig, because they usually involved a handsome cash tip from the families. That's what church is all about, right? The $$$?

As I was saying, the proceedings under Msgr. Seidl's reign were very august. The mood was very somber, with a deep sense of respect for the dogma of the mass. That's when I learned my trade. Handle the water and wine, hold the book, ring the bells, the whole nine yards. Hold a strange long-handled tray beneath the communion hosts (the Body of Christ) as they traveled from the priest's chalice to the mouth of the believer. I definitely enjoyed the theatricality and ceremony of the Catholic mass.

The best thing the altar boys got to do was ring the handbells. The servers would jockey for position to be the guy who rang the bells. Sometimes one guy would ring the bells first and then hand them over so a second server could get a taste of the good stuff. It kinda tells you all you need to know about church if three seconds of bell-clanging is the high point of the action.

Somewhere around my twelfth or thirteenth year, Msgr. Seidl retired, and a new priest, Father Tony, came. Father Tony was a fashion plate, by comparison, whom I remember as seeming very "Rat Pack." He was very Italian and an urbane city guy. He had cool horn-rims and a panache that was not of our small town. I was a fan, and I learned the feeling was mutual when he graduated me from altar boy to the role of the lector, a position usually assayed by an older person. I would recite the gospel readings before his sermon, and that was really where I commenced to having an effect on an audience for the first time. I did care about the quality of the storytelling in my readings, and I sincerely wanted to impart the day's lesson and help get it across, but at the same time, I would maybe just stress certain words that I thought were interesting, such as "Jesus did come hard upon Lake Gennesaret."

I would linger ever so slightly upon words and phrases that I found humorous, so that my cousin Ryan and six other friends would crack up, but no one else had any idea I was being hilarious. As discussed, I believe it's where I first learned to hone the art of dry humor.

I became somewhat the hired hand of St. Mary's. I was the go-to kid, hired to cut the grass and stock the shelves and wax the pews. My cousin Ryan played the trumpet and I played the saxophone, so we also started making some extra bread on the side by playing weddings and such. Again, church seemed pretty cool, with a couple of sweet Alexander Hamiltons in my pocket. The mystical conversion that occurs in every Catholic mass, in which the blood and body of Jesus Christ (our Lord) become wine and, inexplicably, little round white bread wafers, respectively, is known as transubstantiation. Turning my devotion to the church into cash seemed like a much more appealing transformation.

I performed a lot of yard work for Father Tony. He had a house on the Kankakee River, an hour or so south, and he would take Ryan and me to the river to perform yard labor—split firewood and whatnot— and then take us waterskiing behind his boat (not a euphemism). I am sincerely grateful for that time, in which our priest appeared "on-stage," as it were, perhaps as one of the more exciting characters in our community, what with a speedboat and fancy eyeglasses.

We had our version of Sunday school, called catechism. It was terrible, just the worst. By the time you're seven or eight years old, you get it. I understood the stories of Jesus and his disciples and the values I was expected to glean thereof. Now, there are things I like just fine about church, and I don't just mean making money. The notion of getting together as a community to remind ourselves why we shouldn't behave like animals is a fucking great idea. Church was also the place to get a look at all of the young ladies in the other families, the better to determine whose young chests you'd like to target with your clumsy fumbling. It's all the other shitty parts—like when priests tell you who to vote for in a presidential race, because they're personally opposed to a woman's right to choose—that irk me. That's where church crosses my line. When the clergy get too big for their britches, they take these wonderfully benevolent writings from the Bible and crumble their intended integrity by slathering them with human nature.

I remember sitting in my seat at the far stage-right side of the altar while the congregation would slog through group recitations like the Nicene Creed ("We believe in one God, the Father Almighty, maker of heaven and earth . . .") in the most Pavlovian way. The cultish, soulless tone in which this group of two hundred people would repeat this creed of purpose, meant to resonate like a mission statement, lent no fervor to, nor even indicated any apparent awareness of, what they were saying. *"Now we say this part . . . We get the talking over with so I can get home to the football game."*

One Sunday in my midteens, I really heard them droning on, and I found it quite upsetting. I thought, "Listen to what you're saying—you're repeating this supposed profession of your faith and I'll wager you literally couldn't tell me what the fuck you're talking about right now. The words of the creed, as well as this whole notion, are so profound, to re-up your faith week in and week out, but the meaning is utterly lost on you. This is not working. This mass is not working for these people. I'm not interested in taking part in this, because it doesn't seem to be working."

In eighth grade, the church community was all abuzz because they were bringing in this hotshot nun, Sister Gesuina, to teach our catechism class. It was very exciting and potentially scandalous because the word was she had unorthodox teaching methods, which included playing us the Billy Joel song "Only the Good Die Young" and explaining that while this popular music was catchy, sure, it disguised a nefarious, satanic message. "You might think he sounds logical and modern, but, Virginia, he's just trying to get in your pants and knock you up."

And a hundred times better than even Billy Joel, she also brought in *Playboy* and *Penthouse* magazines! *What? Penthouse* shows pink, in the vernacular of porn mags. *Playboy*, by comparison, does not show pink. *Penthouse* will teach you much more about the biology of a lady's privates. But believe it or not, she brought in porn magazines. To church class. And she passed them around.

All of us boys thought, "You are easily the fucking greatest nun I have ever even remotely encountered, but you're also a complete moron if you think you're going to turn us teenage boys in the throes of puberty *off* to porn by showing us this nice lady's utterly amazing bush. Holy Lamb of God, I'll stay at this church class all day long."

It just dawned on me as I wrote this that all of these people simply didn't have their shit together, which is understandable, since their task was not (and is not) easy: trying to keep this eldritch, tired dogma relevant for the youth of modern society. All things considered, I really had an amazing time at St. Mary's, despite the religious parts. The good part about the church, for me, was the people. And the *Playboys*. Father Tony gave me the opportunity to get up in front of people to begin to fine-tune my subliminal messaging, and he nurtured (even unwittingly) my need to perform. In high school, when I figured out that I would be attending theater school to pursue stage acting, he said to me, "I understand this decision and I think it's something you might have a shot at. I just want you to be careful, because in the world of show business there's going to be a lot of drugs and a lot of sex. There's going to be a lot of temptation."

And I said, "Yes, thank you!"

Horse Sense > The Bible

The holy Bible. This "good book" is a book of fairy tales. *What?* Yes, folks, for a fairy tale, by definition, is a fictional story that contains some sort of supernatural creature or occurrence. The Bible is chock-full of both. I don't feel the need to quibble about Old Testament or New, the Gnostics, or any of that crap. My issue is with the exploitation of the entire Bible.

Now, some of the more prevalent supernatural elements in the Bible we are all pretty familiar with: an all-powerful deity called "God" and his charismatic boy, "Jesus" (who has some superpowers like self-resurrection and some cool action like the Wonder Twins, turning sticks into snakes and greatly multiplying bread loaves and fish sticks until history's first all-you-can-eat experience was invented), plus a burning bush, a cool sea that has a secret hallway that opens and closes for you depending on your race/religion, and your usual mountebank sleights of hand in revival settings. Healings, etc. MAGICKS.

This book of fairy tales has proven to yield a wealth of lessons for people who study it. You know the form; it's old-school cautionary tale: "Jahedickus did walk him to the woodpile after dark to fetch some wood so that the women about the place could cook for him and the men some whey-cakes, so long as the women be clean and their flowers be not upon them, which would be super gross. Because of the darkness, Jahedickus did notice not the woodchuck resting on the woodpile, until it did bite of his hand flesh. When Jesus heard tell of this in the marketplace, he did laugh his ass off, and then Jesus spake unto the peoples,

'Gather ye not your fire from the darkness, but instead seek it in the light of day.' Then Jesus said to his apostle Steve, 'Steve,' he said, 'go thee to the woodpile and put the woodchuck to death, taking care that it not nibble at thy hand.'"

There are at least twenty-seven good metaphorical ways to interpret this famous scripture from the book of Nick, and they're all sound. Father, by all means, teach me philosophical methods based upon them. I love philosophy; I love to learn creative ways of viewing the world and mankind's various dilemmas and triumphs. Just don't fucking tell me we should kill all the woodchucks because the Bible says so. That's it. That's all I'm driving at. It's a book of stories that should be treated as suggestions. It is not a book of rules for the citizens of the United States of America. Do me a favor and read that last sentence again.

A step further. Creationism. If you want to go in so deep as to ignore all of the advances and hard facts that SCIENCE and LEARNING have provided us in the field of biological evolution and instead profess that the creation story, written by men from their holy visions, about how the Christian deity spinning the world together out of the void in the magic of Genesis describes the true origin of the universe, that is your business. Terrific. It's a cool story, don't get me wrong; I love magic. Check out Madeleine L'Engle's A Wrinkle in Time, which won a Newbery Medal. For the record, I don't believe the book of Genesis ever won one of those.

You and your fellow creationists profess belief in a magical story. You are welcome to do so. Sing and chant, and eat crackers and drink wine that you claim are magically infused with the blood and flesh of your church's original grand wizard, the Prince of Peace. I personally think that's just a touch squirrelly, but that's your business, not mine. You will not be punished for those beliefs in our nation of individual freedoms. But I do think the vast majority of your fellow Americans would appreciate it, kind creationists, if you silly motherfuckers would keep that bullshit out of our schools. Your preferred fairy tales have no place in a children's classroom or textbook that professes to be teaching our youngsters what is REAL. Jesus Christ, it's irrefutably un-American, people!

Let's take a brief glance at Thomas Jefferson's letter of 1802 to the Danbury Baptist Association. In his letter, making reference to the First Amendment to the United States Constitution, Jefferson writes: "Believing with you that religion is a matter which lies solely between Man & his God, that he owes account to none other for his faith or his worship, that the legitimate powers of government reach actions only, & not opinions, I contemplate with sovereign reverence that act of the whole American people which declared that their legislature should 'make no law respecting an establishment of religion, or prohibiting the free exercise thereof,' thus building a wall of separation between Church & State." Okay. All right then, I thought I had coined the phrase "separation of church and state," but apparently this periwigged joker, this "Jefferson," got there before I did. Why haven't "we, the people" remembered it? It seems like a cool idea.

The First Amendment, by the way, states that "Congress shall make no law respecting an establishment of religion, or prohibiting the free exercise thereof."

What does all of this terribly written gobbledygook mean? I'm glad you asked. The first thing I'll point out is Jefferson's correct assertion that "the legitimate powers of government reach AC-TIONS ONLY, & NOT OPINIONS" (emphasis mine). Check it: If you subscribe to a group that worships a piece of fictional writing—say, I don't know, the holy Bible—then that is your business. Go for it. Create ceremonies full of symbolic magic tricks involving the transformation of a long-dead spirit's body and blood into a cracker and a sip of wine. Sing songs about it. Rejoice at the magic. In America, you may do so, with absolute impunity. However, should you try to bring your beliefs into a public argument of any sort, those beliefs can hold no water. Here's why—as discussed earlier in this book, the stories of the Christian "God" and all of his purported works are merely a collection of stories, and if you choose to have "faith" in the truth of those stories, regardless of right or wrong, your belief that they are true is your OPINION. You are welcome to it.

Secondly, the First Amendment is telling us that there shall be no laws favoring any churches and also no laws prohibiting whatever you might want to think about or preach in your respective churches. Change the cracker to a pickle! You can! It's a First Amendment right!

I love my country. Holy shit, do I love America. In many ways, it is the glorious result of some very open-minded thinking on the parts of our forefathers (and the ladies advising them) a couple of centuries ago. But that right there's the rub, y'all. We're a group of human beings, which means we can never be done trying to improve ourselves, and by default, our systems, including our government. Now, here's the deal: Invoking the Bible in any public school or at any government function? Un-American. Making a witness in a court of law place his or her hand on the Bible? Un-

American. Disputing legislation based upon what it says in your holy book? NOT PATRIOTIC.

Where does this holy book come from, after all? Let's imagine a conversation. . . .

Me: So, Father Mark, why should we do what the Bible says?

Him: Well, that's easy: because it's the word of God.

Me: God?

Him: Yes, God the Father. The creator of heaven and earth. Of all that is seen and unseen.

Me: That's trippy.

Him: It is.

Me: So God wrote the Bible?

Him: Well, in a manner of speaking. God spoke to the men who wrote the Bible and told them what to write, and so I guess—

Me: The Bible was ghostwritten?

Him: Well, it's a little more sacred than that.

Me: How so? All dudes, right?

Him: Excuse me?

Me: Only men, no female ghost-scribes, correct?

Him: Well, yes, that is so.

Me: Okay. Does God prefer men to women? Are men smarter at Bible stuff?

Him: No, no, it's just, well, there weren't really even women who could write in the time of the scribes. It was a different time.

Me: Hm. Okay. Seems a little thin. Anyway, so, here's what I can't seem to puzzle out—if these guys wrote the Bible chapters, based on their divine visions, or what have you, what evidence can you show me that they didn't just make it up? I'll be honest: When you invite me to your church and gently suggest that I "tithe" ten percent of my income to this sort of "Bible club," it makes me wonder a bit. Was ten percent the number God suggested? Is there a religion wherein gratuity is included?

Him: I'm glad you asked me that, because that question is really the lynchpin of our faith. There is absolutely no proof—how could there be—that these scribes were given supernatural messages from a power greater than anything they could know. . . . It actually sounds pretty crazy when I say it like that.

Me: You see?

Him: No, but that's what I was saying—it is because we believe in this truth that we can build our entire church upon faith.

Me: Given that statement, isn't it a little generous to refer to that information as the "truth"?

Him: Not to us. We are believers. In John 14:6, Jesus says, "I am the way, the truth, and the life."

Me: Again, the proof you're citing is that a man spoke this to another guy, who then reported it. You really trust the reporter? Have you seen *TMZ*?

Him: The Bible, as a collection of holy texts handed down directly as the word of God, has to be considered above the uncertain scrutiny of we mortals.

Me: Wow. Okay, I get that. But to the rest of us Americans, who aren't "believers" in your ambitious claim that these writings are actually true using the definition of *true* that involves factual reality, can you see how it would seem inappropriate to us for followers of your book of stories to attempt to bring

their faithful opinions to bear on real-world issues like legal
policy and public programs and school curricula?

Him: [chuckle] You sound like you're writing a book.

Me: It's a "humorous" book, which is sweet; it means no research.
Are you avoiding my question?

Him: No, I'm sorry. The answer to your question can be found in
the Bible—

Me: But that's what I'm saying. For all of us who don't want to
adhere to the stories upon which your religion is founded, isn't
it fair to ask you to leave it at church? How would you feel if
all the Buddhists began insisting that some Zen koans were
recited every morning before class in our public schools [not a
bad idea]? I think what the First Amendment is driving at is
simply that our American policy ensures a fair shake to all
citizens, to consider and choose whatever religion, if any,
they wish to take part in. If we pray to the Christian God in
schools, we offend the Muslims and the Buddhists and the
Hindus, and certainly the SubGeniuses and countless others.
If we sing our fealty to Krishna before major league baseball
games, then the Hindus might be tickled, but again,
everybody else will get their panties in a bundle. Ostensibly,
the goal of any religion is to improve the character, the moral
fiber, of its adherents. We are all just seeking to become
more decent, right? Why not, then, engage in these
improvements whilst in private, at home or at the
denominational gathering place of our choosing, bolstering
our individual virtues with solid consistency, then simply bring
that improved *character* to bear upon public issues? As in,
"Wow, Senator Torgelman, you make really honorable

decisions. How do you do it?" Senator Torgelman may then pound his heart twice with his fist, kiss two fingers, and point to the heavens, or he may just as likely press his palms together and bow, uttering, "Namaste," or even lightly caress the war hammer hanging from his belt and declare clearly, "Praise Odin."

Him: It smells bad in this truck.

Me: Sorry. Pulled pork.

Him: Mind if I take off?

Me: Be my guest.

Him: [trying door handle] It won't open.

Me: Psych.

Him: Hilarious. Thanks for the weed. [exit priest]

Me: Thanks for the money . . . Dad. [I weep and stare at my reflection in the rain-jeweled windshield.]

I'm going to type this in boldface to try to make it as clear as possible: If you read the Bible and go to church, or subscribe to any other religion, that is fine with me. I like nice people, and if you are endeavoring to be one, I say, "Great!" I, too, am endeavoring to be a nice person. The thing that makes me mad is when a person suggests that I CANNOT be a nice person or live a life of goodness WITHOUT reading the Bible and attending church. To sum up—churchgoers: fine and dandy; those who try to force it on me and my fellow Americans: assholes. Areas in which "they" try to force it on us: premarital sex abstention, abortion laws, birth control, gay marriage. The fact that

creationism can even be a conversation is a goddamn shame and blight upon our nation's character.

Jesus was a great and wise man; we get it. His teachings are an excellent set of guidelines by which to conduct oneself; copy that. But you don't get to bring your church book into the city, county, state, or national policy discussion! Put that shit away! Why? Because it's simply not fair. It's not how we play in the old US of A. Muslims are not slinging their shibboleths down on the congressmen or -women's desks, nor are they the insane freaks committing violence upon abortion clinics shouting slogans from the Torah. The Koran is full of wisdom. The Tao Te Ching is an amazing resource of life lessons. Why do I have to be having this argument in this day and age? For fuck's sake, you use your religious (or not) writing of choice at home, or in a place where people gather to imbibe your religion of choice. Hopefully, this practice teaches you decency, common sense, and goodwill toward your fellow men and women. THEN, you take that decency and put it to good use when drafting legal policy! Leave your church out of it! If I were to coin a phrase, I don't know, I might suggest A SEPARATION OF CHURCH AND STATE, just like old Tommy Jefferson did. Time to re-up that shit. Forgive my eloquence.

3

Der Ubermann/Offermensch

When people ask me, "From where did you come up with Ron Swanson? What is he based on?" the main answer, after properly crediting Greg Daniels, Mike Schur, and our show's writers, would have to be that a great deal of him comes from my dad, Frederic "Ric" Offerman. He has been such a hero to me and such an incredible teacher. A stoic, stern, hardworking yet caring man.

I didn't always feel this way. Nothing will piss off a kid more than a dad who wants him to go out and split firewood when he's otherwise employed. I did a lot of whining. "It's Saturday morning. My cartoons are on. Are you insane? It's *Super Friends!*"

He would not reply. I would not continue arguing. Having lodged my complaint, I would dutifully hustle out and try to get my chores done as quickly as possible so I wouldn't miss *Grape Ape*.

I loved my dad when I was a kid, just as I do today. I idolized him and followed him around, emulating his every move. But he was also very much the disciplinarian in the house. He took matters very seriously because he was providing for a family of six on a junior high school teacher's salary. There wasn't a lot of room in his day for fucking around.

As far back as I can remember, my dad has been teaching me lessons about decency and manhood. One of the first things I can recall is him standing next to me to pee, me standing up on a stool (because I was four years old and tiny, not because my hog was so long that I needed a stool to pee over the rim), showing me how to hit the porcelain bowl above the water, so you don't make a lot of noise to upset the ladies, but below the rim, so you don't splatter outside of the targeted area. Aunt Dee had a hand-painted sign in the bathroom off her mudroom: IF YOU SPRINKLE WHEN YOU TINKLE, BE A SWEETIE AND WIPE THE SEATIE. As a child, I always felt bad for anyone who would be so crude as to need that advice. They clearly didn't have as kick-ass of a dad as me.

My father has always been so conscientious, and is such an all-around good guy, that I, of course, bridled against most of his lessons and didn't allow myself to acknowledge them for years. All through my childhood he was teaching me to use tools and how to fix things. My brother and I are two of the only people I know in our circle of friends who can fix any problem at all with a toilet, down to replacing it. Dad's lessons were very clear. "Respect the machinery. When someone is driving a machine they can't always see you and they can't hear you. Know what the machine is and what job it's doing. Whatever it is, it can crush you, or at least hurt your feelings."

I remember once, down in Dad's basement shop, trying to hammer a nail into a board that was resting on my leg. He showed me that when you put the board on a solid surface you're taking away the "give" in your joints and your flesh. If you anchor your work, especially with a clamp, or at least rest it on a solid surface, then all your force is working on the nail and none is being wasted just holding the board still. Such a great lesson. When you're aiming to apply force to a job with a tool, you have to isolate the focal point of your work as much as possible. Driving a nail. Opening a beer. Breaking loose a lug nut when changing a tire.

Everywhere we went there were lessons. The hardware store, the grocery store, church, school. In hindsight, the care he took with all of his kids, the four at home and the dozens and dozens that he taught every year at Channahon Junior High, was amazingly generous. He used all of the considerable powers at his disposal to turn us into the best possible citizens and hardworking contributors.

Being the athlete that he was, combined with the dad he was, he would come to all of my sports games, where he had a great technique for communicating his advice. So many parents come and sit in the bleachers at the basketball game and just scream, "Are you crazy? Are you blind, ref? Kimmy, watch the post-up down low! Aghh! What are you doing?! Watch the baseline!!" (A note to parents at sporting events: DERIDING your child is not going to help anyone but will make you look like a real fuck-nut.) My dad would sit closer down to the floor and he would wait until I ran in close proximity to him, and he would say, "Watch that number fourteen down by the baseline. Bend your knees, will you please?" His voice would come in underneath the cacophony. At the time I thought, "Dad, shut up, I know, I can see him!" and I would bristle, but I had to admit his advice had a great success rate, goddamn it.

One night we were driving home after a game in Joliet, where we had played against Washington Junior High School (and lost), and it was snowing. We were in my dad's old blue Chevy on our road, a graveled country lane called Bell Road. We stopped in the empty road a few miles from home, right by the Larkins' farm before Jughandle

Road. Dad was trying to explain something to me about playing defense and was moved to demonstrate what he meant, right then and there. We got out of the car in the thick snowfall, and by the light of the headlights he showed me what he was trying to explain. It was about keeping my knees bent and keeping my focus on the center of the player that I was defending by watching his solar plexus. "He can fool you with his head and his eyes and his arms and his legs, and even his fanny, but if you stay with his center he can't fool you."

At the time I thought, "Dad, it's nine forty-five P.M. I have homework. I'm tired. It's snowing."

But that scene stuck with me so deeply. I'll be surprised if I don't end up filming that moment at some point because it's just beautiful.

A lot of Dad's coaching had to do with the "fanny," or one's caboose. When you throw a baseball or swing a bat, certainly when you block out for a rebound or set up a jump shot, it's all about how you are disposing the weight of your fanny. Ric Offerman was the kind of ballplayer about whom Malcolm Gladwell could write a detailed study. In his book *Outliers* Gladwell posits that one cannot achieve mastery at an exceptional level over any skill until one has logged ten thousand hours of fundamental practice in that skill set. If that's the case, my dad was probably a master of dribbling and free throws by the time he was twelve. When we would play H-O-R-S-E with him, the rest of us kids would fall over cracking up at the ridiculous shots he would sink, making the net snap as the ball rifled through its exact center. He was so good, it was funny. I can still shoot free throws myself, thanks to him.

We were shooting a *Parks and Rec* episode in which Ron and Andy are coaching boys' basketball, and during a break, I toed up to the line, and although I guess I was forty that year, it was just like Ric was

BASKETBALL

standing right there with me. Give it a dribble. Weigh the ball. Bounce it with backspin. Dribble. Weigh it. Shoot. For cryin' out loud, follow through.

It took me a few tries to find my distance, but then I couldn't miss. I made a long string of them in a row, maybe twenty, and I just thought, "Amazing. Look what my dad did." If he had been there, he would have simply said, "Well, everybody gets lucky once in a while."

As a teenager I would frequently revolt against my dad, as sons will do. I really had bad feelings toward him. Resentment. It was all because of his hectoring, which seems totally unfair now, since his hectoring usually consisted of statements like, "Please be decent today. Please mind your manners at school. If you're gonna do a job, do it right."

He kept telling me to be decent, but I was full of mischief at school. I caused a lot of minor trouble but always found a way to get away with it and come out smelling like a rose. My parents are the best people I've ever met. And I'm not biased—they must have some small failings somewhere, but I can't seem to catalog them. They're just very humble, hardworking, and honorable people. Their families as well. And funny. Maybe we drink and eat a little more than we should. They make mistakes like anybody does, but they are the most decent goddamn people, and somehow my nature was to see what I could get away with on their watch.

I thought, "I understand what you're saying about following the rules and having good manners and telling the truth . . . but let me see what I can get out of this system." At school, I stole Matchbox cars from other kids and would then get caught and have to fess up. When I was little enough to sit in the shopping cart at the store I stole some gum from near the cash register. By the time we got to the car I had exposed it somehow. My mom said, "What the heck?" (a two-dollar cuss word for her), and I had to go back inside and apologize. But somehow, I kept doing it. I was a pilferer.

I would lie at school, for show, mainly. I remember—I think this is the beginning of whatever the need was for attention, or the need to be told I was special—in grade school raising my hand and telling stories. They'd be somehow relevant to the day's proceedings. The teacher might say, "Today we're going to watch a documentary about how soda is made and bottled," and I'd raise my hand and say, "My uncle once found a mouse in a Coke bottle." I remember getting caught in lies. The school would call home and my parents would sit me down that night and talk to me. My parents would be very civil about it, shaking their heads and saying, "I don't understand what we're doing wrong. All you have to do is tell the truth. If you tell the truth, then no one can ever hold anything over you."

Whatever it was in me, I was certainly not cognizant of it. Sure, I'm embarrassed by it, but I can recognize that it was simply in my nature, own it, and move on. OR IS THAT A LIE?

I continued to try to put one over on people, but I got much better at it. In high school I would still famously lie about things but now mostly to the administration. My cousin and I would commit small acts of graffiti and then I would pin it on other people. The funny thing was, I was actually in charge of the committee to clean up the graffiti and I would get out of class to do it. I was definitely very Machiavellian about it.

My mom and dad had instilled enough character in me that I was still an A student, and I was still very productive in my endeavors, but there was maybe 10 percent of my personality that still wanted to somehow trick the world into giving me some sort of get-rich-quick lottery ticket. I suppose I had to learn on my own that there are no shortcuts to anything, be it success or just winning people's attention for the right reasons. Because I'd eventually learn that nothing beats hard work.

Once I got to college and realized, "Wow, I'm on my own. Criminy. I have a checkbook and I have to pay bills," I immediately got over the 10 percent bullshit fraction I had fostered as a teen, thank goodness. Life is hard enough when you're operating 6-2 and even, which is one of my dad's favorite phrases (it means a racing horse's odds are 6-1 to win, 2-1 to place, and even money to show—which I always interpreted to simply mean "decent").

Fortunately, as a young Illini, I was quickly rescued by my passion for theater. I had always been an A student, as I said, but I would do only just enough work to get ninety-threes and ninety-fours. I didn't care about getting 100 percent. I ended up graduating in the top 10 percent of my class. I was in the elite group, but I didn't give a shit beyond maintaining my place with the smarty-pantses. Once I got into theater school, that changed overnight. I wanted to be at the top of my class. I wanted to excel. When I got to this new world of, well, sincerity, I thought, "Holy shit—I have a lot of work to do, and I can't wait to do it. I have a system—by god, I have the tools; I can do this! Hecate's girdle, I WILL PERSEVERE!" It was drama school; go easy on me.

And it started working for me right away. About a month into college I was walking across campus, and I had to stop and call my dad from a pay phone, and I said, "Dad, I just want to say that everything you've taught me has just landed. I get it all. I'm really sorry I was a bit of a dick to you for the last five or six years. But I just want to say thank you. I'm going to make a good go of this. Everything you and Mom have been quietly instilling into me, despite my resistance—it worked."

How to Be a Man

Step One: Eat a steak, preferably raw. If you can find a juicy steer and just maw a healthy bite off of its rump, that's the method that will deliver the most immediate nutrition, protein, and flavor. Make sure you chew at least three times.

Step Two: Wash it down with your whisky of choice, preferably a single-malt scotch. My two favorites are Lagavulin and the Balvenie, but I won't turn my nose up at Talisker, Oban, Laphroaig, Ardbeg, and many more. The Glens. Caol Ila. Dalwhinnie. Cragganmore. Delicious. Just speaking their names aloud will put hair on thy chest, laddie. Or Irish whisky—I mean, goddamn, Jameson, Bushmills, Tullamore Dew, Redbreast, Midleton—or come on, what about the ridiculous amount of good bourbon available right here in the good old US of A? Your Woodford, your Bulleit and Blanton's, Pappy Van Winkle's and Four Roses, and there's frankly not a damn thing wrong with Maker's Mark. Not a goddamn thing. Then there's rye. Then there's corn. What a wonderful world in which to call oneself a man.

Step Three: Find a socialist and punch him/her in the face.

Step Four: Craft a small wooden watercraft from cedar (for the hull) and domestic hardwoods, like ash or walnut or white oak (for the gunnels and other trim). Carve a paddle from cherry and Alaskan yellow cedar.

Step Five: Make sweet but powerful love to another human, most preferably one who is welcoming of your advances. If you have adhered to steps 1 through 4, how could they resist? Upon climax, unholster your enormous pistol and empty the cylinder as you fire rounds laced with double entendre into the night sky dripping with stars.

Or not. Sorry, everybody, totally just kidding (except, of course, about the whisky and boatbuilding). I feel like these are some ideas that are somewhat mis-associated with my public persona, as well as with my TV character Ron Swanson. While I firmly adhere to much of this list, these are not, in fact, what I truly consider to be the steps one must tread if one seeks to attain a quality in life leaning toward what we're here calling manliness. Most of this list pertains more to what I would refer to as the slaking of one's animal thirsts, or just achieving some of the more delicious base pleasures in life.

Okay, so here we are. As I mentioned, I seem to have been associated with certain traits of machismo in the zeitgeist, at least for this brief, golden moment. I find that fact to be somewhat embarrassing, given my firsthand knowledge of my personal failings and propensity for jackass behavior, but I get it, based on superficially perceived signals of manhood, like a full, thick moustache and the ability to use tools. When people ask me questions relating to my "manliness," I like to remind them that I am primarily an artist as an actor, writer, and woodworker.

It's worth mentioning that the two best woodworkers in the Offerman Woodshop are women. Beefy, mannish women? No, nothing of the sort. Lovely, talented, strong, young, and smart ladies, who continue to learn and profit by the time-honored crafts of handmade wooden furniture and boats. Lee and Michele are full-time woodworkers. Me, on the other hand, I'm pretty sensitive. I am an entertainer, and I believe that "entertainer" and "artist" are not the usual vocations that spring to mind when we picture our idea of the classic "man." I am studying at the same school as Lee and Michele, but they make it to class a hell of a lot more than I do.

Even in my family, I'm not the one you'd call manly. I'm the one who went away to theater school. I took two semesters of ballet, for Christ's sake. Sure, my incentive was that it was the elective in which one could look at girls the best, but still. Come on, I wore tights and busted out an *entrechat quatre*. In layman's terms, that's when you spring straight up in the air and twiddle your pointed toes like scissors four times before you land. The talented dancers could achieve an *entrechat six*, so even in ballet, I was out-manned.

In most of the country (and the world), there are teenagers who could whip me in most contests, because they are working hard every day of their lives, swinging an axe, hauling buckets of water, wrangling herds of cattle, hogs, and horses. Conversely, I memorize written lines of (brilliant) dialogue. Then I go to a trailer where my hair is coiffed and MAKEUP is applied to my face. After that, I squeeze my beefy corpus into specifically unattractive garments before heading into the set, where I then deliver my prepared scenes with all the deadpan élan I can muster. If hungry, I can request a sandwich fixed to my liking. My mewling is easily silenced with a bottle of water or a cup of corn chowder.

Please don't misunderstand me. In my life, there are and have been times when I do and did work like "a man." I have engaged in seasons of labor on my family's farm. I have framed houses. I worked two summers on a blacktop crew, paving parking lots and driveways in the Illinois humidity. I did some roofing in Chicago. I have known and enjoyed hard work for many of my prime years. But now, I am a clown who occasionally gets to mill a tree into table slabs.

Having thus established my current meager rank on the great tourney bracket of manliness in life, let's begin this chapter in earnest. First of all, let's change up our semantics. I wish to examine some human attributes that I think of as, yes, "manly," but I would also like to touch upon some personality traits that I feel are charismatic in people of all sexes, that many readers might instinctively think of as "manly" but I will simply call "capable." I will perforce be indulging in some gross generalizations here, like "all men have strong arms" and "women wear high heels," but this is obviously not the case for everyone. Just making conversation.

For the menfolk:

Chivalry: In a nutshell, there are certain situations in everyday life in which we fellas have the opportunity to behave, well, decently. The initial "women's lib" movement brought the role of modern-day chivalry into question. "If you ladies want to be treated as equals, then shouldn't you be able to open your own car door?" The answer to that is, quite simply, "No, dude. You're an asshole." Women are, quite clearly, powerful and smart, quite often more than us bros. Their literal bodily connection to the forces of the moon's gravity and resultant tides, not to mention their quite regular performance of the medicine-ball-through-a-needle's-eye MIRACLE of childbirth, renders them superior to men in many important ways. However, when ladies like to wear shoes that are difficult to move around in, or perhaps a foxy skirt that limits their choices in sitting positions, then it's simply nice to lend them a sympathetic hand. We men generally weigh more than they do, so the wind doesn't prove as much of a threat to us. Perhaps we're not as worried about our hairdos, so the rain is not as big of a bummer. Whatever the adversity, if a man is on hand to provide ease to a lady's cause, I think he's a shitheel if he stands idly by when she could use an umbrella, a handkerchief, or a steady arm.

Of course, this is applicable to all people, not just ladies. There are a lot of daddies out there who sometimes need a little aid as they try to change a diaper whilst juggling groceries and a latte. I suppose that's another part of being "manly," or more accurately, "like a man." I am speaking of our tendency as humans to try to do too much. People love to bite off more than they can chew. I consistently arrive at the grocery store for maybe five or six items, so I get the two-handled plastic basket instead of the cart, and I invariably see seven more things I need, including sixty-four ounces of cranberry juice, and, oh, I really should try this new craft beer from the Russian River Brewing Co., and on and on, until I am testing the limits of both the thick-gauge-wire basket handles and my arms and fingers. Why don't I go get a cart? Go fuck yourself. Why don't I ask for directions? A topic much masticated by many before me. "I know I'm lost, I *know*, but I will be *goddamned* if I'm going to stop and ask someone in a gas station for help." Behave like that, and I'll be much more quick to call you "manly" than if you win a boxing match.

Grooming: Again, who is making the rules? How does a "man" groom himself in this modern age? As a character actor blessed with a thick head of hair and a thicker thicket of bracken upon my face, neck, and lip, I have enjoyed excessively utilizing these accessories in every possible permutation I could muster. I have done Mr. T's majestic hairdo in both brown and platinum white. I often shave my head bald. I have exploited my whiskers for beards, goatees, Vandykes, muttonchops, and of course all manner of moustaches.

Working in the live theater or on a television series can mean maintaining a certain look for months on end, which means if I'm playing a person with a douchey hairstyle (for Christ's sake, Ron Swanson's coif is called "the full douche") or lame facial hair choice, then I might be stuck with said shrubbery throughout my real life, at the lumberyard, at a Little League game, at the post office, you name it. It's been fascinating over the years to study how I am perceived differently by strangers depending upon my current hair/whisker style. I certainly have rolled around town in a Gucci tuxedo or other fancy Sunday clothes. I have also swaggered about even more in dusty Carhartt pants and jackets (for my money, nothing beats denim and work boots), but whatever the case, people tend to look at you and judge you differently based upon the cover of the book.

I say, who fucking cares? Sure, I think we should do our best to keep ourselves clean, for reasons of health as well as politeness. If you want to attract a conservative person, then get a square haircut and a clean shave. If you long for a Phish fan, well, I don't know what they typically look like, but I'm betting it's more laissez-faire than most. Let your freak flag fly, friend. Do your thing, however it looks, keep the hygiene up, and tell everybody who doesn't like it to kiss your tattooed ass.

Another thought that I think goes for everybody, but men especially: **Be Handy.** For Pete's sake, I know not everybody can build a canoe, or even a Popsicle stick. That doesn't mean you need to throw your hands in the air and say, "I'm useless." There are many facets of our daily lives that entail minor tool use, which damn near any idiot can master. A pet concern of mine: changing a tire on your vehicle. I know, I know, AAA is great, they really are an amazing service, but don't let the security blanket of their service make you soft. You just might get caught out in the cold without your blanket. Every modern car and truck comes with a full kit for changing a flat tire, and I highly recommend you give it a few practice runs in the safety of your own driveway or street, before you're stranded in the hills on your way back from Bonnaroo with no cell phone service and a pancaked tire.

You can use a screwdriver. You can use a hammer. Trust me. If you want to fix a broken closet hook or doorknob, you can! Take your time, read about it online, or better yet, ask someone handy that you know for advice. I can't describe the richly deserved feeling of accomplishment you'll glean from nailing up just one fallen fence board. Your genitals will expand exponentially. Men have been known to gain up to seven-eighths of an inch in length, and a burgeoning nine-sixteenths of an inch in girth! I've heard tell of ladies who increased their vaginal volume by almost a half liter! Don't take handiness lightly, especially if you hope to increase your manliness, particularly by means of an enlarged vagina.

I cannot wrap up this chapter before touching base with one of my all-time paragons of manliness. I speak, of course, of Theodore Roosevelt, aka "number 26." Here is a piece he wrote to adorn the wall of the lobby at New York City's magnificent Museum of Natural History:

MANHOOD

A man's usefulness depends upon his living up to his ideals insofar as he can.

It is hard to fail but it is worse never to have tried to succeed.

All daring and courage, all iron endurance of misfortune, make for a finer, nobler type of manhood.

Only those are fit to live who do not fear to die and none are fit to die who have shrunk from the joy of life and the duty of life.

Oh, right, just in case we might have forgotten why he was the baddest mofo ever to sit the Oval Office bareback (we haven't), this should firmly remind us. I would especially like to echo his sentiment that "it is worse never to have tried to succeed." I would equate this notion with manliness, or, more correctly, capability. Damn it all, you have been given a life on this beautiful planet! Get off your ass and do something!

It is far too simple these days to lazily coast through an entire lifetime, performing adequately at some thankless job, so that one can purchase a roof, a television, a video game console, and a crappy vehicle, only to find oneself in the final days with absolutely nothing to show for the squandered years. My dad always told me, "If you're gonna do a job, do it right," and "Just always do the best you can, and then nobody can fault your effort."

Those simple adages saw me through a great many times of adversity, lending me the necessary gravel for finding gainful employment, so that even when I couldn't land an acting job, I could find carpentry work, which paid me dollars that I could then spend on beer. When the storm clouds hit, with a little gumption, life can begin to look rather sunny pretty quickly. If you like beer. Which men do. Just kidding. My sisters Laurie and Carrie can drink circles around me. Not sure if I mentioned that they're also talented belchers.

You'll notice that Mr. Roosevelt doesn't mention punching anybody in the face or firing a weapon of any caliber in his description of manhood. This from a man who so famously led the Rough Riders in their conquest of San Juan Hill and punched a fellow assemblyman in the face during an argumentative session of the New York State assembly. He does suggest that quality can be found in a chap who lives "up to his ideals insofar as he can." This, to me, is another arena in which men and women can prove their worth. **Loyalty. Honor.** Have a set of rules, a code of ethics, that you will do your best to uphold and defend, whether you're on horseback in Cuba in 1898, or at a school board meeting next week, or merely at the water cooler with your coworkers. Pursue decency in all dealings with your fellow man and woman. Simply put? Don't be an asshole.

4

Football Troubador

1984. My hometown, the village of Minooka, Illinois, was rather devoid of anything but the most homogenized popular culture. To this day, I don't know where the good independent record store or bookstore is. I'm certain they must exist, perhaps in Morris, the nearby town with a movie theater, but I just never had occasion to find them.

My older cousin Angie and my sister Laurie could legally drive to town, enabling them to traipse the twenty minutes to the Louis Joliet Mall in the nearby metropolis of Joliet. There Duran Duran records could be obtained, as well as the other glittering apples of their teenage-girl eyes. George Michael and his sassy young band, Wham! UK. Cyndi Lauper. Adam Ant. Madonna. In fealty to these musical phenoms, the girls also would purchase multicolored bangles with which to festoon their wrists; all well and good for them.

But there was little opportunity for a future weirdo like myself to discover the bands that would have thrilled me to pieces, like Talking Heads or Elvis Costello, not to mention Tom Waits or Laurie Anderson. If I wanted to experience popular music, I had but one apparent alternative, and that was to accompany Laurie and Angie to the concert of their choosing, which in 1985 happened to be George Michael and Wham!. Was Mr. Michael a bewitching singer and captivating dancer? Certainly. Was I as intoxicated by the lights and glamour as I was terrified by the wilding crowd of screaming, drooling housewives at my first large-scale music venue? You bet. Did any of that make me the tiniest bit inclined to answer in the affirmative when George Michael shouted, "YOU WANNA SEE MY BUM?!"? It did not, no.

Clapping along to his dance hits did not induce in me any urge whatsoever to enjoy a peek at his buttocks, as impressive as they must have been after all that "wake me up before you go-go"–ing. Experiences like this one certainly must have nurtured any developing feminine or "sensitive" side I possessed, so perhaps I entered high school looking for ways to round out the testosterone contingent in my hormonal congress.

In the 1980s there was really not much to do in a small Midwestern town. This recreational vacuum made team sports an incredibly important and prevalent part of our everyday lives. We worshipped the Chicago Cubs with a fervor now reserved for things like *Downton Abbey*. My older sister, Laurie, and I would compete on car rides in the arena of baseball statistics, quizzed by Dad at the wheel, which we could call up from our encyclopedic mind-vaults like Rain Man. Keith Moreland triples in 1982? Two. Fergie Jenkins's last wild pitch? Nineteen eighty-three. Easy.

Laurie and I mowed the front yard on a tractor mower. It was about eighty yards to the road and back. Two laps would take ten minutes, so we'd take turns, one of us watching the Cubbies while the other mowed. We got so good at it, we'd never stop the mower, just supplant each other while in second gear. Cubs fever? . . . We caught it!! This obsession bled liberally into our own participation in baseball and basketball for me, and in softball for Laur. At about eight hundred students, our high school was small enough that we could participate in almost every activity we desired, meaning sports and then some. Thus, I immediately signed up for band, jazz band, drama club, football, baseball, and basketball. I also was on the student council, eventually serving as its president. In other words, I was an asshole.

I had already played my first dramatic villain by this time, dastardly sheriff Black Bart something-or-other, in our eighth-grade play, *Trouble in Sinnimin City*. My friend Joe Frescura—a strapping Eagle Scout of a lad—played the protagonist. I suppose he was named "Tom" or some other bullshit hero name. This was several years before I would learn the efficacy of stage combat, so we opted for full-contact face punches in the show's climax so as not to appear weak before our thirteen-year-old castmates. In hindsight, the fact that Joe let me leave the stage on my feet with all my teeth speaks to his quiet generosity of spirit, because he could have laid me out with a single clout from his well-fed Italian knuckle sandwich. Joe went on to become an exceptional army major in the Special Forces. I became an actor, and not just an actor, but a thespian.

I didn't have a chance to play football before arriving in high school. I'm not sure I had any business getting into it even then, but I was a decent-to-good athlete, and I was willing to buy into the whole romance of high school and homecoming and, well, cheerleaders, so I signed up. At age fourteen and fifteen I was faster than I was tough, so I started out as a receiver and a defensive back, and those first "double days" (two conditioning practices a day) in July and August 1984 left me so stiff and sore that my uncle Dan would chase me around giggling at the pain my aching muscles were causing me. Halfway through the season I broke my collarbone diving for a pass, which was admittedly pretty badass. At least it was until I started sobbing openly while my mom drove me to the hospital in Morris. We would laugh/sob every time she hit a bump because it hurt so goddamn bad that it was funny. When things get bad enough, all you can do is laugh. I feel like my mom saved my fanny like that about once a week throughout my childhood.

That injury put a damper on my football career for a while and allowed me to focus on my life in the arts. Namely, playing the saxophone in band and jazz band, kissing girls, the theater, and more kissing girls. Band was overall a really great experience throughout my school career, but it was also a place for me to explore my inner smartass. I would offer my belated apologies to our band director, Mr. Wunar, who had to put up with way more "hilarious" tomfoolery than any human should ever have to countenance. It was in band that I was able to learn how to carry myself as a leader with a sense of humor, whilst indulging my propensity for high-grade jackassery.

The key was in discerning just how much mischief I could get away with. The percussionists, for example, took things too far. They drank vodka and beer to excess and then allowed their alcohol to fuel some pretty flagrant insubordination, ultimately finding themselves in the principal's office. I was interested in the grab-ass but not the consequences, so I focused on making people laugh without having my techniques detected by the administration, in this case Mr. Wunar. Apparently, I became rather adept at playing both sides of the fence, earning A's in class while firmly establishing myself as a miscreant purveyor of chuckles.

I also, quite understandably, took to the stage whenever I could. As my involvement in the arts expanded, I found myself being cast as more bad guys or antihero protagonists, such as Jud Fry in *Oklahoma!*

and Joe Ferone in *Up the Down Staircase*, and I really began to enjoy the therapeutic aspect of getting to play some version of an asshole. All of the weak human inclinations that I had been raised to eschew were qualities in which I could revel onstage, and I could even win an audience's love through misbehaving! This was big, big news. As I worked as a professional on the stages of Chicago in later years, I continued to find that people were willing to reward me for acting like some of the jerks I had grown up around.

To wit: football players. Thanks largely to my dad's genes and his coaching, I was pretty good at sports, but I was like the fifth-to-seventh-best guy on any given baseball or basketball team. I was a solid contributor, but I was never the star. I often batted second or sixth. I'd win "most improved" or "best sportsmanship," if anything. I would be among the team leaders in rebounds or assists, perhaps. But by junior year of high school I had started to fill out, and through no fault of my own, I ended up being one of the hardest hitters on the football team. There were guys on the team who were much more imposing Mack trucks of young men, like Todd Reische and Brian Edge, to name a couple of hulks, but some badass instinct was awakened within me. By senior year I was the "headhunter" on kickoffs, which meant I was the guy who ran in front of everyone else to reach the receiver of the kickoff and exact as much punishment upon him as possible for having the temerity to carry MY FOOTBALL.

This was insane. I was a former member of swing choir (our version of glee club). Now, out of nowhere, *I* was the scary one. Instead of relying solely upon my speed, as I had in years past, to avoid confrontation on the field, I now realized that I could fucking decimate these other guys. Except Reische and Edge. And maybe Lance Pelton. (We cool, guys?)

Poor Todd Reische, most likely our school's best athlete during my tenure, who would have definitely been sole captain of the football team in any other year, had to arrive during a year when the coaching staff had determined to have three "cocaptains" instead, and so Todd captained the defense from the middle linebacker spot, Tommy Morris captained the offense from the quarterback position, and I captained the secondary defense and special teams. If I could go back and remove this indignity from Todd's shoulders, I would goddamn not. Are you kidding?

"Most improved rebounder" Offerman was now a cocaptain of the Fighting Minooka Indians?! I wouldn't trade those months of athletic prowess, however specialized, for the world. In those golden moments on the football field, I was revered as a frightening, manlike teenager, and I have never forgotten the Bronsonlike confidence this instilled in me. In their defense, many of my teammates were better at sports than I was. In my defense, I set a school record for interceptions in a season. Everybody gets lucky once in a while.

Hustling to football practice from, say, a rehearsal for *Oklahoma!* created an interesting situation. Of course, some of the team members were macho, homophobic guys of the sort that have come to be considered the norm for American high school football players, also known as "bullies." But in reality, most of the team was comprised of really nice guys with whom I had grown up playing sports. However, I do remember one specific bully, a guy my age named Biff, who wanted everyone to know that he was the dominant male in any given situation. Sadly, even then, we all knew that Biff's family had undergone some turmoil at home, of the sort that was most likely the source of his Steven Seagal–style posturing and preening, but that didn't make them any easier to swallow.

Suffice it to say, ahem, that Biff was not happy with the choirboy-cum-cocaptain headhunter. If you read back a paragraph, you'll notice that *Biff* was not the name of any of the three cocaptains, even though our Biff had been excelling at football since he was in something called Pee-Wee. Biff worked his tail off, a strong, fast, and gifted running back, but his fate was such that he was maybe the number five guy on the squad.

Now, this may be distressing news for Ron Swanson fans, but I have never in my life been in a fistfight. Really never even close. The closest I ever came was being taunted by Biff in the locker room or at a couple of barn parties. By the way, Biff was and still is a good guy, overall. In the hallway between classes, we were friends. He recognized his antagonizing tendencies even then, but, like an alcoholic or a fan of the Dave Matthews Band, he ultimately couldn't control his self-destructive addiction.

My dad had taught me to never throw the first punch, and so when Biff would want to unload some rage onto my face, I would simply suggest he go ahead and do it. I would say, "I'm not going to fight you, Biff, so you better just beat me up," while silently shaking in my boots.

Biff was the kind of person who used the term *faggot* rather liberally, and really never to describe a smoldering bundle of sticks in the fireplace in a Victorian novel. Biff had a violence in him that was frightening, and I'm very thankful for my dad's lesson, because if I had ever engaged young Biff in fisticuffs, I fear I would have been very seriously, well, fucked up by him. Instead, he would say something imperious and admonishing, ending with "I thought so, faggot," before heading back to the keg or his locker, depending on the location. This happened, I believe, three times over eight months or so. It is not the stuff of a coming-of-age film, so, Disney, please don't option this chapter. It's just the closest real-life experience I had to some of the violence I now love to pretend to in my day job.

I was to learn later in theater school of Aristotle's observation that theater is the mirror held up to society. But I was already inadvertently picking up on that heady notion by mere good fortune. By and large, I was learning to be decent to people in real life while engaging in delicious human indiscretions in my performances. Think about it: If you perform *A Clockwork Orange* onstage, you can be paid cash money to indulge in both ultra-violence *and* a bit of the ol' in-out-in-out!

Meanwhile, I was beginning to get an inkling of what I wanted to be when I grew up. Sophomore year I was in this horrible play called *The Prime Time Crime*. It was a "wacky caper" play starring Inspector Clouseau, the Pink Panther, Kato, Starsky and Hutch, Kojak, Baretta—it was truly ungodly. Why must high school plays be so ham-handed?! There is so much excellent writing available that must certainly be acceptable to any school board, even creationist idiots. *To Kill a Mockingbird*? *The Crucible*? Jesus, I'll even take some Neil Simon over *The Prime Time Crime*! The first good play I was in was *Up the Down Staircase*, from the sixties, in the vein of *Blackboard Jungle*. I played the sort of brooding James Dean role. It was funny—I took a lot of shit from the football team because I'd have to miss practice to go to a speech competition or band performance, but then those same meatheads (except Reische and Edge—totally cool dudes—not meatheads!) would be screaming and cheering at the curtain call. It seemed that in my small pond I was halfway decent at entertaining people from the stage. That was enough to send me on the road to theater school, where I promptly learned that I sucked. I hadn't fully discovered the value of my own unique voice.

One wasn't allowed to take speech or creative writing classes until junior or senior year, but I really took to them once I got there. I was also a very proficient sax player, but my teachers never took me to the point of inspiration, inspiring me to create my own sound. They simply taught me to read off of sheet music as well as I could. In jazz band you'd get the music for, say, "Sweet Georgia Brown," and there would be a tenor sax solo for sixteen bars, a suggested solo written in and then chords as well, so an adept improviser could just jam his or her own solo based on the provided chords. No one ever suggested that to me, and I needed the suggestion. I didn't think to try it on my own, nor did I possess the natural ability, so I'd just play the suggested solo in a kick-ass way (as far as I could tell).

I got more weird in speech class, where I'd do odd comedy bits for my speeches. The video camera was new on the scene—this was '84 or '85, and, stupidly, teachers would let you do a video report instead of writing a paper. Which I think was just idiotic, because we took full advantage of the opportunity to shoot a ten-minute video instead of spending hours writing a dreary report on some boring topic.

My cousin Ryan and I did an infamous joint video project for French class. I wish I still had it; someone from the class—I think a girl who was sweet on Ryan—stole it (looking at you, Jennifer Groot). It was the two of us in different scenarios, like me sitting in a chair in front of a roaring fireplace with a dog, a newspaper, and a pipe. I'd say in French, "Welcome. You're probably wondering why I'm sitting in this domestic situation with my pipe, my newspaper, my dog, and a fire. Let me explain. . . ." Then Ryan was happily making pasta at the stove, then he was in the shower, then I was vacuuming, all the while laying out clear French exposition. It was all very deadpan—"Oh, *excuse-moi*"—as we pleasantly described domestic tasks and personal hygiene. *C'est hilarant!* Hilarious!

So we were into making these weird, random comedy videos, but we were about two decades away from understanding that was a thing. It was just us being funny for a class and, more importantly, for ourselves, which is a significant flag by which one can navigate toward one's "voice," a flag entirely outside of my comprehension at that point.

I remember attending these speech contests where I tried the "Extemporaneous" category on for size. There was a kid from the suburbs of Chicago—I think his name was Bix—and he was a very flamboyant, queeny kid who was very, very funny. He was basically doing stand-up at age fourteen, with this incredibly sophisticated, fully written show (hardly extemporaneous, but who's counting?) with a character based upon Robin Leach from *Lifestyles of the Rich and Famous*. Only it was a swishy version, like a Bravo show this kid had created. It was, in a word, amazing.

Little me, a literal freshman in this arena, thought, "Holy shit, this kid is ready for the big time. He's like the Uncle Miltie of Grundy County" (if I'd known who the hell Uncle Miltie was). I was presenting material like "Welcome to the Sandwich County Fair. Get ready for the Spitting Contest!" and then I was enacting a spitting contest. I don't remember the setup, really, but I remember that "wind was an issue," and at one point I kept "catching the spit on my hand," which involved some kick-ass mime and sound effects, or "Foley," work. I was trying to draw from my own strange experience but had yet to learn the lesson of applying hard work to my act, to persevere in the face of the damning criticism of a central Illinois high school speech contest. My bits were certainly unique, but I interpreted those first flops as the ultimate judgment of my voice, so I didn't try again with that brand of wisecrack for many years.

Enter Mr. Pat Luther, or "Lex," as we obviously would have called him. A term of great affection, for remember, kids, this is back when Gene Hackman permanently endeared himself to audiences as a subway-dwelling, bald-headed, charismatic-as-shit Lex Luthor. Mr. Luther was the top-tier English teacher at Minooka, and it was in his creative writing class senior year that I really enjoyed a first taste of what my weird voice could achieve. (PS: He's the first person who ever said anything to me like, "You should check out the Royal Shakespeare Company. They do this play called *Hamlet*." A hero.)

One day near the end of the year, we assembled in his class for our final exam. He took a one-page essay, printed in a large font—long before we knew the term *font*—and taped it to the wall in front of the class with about an inch of masking tape. He said, "Here is your subject matter. You have ninety minutes to compose an essay on this." I did not even read the posted text. Instead, I immediately shat out an entirely fabricated history of masking tape, starting with some Native American origins involving applying sorghum to the leaves of the sumac tree, and so forth. I confidently handed it in and strode from the room.

You might expect that the next day I would have received some sort of admonition from my man Lex. But if so, you'll be disappointed, because really for the first time in my life, someone got me! I was seventeen years old, and I knocked the old tea head on his ass! He praised my paper and read it to the class, celebrating my initiative to think outside the box. I'm sorry if this is a little braggadocio, but I believe this to be a noteworthy moment, the first tangible triumph of my nonconformity!

I had a good season of football, and then I was a smart-ass, and I got an A, and I was singled out by the teacher. Two accomplishments in seventeen years. By god, I was on my way.

Don't Be an Asshole

I find it consistently difficult to get around the notion that we are all, in our very natures, assholes. I am an asshole. I'm afraid you are also. That's why the conversation about good manners even exists in the first place. We're cognizant, curious beings, capable of philosophical thought, nuclear physics, repeating Nerf weapons, global consciousness, Glade air fresheners, and sentient automobiles. But we're assholes first.

This is because before we can begin to argue mortgage rates and tuition hikes, before we can roll up our sleeves and thread a perfusion catheter into the cholesterol-choked artery of today's society, we, every one of us, must first replenish our mammalian bodies with food and water, whilst establishing and maintaining a comfortable climate around our bodies through the employment of garments and heating/cooling systems. Before we can arrive at the office to resume our efforts to improve, say, worldwide Muslim-Christian relations or the infrastructure of the Haitian public utilities systems, we must commune and, more to the point, commute with thousands of other animals upon ever-increasingly crowded roadways and public transit vehicle systems. It is during these more basic, elemental steps in our day that we reveal our true colors. As assholes.

Our bodies tell us frequently, in no uncertain terms, to do things that society has deemed inappropriate, or, quite often, illegal. I'm talking about the animal voice deep inside us all that we've learned to repress through socialization. "Hey, Dave. Look at that ripe, young female cheering for the sports team. You should make some babies occur." Or "Excuse me, Jorge? That other family is in front of you in line at the Reuben Truck. Your own family could claim all of the delicious sandwiches and grow stronger if you simply kill that first family." We humans contain within us instinctual signals, influencing us toward the perpetuation of our species, specifically our own tribes or family units, often to the detriment of others. That's just how nature works. What's amazing is that we have largely contained these urges to the point of successfully checking out of a crowded Whole Foods without decapitating that crunchy, granola-haired hustler dude trying to squeak fourteen items through the express lane WHEN THE SIGN CLEARLY STATES "TWELVE ITEMS OR LESS." YOU THINK WE AREN'T ALL GOING TO BE COUNTING YOUR FUCKING ITEMS, BRO?! But we don't strike. We take a deep breath and feel better for another day of carnage-free foraging at the grocery store.

As civilization developed, we learned to establish some rules and guidelines—"laws," if you will—to convince ourselves that it's not right to heed these animal urges. "Okay, everybody, I know we used to just rip one another's throats out if we wanted to claim, say, a certain hunting territory for our own, but we're all deciding, in this new committee, or let's say 'congress,' we've formed, that that's not cool anymore. We're going to lay down some notions about personal property and the ways in which we can violate those notions, and we're going to establish some punishments to hopefully deter us from, you know, raping and killing one another. Mostly, the weak people."

Over the centuries, we have continued to evolve these notions so that every citizen receives a fair shake, and by god, we're still working on it. For you see, gentle reader, it's complicated. In a society where "to the victors go the spoils," it can be difficult for said victors to wrap their heads around fair treatment or "rights" for all the people, especially those who have been defeated or dominated in one sense or another.

For example: slavery. Although versions of slavery have been prevalent all over the world throughout history, I'll focus on American slavery during the last few centuries. We "Europeans" were caught up in a system that entailed the brutal, inhuman capture and transport of brown-skinned Africans to the United States, where they would be sold like work animals to perform labor in the fields and houses of farms and plantations. Full-on flagrant, fucked-up assholery. Unthinkable.

This horribly criminal system existed for hundreds of years before the white folks finally copped to its being not super cool. It took a long time for the whites to wrap their heads around the idea of sharing this nation (which, incidentally, was brutally stolen by them from the indigenous tribes) in equality with the dark-skinned people whom they had once owned like mules. How did this ever occur? Assholes. The rules were being made by assholes. These decisions were handed down from assholes on high and carried out by, you guessed it, assholes. So, thankfully, we got that bullshit straightened out on paper, but we're still trying to heal the wounds of that and countless other genocides and discriminations and ass-fuckings that we humans have handed one another over the years.

The early transgressions that our "laws" sought to prohibit involved a violating poleax or spear of one brand or another. Many crimes of action required a sharp bladed weapon with which to pierce the skin or property of the victim, or an actual penis, with which to violate another in the most intimate of breaches. By now, civilization has done, it must be said, a pretty stand-up job of reducing these more overt asshole moves with the promise of strict repercussions. Prison, death, what have you. Terrific. But, folks, we have got us a very long way to go.

I here proffer my opinion that we, the people, are still being raped on a daily basis, but it's a much longer, much slower fucking. The aggressors are the lobbyists for big tobacco and for guns and for pharmaceuticals and for agribusiness, and their filthy, turgid cocks are enormous, probing ram-shafts made of money.

But wait, I thought this book was a lighthearted look at living one's life deliciously? That's all well and good, fat boy, but you cannot just blithely drift through life in your canoe whilst turning a blind eye to the bullshit going on around you.

Really, all religious teachings can be boiled down to: "Just be cool. Don't be an asshole." The teachings of Jesus, of Muhammad, of Buddha, of Yahweh, Dionysus, Oprah, Yoda, and the rest. Confucius. All we need to be told is that we are all presented with a similar challenge in life, which is, "You will encounter tests every day. You can serve yourself, or you can serve others." Now, before I dive headfirst off a self-righteous cliff like a motherfucking juggernaut, let me point out that I count myself as not only a human, but a fucking American white guy with a decent brain and set of life skills, which means I am, by birthright, a major asshole. I come by it honest. It's the first rule of Fight Club. Admitting you're an asshole. Once I saw this truth and swallowed it, an excellent technique developed, one that I believe makes my life much more calm and much less desperate—therefore, much more *delicious*.

The technique is: Let the others go first. At the airport, at the grocery store, at the Pleasure Chest (hey-o!). The calmer I become, the more I enjoy my day. The more I enjoy my day, the more people enjoy me and the more they want to see me in my enjoyment. Eventually, they want to see me enjoying my day on the set of their film playing Holly Hunter's husband for Diablo Cody. BOOM. Turns out all I had to do was keep my cool.

I can hardly dive into this topic without immediately citing the storied heavy traffic of my hometown of sixteen years, Los Angeles, California. Crosstown trips continue to take longer and interminably longer with each passing year. In the arena of the streets of LA a great many motorists reveal themselves to be lacking in moral fiber. Their integrity is questionable at best to begin with, perhaps because Hollywood, more than any other American community, is the city of dreams. Los Angeles County is choking with these supplicants to glittering visions, like that of impressing one's handprints in the cement sidewalk outside of Mann's Chinese Theater or delivering a sexual pleasuring to a studio head. Of course, most of us will never realize even the first flirtation of such a lofty climax, and the frustration with that status quo can foment quite a bitter, impatient, aggressive driver.

I can speak to this sensation, as for my first years in LA, I felt like I was in an invisible queue, bombarded daily by reports of all the goddamn guys in front of me, succeeding by inches, wedging me out of TV pilots and film roles. When I learned to ignore the business and instead focus on woodworking and my LOVE LIFE, I merely calculated my drive time, adding a fifteen-minute cushion for chilling out, and Christ almighty, did my mood improve.

5

Walking Beans

Because I ended up his spitting image, my dad gets a lot of screen time (page time?) in this book. A lot of ink. But as a kid growing up in a very simple and happy household (which I learned later was a very modest one)—an honest, salt-of-the-earth household—my mom was also one of my heroes. Big time. It must be said that the ladies on any farm—the housewives and the farmer's daughters—are out there swinging the axe and the hoe with the fellows. It didn't occur to me until later how equally heroic, and perhaps even more so, the women of the farm were. Because at the time I saw the guys drive the tractors and thought, "Who's in that big goddamn tractor? The boss, that's who. That's what I want to do."

Around age eight or nine I began having "coffee with the guys." With plenty of milk and sugar and just a dollop of coffee, of course—I didn't start drinking it black until I was eleven or even older. As I mentioned previously, by a mere six months over my cousin Ryan I was the oldest grandson in the family. That did—and still does—make a difference on a farm. Of course, Ryan's folks, my uncle Dan and aunt Dee, were running the Roberts farm by then, so he had a distinct advantage in being a full-timer. I lived six or seven miles away, so I was a guest laborer.

At home, I was taken outside and taught to use the tools in a way the girls weren't. They learned possibly more valuable skills, cooking and feeding the family and sewing and whatnot. It was a very fair household, though. I did some cooking and sewing, and they cut some grass. We siblings and our cousins all had our turns baling hay and chopping firewood and making bean soup, but all I wanted to do was go out in the field and work with the guys.

The first step was to travel out to the crops and ride on or in the tractor and the combine with the guys, meaning Grandpa Mike, Uncles Dan and Don, and sometimes my dad. It was amazing. Pretty soon, Uncle Don would let me steer when we'd drive the tractor together. And when I could reach the pedals, he'd have me drive the combine. It felt like undergoing some sort of cowboy training right at home with my family. Uncle Don was always encouraging Ryan and me to drive, on a motorcycle, snowmobile, go-kart, truck, or tractor. I guess that's how you do it on a farm. You get next year's labor trained as soon as possible.

I hung around them and did everything I could. When Ryan and I were old enough to start earning wages, there were two things we could do. Number one is called, simply, "picking up rocks." There's not a lot of embellishment in that title. When you cultivate field dirt, you're constantly turning over the top foot or sixteen inches of the topsoil. As the earth continues to shift and erode, the larger stones constantly come to the surface.

When you're big enough to pick up rocks, you're sent out with a little tractor and a little cart and a buddy, and you canvass the entire field to pick up rocks and take them to the rock pile. One of the fun parts is that you find a lot of arrowheads and Indian artifacts. My uncle Dan has an amazing collection of arrowheads. He spots them from twenty feet up, on top of a combine, even though he has lousy eyesight. Both of my uncles have seemingly no end to their superhero abilities, and they're also full-on MacGyvers. They wear vise grips on their belts as well as about eighteen other tools about their person at all times.

The other remunerative chore one could perform was called "walking beans." I started walking beans in the late seventies. When soybeans are full grown they go up about to a child's sternum, but when they're half grown they only reach your thigh or your waist. You head out with a garden hoe or a machete, which we called a corn knife. Grandpa Mike taught you how to sharpen the steel blade with a file. You'd get a very strict safety lesson, because it's easy to lop off a toe or put a considerable dent in an ankle with a corn knife. We learned at a young age to respect machinery and sharp steel, an education that continues to serve me well in more than one of my walks in life.

We had a great crew on the Roberts farm once the grandchildren came of age: myself and Ryan, his older sister, Angie, and my big sis, Laurie. We would go out and walk beans. Uncle Don, who was then in his late teens, would be the captain of the walking-beans team, and we'd sometimes bring in a neighborhood friend or two from the local families to round out our numbers. We got paid, but I can't remember how much. People from my dad's generation would remember the details, I'm sure, because they grew up much nearer to the Depression. They remember what they got paid for any job, down to the penny. I don't, to my detriment, remember our starting wage in 1981. We were probably making a dollar an hour, a considerable improvement over zero dollars an hour, and so nickel raises were a big deal.

By August it was a buck twenty-five. On Sunday after church, if you could afford a Snickers bar and a Coke at Ralph Hibner's Grocery Store in town and still have sixty-five cents in your pocket? That was walking in pretty tall cotton.

We walked beans and I loved it. I was out in the sun (or rain, at least until it got too muddy) all day, walking up and down the field. We would take a crew of six, and each person would take four rows on either side. We'd then walk all the way down the length of the field, hustling to try to keep up with the older kids, and simply kill the weeds with a hoe or a knife.

Certain weeds, if you could, you'd pull them, roots and all. There were promiscuous weeds called buttonweeds and milkweeds that were very prevalent. In the soybean field you also run into a lot of corn, because the crops are switched over, so maybe last year's corn left some random seed in the ground. Then there was black night-shade (such a satisfyingly evil name), which we would do our best to pull out by the roots if we could. Some weeds are so tenacious that they grow to seem like a small tree in a matter of weeks, stealing precious sunlight and water from your crop. Even if we'd cut them off at the ground they'd grow back in a week. Generally speaking, there were different degrees of death and dismemberment that were doled out to the weeds, commensurate with that weed's ability to inflict damage on our soybeans.

At the end of the row, there would be a cooler jug with water or lemonade, and all things considered, it was a good time. I think many modern urbanites would find this activity repugnant or even impossible, but in our family we always had the ability to tuck into tedious work with a positive attitude and the knowledge that a cold soda pop or beer was waiting at quitting time.

Walking beans evolved into something even more idyllic over the years. Uncle Don got us this huge steel bar that attached to the front of a tractor that had maybe—I want to guess—four seats on the twenty-foot bar, two on each side of a thirty-gallon tank. Each seat had a spray gun on a hose, connected to the tank, which contained a minor herbicide. So walking beans became shooting beans. The guns had adjustable nozzles that you could set to "spray" or "stream," so we became sharpshooters. They'd just come out with Roundup herbicide, which has turned out to be the bane of biology, but even in '84 or so, we knew enough to keep it in a separate little bottle. We'd reserve it for plants like jimsonweed or black nightshade, and—this is how scary this shit is—we would just place ONE DRIP on one leaf of a weed as we drove by on the bean bar, and when we came back around the loop maybe ten minutes later, that plant would be a shriveled corpse. The stuff is like napalm for plants.

Maybe by the time you read this book, we'll have finally voted that poison out of our fields, but something sadly tells me it's going to take rather longer.

Thus walking beans was now riding the bean bar. We would take turns driving the charismatic, old Minneapolis Moline 602 tractor from the sixties, which Uncle Don kept in perfect running order.

Our fields were twelve miles apart, so at some point one of us would have to drive the tractor twelve miles. The 602 does twenty-five, tops, on the road. So I'd be on a tractor, everybody passing me, waving, and I'd be out in the sun with the wind in my hair, some Doobie Brothers on the ancient radio. I've never been happier than just getting to drive farm equipment between fields. Being out in the weather was such an incredible part of engaging in the privilege of rewarding work. Even if it was raining, we'd just work in the rain.

After weeks in the July and August humidity, it could be mighty refreshing. Working outside instilled a toughness in me, my siblings, and my cousins that I'll always be thankful for.

It was hard work, sure, but I don't remember any shortage of playing baseball or going swimming. Jumping in the pond was that much more delicious when you'd been out working in the sun all day. And I had sixteen dollars in my pocket to boot. Six or seven of those days and I could buy a motherfucking Walkman. To arrive at the age at which you could buy a Walkman and the new George Michael record on cassette with your own earnings—if that wasn't heaven, I don't know what was. Although I wish, in hindsight, that somebody had pointed out Talking Heads to me.

Throughout the years, Ryan and I especially enjoyed each other's company, and walking beans was a way to spend all day together. We'd screw around just enough to have a blast, but just little enough to still do a good job in the bean field.

Ryan and I really benefited from being the young men in our farming circle. We were attempting to come across as "good-looking" teenagers, which means we *thought* we looked awesome, but we really looked a bit like teenagers trying too hard, especially me. Ryan was always the more modest and decent of the two of us, and now he's a paramedic, and I'm full of shit for a living. Amazing.

In the summer we would sell sweet corn at a stand near the main intersection in town. We'd put Sun-In in our hair and listen to music and hope that girls would come by to buy a dozen ears for their family dinner. You can bet your ass we gave them a baker's dozen. It was a dream life. A couple of times during the harvest season (also the homecoming season, lucky for us), the cheerleaders would hold a car wash at the nearby gas station. It goes without saying we were happy as pigs in shit.

Eventually, as we grew into our teen years, Ryan and I started running the walking beans crew. We became autonomous, because we had the system down. Sometimes it was just the two of us, sometimes we had a crew of six. We spent a lot of time by ourselves in the field.

It was 1984 or 1985, and break dancing was becoming a huge sensation all over the country. Unfortunately, we really had a hard time finding appropriate music in Minooka. I'll remind you this is decades before the Internet, let alone the iPod, but we were aware of the whole movement because of the break-dancing movies we could rent at the video store. We just couldn't find the music for sale. Our favorites were Grandmaster Flash, Run-DMC, Melle Mel, Newcleus and songs like "Rapper's Delight" and "Jam on It." We knew that in the cities this exciting new culture was happening, but we were just too far removed to even begin to know how to get to where it was. We'd listen to these late-night radio shows out of Chicago on which they'd play break-dancing music, and we'd record tracks off the radio onto what were quickly rendered our most prized cassettes.

Ryan and I had a two-man break-dance team that would practice in his basement, in front of a mirror, on the requisite large sheet of cardboard. We'd take our fly stylings to the Channahon skating rink on weekends and take part in competitions. We had break-dancing names—I was Tick-Tock and he was Flip-Flop. Tick-Tock was named because of my propensity for popping and locking, and Flip-Flop did flips and the hard moves on the floor, like the helicopter and whatnot. We dabbled with a cool team name like "the Minooka Crew," but I don't think we ever had a name that stuck. For some strange reason, we never could fully reconcile our farm flavor with the hardscrabble aesthetic of inner-city street dancing.

Out in the fields we would write raps about ourselves, touting our prowess and our manhood. How our dope-ass moves would attract the ladies like bees to honey. In hindsight it was really funny (I'm told), but it was sincerely a big part of our coming-of-age. We carried ourselves at school like some kinda badass street thugs, like we knew the ways of subway trains and the back alleys of Harlem.

It was a quick phase, though. It came and went like our parachute pants. We each had one pair of said pants, from Sears or Chess King, perhaps, and we'd accessorize like Michael Jackson and Adam Ant. Of course, we inexplicably drew the line before donning the scarves and bracelets of Boy George and George Michael (because their effeminacy was somehow more girly than Michael Jackson's? Or Adam Ant's?). There were other dudes wearing bangles, but they were okay because they were New Wave, which, again, could be tough to pull off. A Flock of Seagulls? Duran Duran? Kajagoogoo? These are guesses. I don't know much about New Wave. The Smiths? Lots of people dug them, but I never did hear them, at least not at the time. Before I wander too far afield, I had better get back to my element. The break dance.

Our parents were really very generous about it. We would show them our moves and routines. They understood that even though they didn't appreciate the break-dancing movement, we were exhibiting prowess. Ryan's mom and dad, Dan and Dee, had undertaken an earlier disco phase, after all.

Many years later, in 2006, I did a show on Comedy Central called *American Body Shop*. Pete Hulne, who is a great, underappreciated

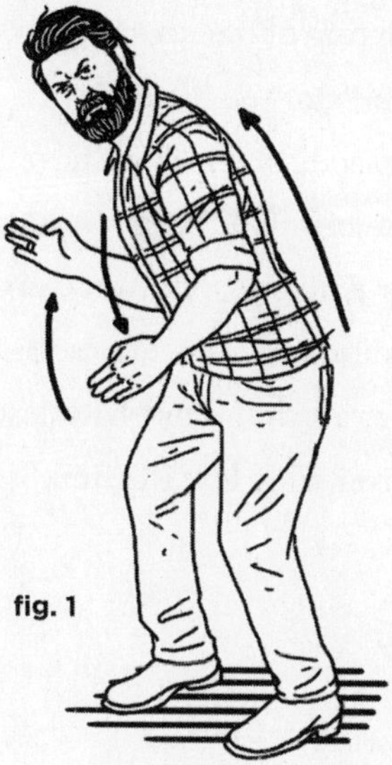

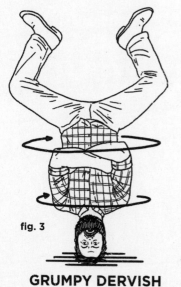

fig. 1

C-4PO

fig. 2

PERINEUM'S BANE

fig. 3

GRUMPY DERVISH

fig. 4

THE PIGFUCKER

BREAK DANCING

comedy actor, and I had both brooked a very similar break-dance experience in the eighties, and late in the shooting of our series, we realized it. I was astonished: "Wait, hold the phone. You break?"

So we convinced the team to write an episode in which we have a rather middle-aged break-dance competition. We were in our midthirties and quickly learned that this dancing style was very much a young man's game. I could pop and lock, but I could no longer get on the floor and execute the spinning moves. I may have lost a step, but I also discovered that one can never truly lose the funk.

Work Hard, Work Dirty

Choose your favorite spade and dig a small, deep hole, located deep in the forest or a desolate area of the desert or tundra. Bury your cell phone and then find a hobby.

Actually, *hobby* is not a weighty enough word to represent what I'm trying to get across. Let's use *discipline* instead. If you engage in a discipline or do something with your hands instead of kill time on your phone device, then you have something to show for your time when you're done. Cook, play music, sew, carve. Shit, BeDazzle. Maybe not BeDazzle.

The arithmetic is quite simple. Instead of playing Draw Something, fucking draw something! Take the cleverness you apply to Words with Friends and utilize it to make some kick-ass corn bread. Corn Bread with Friends—try that game.

I'm here to tell you that we've been duped on a societal level. My favorite writer, Wendell Berry, writes on this topic with great eloquence. He posits that we've been sold a bill of goods, claiming that work is bad, that sweating and working, especially if soil or sawdust is involved, are beneath us. Our population, especially the urbanites, has largely forgotten that working at a labor that one loves is actually a privilege. To be on the receiving end of this gift of a life complete with human body, mind, and heart is to be indescribably blessed indeed, but all of our conveniences and comforts and amazing technological advances have made us completely soft and fully pusillanimous! If a person can simply discern what it is that he/she loves to do with an eight-to-ten-hour day, then a satisfying workday is easily attained.

When asked for advice at colleges, I always give this as my main tenet: "Figure out what you love to do, then figure out how to get paid to do it."

I have lived a somewhat double life between my beginnings in small-town Illinois and storefront Chicago theater and the much more "fashionable" urban intelligentsia in Los Angeles and New York. But in all of these communities, I have known a sizable percentage of people to spend a great deal of their leisure time in front of a screen, be it television, computer, video game, or smartphone. I have also known a somewhat smaller percentage of people who make things in their spare time: artists and craftspeople. Some are full-time fabricators of, say, jewelry, or songs, and some work in an office all day, then come home to paint turtles in calming blue and green seascapes.

I'm not a scholar, and I'm not about to compile an impressive set of statistics for you. I'm just going to proffer this opinion: The people making stuff are generally less wealthy but much happier overall. Less bored, less bitter, more satisfied. The trick is to flush out decades of conditioning by advertisers. We have been taught to watch the media channels and thereby determine how to spend our time and money. Wondering which car to buy? Take a walk and seventeen billboards will tell you which model you prefer. "Do you like pretty women with orblike breasts and a mouthful of pearly white Chiclets? Then, buddy, you're going to love our SUVs, jeans, cheeseburgers, hair dyes, English muffins, and insurance policies!"

The secret is to turn a blind eye to all of that information and look to the billboard in your head. What does it tell you? Mine says, "Hey, Jasper. You should build a kayak and then paddle it in the ocean."

I have come to recognize the extreme value of this message. If I will adhere to its instruction and commit to some months of boatbuilding, I will be feeding my soul a hearty meal of satisfying hand-skill development and execution, appreciation for centuries of cumulative design, and finally, countless hours of reverie in nature, quietly paddling along the coast and enjoying the sea lions, dolphins, caves, and quiet. Not only that, but as soon as I immerse myself in a project, my focus makes it impossible for me to give any attention to the channels of popular culture. Diaper commercials are still accosting the population, but I can neither see nor hear them.

Right now in my community of friends, I count a sculptor who makes human-shaped mountain ranges and then clads them in tiny facets of different-colored linoleum. Another winning gal creates taxidermy animals skinned in camouflage fabric. Another woodworker buddy just made a stool for a modern witch with a hole in the middle of it. Beneath the hole hangs a cauldron in which herbs are stewed and the medicinal steam rises to engender health in the female sitter's reproductive neighborhood. I know a brilliant guy who moved into a decrepit old pipe foundry and learned to smelt and pour enormous bronze statues. My buddy Corn Mo writes gorgeous rock operas and shoots little stop-motion movies. Another pal does needlepoint samplers with a quaint picture of a chick emerging from its cracked eggshell, with the words *Fuck Off* embroidered in a lovely period font worthy of Laura Ingalls Wilder.

Many of these pastimes could be considered strange by the general public, but nobody's asking the public. NOBODY'S ASKING THE PEOPLE WHAT THEY THINK. That's such a nefarious social paranoia—"What will people say?" WHO FUCKING CARES? We engage in these activities because it's what we feel like doing. It's our reaction to modern society, to our time and place, and it is extremely healthy to our dispositions. It's remunerative nonconformity. We are all still aware of television and film and music—in fact we love them—but as an occasional treat between projects rather than how we fill our spare time.

Also, if you love music, there is no better way to indulge in it than by playing it at a healthy volume while you shave a canoe paddle or oil a slab dining table. "Hey, hey, my, my," reverberates in my marrow because of the hours I've spent working hard with that album as enervating score. (Neil Young, *Rust Never Sleeps*, of course.)

Another way to address this idea is to fill one's life with the opportunity for seeing solid, real-life results as opposed to virtual. In my opinion, all of the "living" that people do online, in social networks, elaborate multiplayer games, blogs, and so on, is often merely the facsimile of real life, and so it is ultimately unsatisfying. I'm not speaking in absolutes here, for there is clearly a lot of value in social networking. Even my canoe work is enhanced by the ability to commune with other boatbuilders in online forums, asking and answering questions in areas of specialty that would have been inscrutable a mere ten years ago. What I'm addressing more specifically with this writing is how easy it is for we funny monkeys to waste our precious time on these convenient gadgets. I have always liked to carry a book with me, so during a lull at the dentist's office, or the bus stop, I have something to do that I have chosen. I know that if I'm stuck with only my smartphone, I'll simply browse the unlimited possibilities made available, with no perceivable result beyond providing a diversion for my attention. That's the rub. I would rather get something done.

It's important to me, when I finish any pursuit, to be able to look back at my work and see a tangible result. Obviously, when I complete a canoe paddle, I can hold it and feel it and use it and thereby know the value of the time I spent making it. When I write a song and perform it for an audience and they (hopefully) laugh, I can see and feel the result of my efforts. Beyond that, I feel like the relationships I maintain in my life are so much more satisfying when I am interfacing with my friends and loved ones face-to-face, rather than by text or even telephone.

Social occasions with family and friends are golden treasures, as are leisure-time activities, which for me include fishing, hiking, going to a film or play or art show, playing cards with Megan or my family, or reading. Treating yourself to such desserts is an important part of balancing the meal of your time, so that the entrée of your vocation, your calling, gets its due in a healthy proportion.

In my Minooka, Illinois, family; my theater companies (Chicago's Defiant and LA's Evidence Room); my Offerman Woodshop; and now in the cast and crew of my current job at *Parks and Recreation*, there has always been a strong foundation of mutual love cultivated by the implicit understanding that we would all work hard together to achieve some communal goal, be it a fellowship of healthy households and children, a refreshingly original piece of theater, or a quality television program rife with laughter, heart, and intelligence. I'll tell you how I pick people to work with me, and I get this from my dad's teaching of fundamentals. I just give a prospective apprentice a broom and tell them to sweep. The quality of the job they do tells me a great deal about them. Attention to detail, willingness to go the extra mile, pace, fastidiousness, or lack thereof. If you can, hire the gal or guy who moves the furniture and rugs to sweep beneath them. Their work speaks directly of their desire to contribute to the well-being of the community. They know how to do a job right.

There's no denying that many of the opportunities that have come my way over the years came partially thanks to my willingness to work hard. It's been said that luck is when opportunity meets with preparation, so I will always remember to thank my teachers and taskmasters for giving me the necessary preparation to get goddamn lucky, time and time again.

6

Carnalisthenics

As discussed earlier in this tome, I have nothing bad to say about organized religion in general. I think it's a good idea to congregate once a week in order to remind ourselves of the rules of etiquette that we have established as a society over the years, rules like "Don't kill one another" and "Don't steal one another's shit." This is good. A wholesome practice.

The instance in which religious matters raise my ire is when they cross over out of the doors of the church and into my secular world. I was raised Catholic, and I flirted (and scored) with born-again Christianity as a teenager. I have learned and, yes, profited spiritually from a great deal of Christian doctrine in my life, and I still do. The exact same way in which I have profited from the knots I learned in Boy Scouts, tetherings that still serve me admirably to this day, in securing the implements of my life with the purpose of bearing an ample load.

However, church-wise, I wasn't ever really what you would call a "believer," and ever since I could think for myself, from around age thirteen or so, I've been what you would call an "agnostic," which is a person who doesn't have the temerity to claim knowledge of any specific godlike entity such as the "God" suggested in the Bible.

I like faith. I dig hope, everybody. I'm not an asshole, at least as much as I can help it. I love my neighbor as myself; I get it. Whatsoever I do to the least of my brethren, I do unto Jesus. You bet. Indiana Jones identified the crappy chalice as the vessel of Jesus, because that's the cup of a lowly carpenter. The dogma of Western organized religion is not particularly tough to wrap one's head around, and most of it has its heart in the right place.

So in conclusion, given the miles I've logged, I'm going to go ahead and suggest that you maintain a relationship with Jesus Christ . . . if it is getting you hot sex.

What could I possibly mean by this, you might wonder? Let me inform you. The reason I momentarily dabbled in born-again Christianity, exhibiting a most ardent love of the Savior, is simple. It's because I was obsessed with this cheerleader from Yorkville, who was also a born-again Christian. Hot, right? Wickedly hot.

We became acquainted at the Louis Joliet Mall, the Cookie Factory to be specific, when I was a sophomore. Lynette. She would come over some nights, and we would indulge in Offerman family-favorite videos like *The Sound of Music* and *The Quiet Man*. I was smitten. The only hitch was, one had to become "born again" to date her, which would have been insane. So I did not hesitate to do just that.

I went to the Joliet Christian Youth Center with Lynette and made friends with the other teenagers. I'd say the ratio of kids using Christianity as a cover for illicit activities to kids actually engaging in the sincere worship of our Savior was about three to one. There were drunks and stoners, dope pushers, and, of course, plenty of puberts like myself. A pubert is simply a teenager, usually male, experiencing puberty so virulently that he is hallucinating perverted sexual fantasies all the livelong day. Hence *pubert*.

We would gather in the "fun club" area to play pinball and shoot pool, indulging all the while in cookies and lemonade. Then at the appointed hour, we'd gather and sit in an audience in a small auditorium, usually thirty or forty strong, and listen to a "cool" adult (their nicknames let us know they were okay, like *Smudge* or *Harv*, and to be fair, they were actually pretty excellent) talk about some scripture, very much like a priest reading the gospel and then sermonizing.

Sometimes other kids would get up and "witness," which entailed describing a scene in which they'd had the opportunity to "share the word" with some other lost children, perhaps at the McDonald's or at the football game. "Hey, guys, can I talk to you about the fact that you're going to *hell*?"

On occasion the performer would tear up and the auditorium would be profoundly moved by the recounting of the youngster's attempt at shoving his/her religion down some poor stranger's throat at the mall. Or sometimes the witnessing would just involve the description of a scene in which the supplicant was visitationed by the Lord in some way. You know, as in a miracle? Young Julie was sitting on a footbridge and the sunlight dappled the water in just such a way that she was momentarily blinded, when she suddenly heard a voice inside her head, telling her that she was okay and that Jesus' love was really where it's at.

Once a month or so, kids would be invited to come down to the front and be "saved." This involved a lot of group histrionics, as each teenager gave his or herself over to the saving love of the Lamb of God after a lifetime of depravity and darkness. This "saving" is the moment when you are "born again," washed clean in the cleansing love of Jesus

Christ, etc. Most of us waited until some attention hound put on a big, dramatic show, and then we'd follow them to the front, where we could usually just answer the question "Do you accept the Lord Jesus as your personal Savior?!" with a "You bet your ever-lovin' tits I do!" It was moblike behavior that is most commonly described as "cultish."

So, I got saved and Lynette and I began to chastely date, and after four or five months of devout prayer, song, and fellowship, as you may have by now surmised, we began to fuck. To really get down low and rut like demonic beasts. I was fifteen, she was sixteen, and, by Jesus, we were engaging in fornication.

The first time was in my friend Ed's canoe on the Aux Sable Creek in Grundy County. Ed was not present. We were naked in the dappled, golden sunlight. Yes we were. Were we hearing the planets grind slickly through their orbits? That is indeed what we heard. Was it awkward and clumsy as shit? You bet your ass it was. The canoe is traditionally a very easy boat to capsize, but I am proud to report that ours remained upright throughout all of our carnal calisthenics, or carnalisthenics, only to be dumped over by me after our mortal sin had been notched onto the Lord's paddle, or I guess Satan's paddle. Whichever one of those characters is paddling in the stern (is it any wonder that I have grown to become obsessed with building wooden canoes and luxuriously running my hands along their hulls?).

Our coupling continued with an intense regularity for months and years. Mm. Ahem. If any of you are still young enough to get involved in this kind of heated tryst, I cannot recommend it highly enough. The secret ingredients are sinful anticipation and Christian guilt. Every night she would come over after teaching dance to six-year-olds, sweaty in her leotard, and we would kneel on the living room floor, directly beneath my soundly sleeping parents' bedroom. Because, again, being a born-again couple is the perfect cover for getting away with any iniquities you care to indulge in. ("Mom, Dad, Lynette and I are going to Bible camp for three weeks in Wisconsin." "Okay, sounds good. Gosh, Ric, we sure did something right with this guy. Bible camp!" We would then go to camp, where we would participate in camp activities, like the Jesus log-roll, the Jesus potato-sack race, the Jesus hammer throw, then we'd go sixty-nine in the woods for two hours. Get saved. It's genius.)

Every night, kneeling there on my mother's carpet, face-to-face, we would pray for the strength to abstain from the juicy copulation we so cravenly craved, all the while drinking deep of each other's musk and withstanding the trembling of our lascivious flesh. Our prayers were so sincere and devout that they often elicited tears (not to mention a rather unyielding boner). We would cry. We would pray. And then we would fuck. We would scrump and munch upon each other with ravenous, animal abandon. We did every unholy thing we could possibly think of to each other, on every inch of every piece of furniture.

Sorry, my two sisters, if you're reading this, I know that's where you liked to nap. No longer. That ottoman has been defiled. Granny's afghan has been, in a word, copiously befouled. Let's not forget that teenagers are a limber bunch, with exceptional constitutions. I shudder now to think of the endurance we would exhibit in these Grundy County rug sessions before finally petering out. And then we would cry again. We would pray for forgiveness and hope that we could resist each other tomorrow night. And then sometimes we'd go again. So, yes, I love me some Jesus Christ.

*　　*　　*

To say that I had gotten myself in deep could be considered a significant understatement. When the two of us finally went away to the University of Illinois, we learned that our chosen lifestyle did not exactly blend, especially for me, into the confederacy of hedonists and Freemasons with which I found myself surrounded. Arriving in the theater department as I had, with a born-again long-term girlfriend on my arm, I could hardly just denounce her and the Lord and hope to retain any sort of face with my newfound peers. So I began to slowly and painfully extract myself from the situation like an oak splinter coming ponderously free from deep in one's palm.

Lynette did the same, to be honest. Small-town life had been, among other things, incredibly insular for us, and arriving in the bustling metropolis of Champaign–Urbana was culture shock enough to jar us soundly away from each other. I got lucky (I get lucky quite a bit), for there was a senior in the theater department named Mary who also happened to be on the fence about her status as a Christian and who also happened to be cute as a button. Mary and I picked up the quadrille where Lynette and I had left it off, wrestling with the opposing forces of lust and religious ardor. Literally. She wouldn't go all the way, but she would stand on the porch and sometimes leave a basket of baked goods on the mat, to make a figure of speech.

Our tryst was an appropriate stepping down from my full-on teenage circus, and I am grateful that Mary was there to ease my reentry into the world of reality. She ended up dumping me to run off and marry her preacher ex-boyfriend Todd. I hope she found happiness, because she was torn up about taking that plunge when she left. I know I certainly found it when I fully fell into the embrace of my theater school compatriots, but not before Lynette and I had one final chapter. We'll save that for dessert.

Leviticus Can Blow Me

As I have asserted, much of the Bible holds excellent lessons in the pursuit of modesty and living as a straight shooter, but I would invite you all to investigate the WHOLE DOCUMENT. Leviticus, for example, is commonly referred to as "easily the most fucked-up book in the Old Testament."

I believe it was none other than the Lord God Almighty who instructed us to "Love thy neighbor as thyself." Wise words from the King of Kings. Unfortunately, he spake this phrase smack-dab in the middle of the book of Leviticus, and I think we can all agree by now that when it comes to writers of books of the Bible, the Leviticus scribes are about as nutty as a tree full of squirrels. For example, Leviticus is the book that prescribes all of the punishments for women made "unclean" by menstruation. That's right. When a lady's "flowers be upon her," linens must be destroyed, chairs must be burned—you get the idea. We're then told that these women can be "exonerated by bringing an offering of two turtles to the priest at the temple." Some translations have it as two doves, which is also quite bizarre, but turtles? WTF? I think this is a perfect illustration of the integrity of the Bible in toto, specifically in regards to its applicability (or lack thereof) to modern issues.

Leviticus is also merely but one of the chapters in "the good book" that enlighten us to the fact that homosexuality is an "abomination" (New International Version). "If a man has sexual relations with a man as one does with a woman, both of them have done what is detestable. They are to be put to death; their blood will be on their own heads." Leviticus 20:13. This passage tells us that our fellow human beings should be killed, basically, for engaging in an act of love. Um. Ridiculous and upsetting? No shit, and then some. "Put to death"? Really? Seems just a bit over-the-top, but at least people are finally starting to realize that. If two people want to love each other and build a life together, I say more power to them. Let's encourage solid, loving households with open-minded policy, and perhaps we'll foster a new era of tolerance in which we can turn our attention to actual issues that need our attention, like, I don't know, killing/bullying the citizens of other nations to maintain control of their oil? What exactly was Jesus' take on violent capitalism?

I also have some big ideas for changing the way we think about literary morals as they pertain to legislation. Rather than suffer another attempt by the religious right to base our legalese upon the Bible, I would vote that we found it squarely upon the writings of J. R. R. Tolkien. The citizens of Middle Earth had much more tolerant policies in their governing bodies. For example, Elrond was chosen to lead the elves at Rivendell not only despite his androgynous nature but most likely because of the magical leadership inherent in a well-appointed bisexual elf wizard. That's the person you want picking shit out for your community. That's the guy you want in charge. David Bowie or a Mormon? Not a difficult equation.

Was Elrond in a gay marriage? We don't know, because it's none of our goddamn business. Whatever the nature of his elvish lovemaking, it didn't affect his ability to lead his community to prosperity and provide travelers with great directions. We should be encouraging love in the home place, because that makes for happier, stronger citizens. Supporting domestic solidity can only create more satisfied, invested patriots. No matter what flavor that love takes. I like blueberry myself.

Speaking of flavors, here's the deal—the sexual orientation of a human being is just that. An orientation. It's not like a faucet that can be turned on and off. It's the plumbing itself. The plumbing exists, built into the structure of the house, and is not adjustable. Sure, a body can choose *how much* hot or cold water to express from the plumbing, but the nature of the water itself, hot or cold, sulfurous or redolent of iron, cannot be adjusted from the faucet.

When a person chooses a flavor of, let's say, pie, that human is not choosing their preferred filling lightly. Flavor choice is based upon one's biology, which, in case you've forgotten, happens to be SCIENCE. My own body speaks to me very clearly, in no uncertain terms, about blueberry, and also about pecan, and sometimes the conversation will detour into key lime. My orientation toward one flavor over another is not based upon whimsy or caprice. It is instead directed toward the comestible that my tongue and my belly instruct me to consume. The debate over the semantics of "preference" versus "orientation" is utter nonsense, and if you even suggest to me that one might "pray the gay away," I will kick you soundly in your nuts or your juice box, just like I believe Jesus would have.

Gay people are for real. They are part of our group. That is, "all of the people." When we discriminate against them for their plumbing, we are in the wrong. Let's not forget all of the other atrocities we have mistakenly inflicted upon our brothers and sisters in the human race across history, based upon race or gender or hair color, for Christ's sake. A homosexual has every chance of contributing to our community as a solid citizen just as respectably as a heterosexual, and also of being just as big of an asshole as a straight person. The reason for this is because they are all merely citizens. As long as our purportedly "free" country continues to discriminate against them, in the category of same-sex marriage rights and in general, we will continue to be total dicks. I can spy no distinction between denying two loving people equal marriage rights and refusing to let a black person drink from the same water fountain as white folks. Both are examples of We the People shitting the bed in regards to defending each and every person's inalienable rights. This wrong stems from centuries of tradition based on fear, and I comprehend that, but I am encouraging us all to take a deep breath and have the guts to give everybody a fair shake.

The flagrant double standard espoused in Leviticus should surely be enough evidence for us to take the Bible's trustworthiness out of the equation. When I am instructed by the all-knowing Jehovah to profess an ostensibly "equal" brotherly love within the same pages where I am instructed to murder my fellow man or woman for engaging in a love act, I can't help but look elsewhere for guidance. I am choosing to enlist instead the book of my own common sense.

7

Enter Dionysus

Wendell Berry talks about some of the detriments the secondary education system holds for our youth in regards to teaching our young people to work at a vocation they love. He asserts that we've created a system in which if you want to make a certain salary, you are required to go to college. So our young people think less of working with their hands, which is seldom if ever presented as a viable option. I can't argue with his call for change, especially in this day and age, when a person could be apprenticed at a trade, like that of cobbler or sawyer, whilst still devouring all the information they might care to consume from the Internet or books.

My generation certainly had the mind-set that in order to get a "good job," one had to attend college, but what I've learned since is that many of these so-called good jobs are just a sentencing to a sort of cubicle soul-death with a paycheck attached. That kind of life sounds like pure hell to me. Fortunately, I make my living primarily as an actor, which is what I went to college to study, so in my case, the theory worked. Utilizing my college instruction in the history and the techniques of the theater, as well as my wits, some gumption, and the seats of several pairs of pants (oh, and also a healthy serving of good luck), I have been able to ride my actor's training to a healthy life full of bounty, BUT . . .

There were many years in which I earned little more than peanuts as an actor (the Steppenwolf Theatre actually paid us in almonds, with macadamias on two-show days—always a cut above their competition), and in which I earned more of my living with my tools and the labor of my hands. The skills required by the labor that provided me with my food and rent, both during college and for most of the decade to follow, were learned not in a classroom, but in the yard, in the garage, in the shed, and on construction sites.

When your folks tell you to "make sure you have something to fall back on," don't take it lightly. There are many modern schools of thought and action by which one can educate oneself to conduct some remunerative activity or other, often without the necessity of a crippling college price tag. Good food for thought.

All that said, back in 1987, when I was asked by my elders and my high school to begin the process of choosing a college, I never paused to consider that I might not go to college. It was a foregone conclusion, the only questions being "Which college?" and "What major?" My grades were good but my budget limited, so I was looking pretty exclusively at state schools. I hoped to attend the University of Illinois at Urbana-Champaign, as it was generally the best of several quality choices. I didn't even consider a city school. Less than an hour to the northeast, Chicago might as well have been Oz at this point, a terrifying metropolis, which rendered places like New York and LA entirely out of the reality of the moment.

Furthermore, the pursuit of any aspect of the arts was not on the list of possibilities presented me by our school's guidance counselor, Mr. Juan, whom I would describe in more detail, but as he chain-smoked in his office while one sat with him, marinating together in a thick, poisonous smog, I never did really get a good look at him.

My main interests of the day were playing the saxophone and performing in plays. Neither of those choices came up on the ballot of potential college majors. In fact, nobody in my entire sphere, nor my parents' spheres, had ever attempted a career in the arts by any stretch of the imagination. One local man had studied music in college and gone on to become a high school band teacher, so that was the clear extent of the realm of possibility in the eyes of my adult guides. These were people who had enjoyed responsible lives by playing it safe. They had no idea what to do with a teenager hell-bent on making what seemed to be an entirely jackass move, and I was absolutely stymied by the lack of options. I was beginning to consider agricultural law, as I liked farming, and as my dad put it, I had a good line of bullshit.

As she has many times in my forty-two years, Fate swept in to save my newly hairy caboose. I was visiting the U of I down in Champaign with Lynette, who was auditioning for their dance department. Loitering in the hallway while she pirouetted in a classroom, I happened to meet two students in the acting conservatory program there. THE MOTHERFUCKING WHAT, NOW?!!!

"Yes, we study acting in plays."

"And then what?"

"Well, we hope to work professionally in Chicago, in live theater."

"Excuse me. You're telling me that a person can get paid to perform in plays in Chicago? Like it was London or some shit?"

"Yes. I mean, it's not easy. You don't get rich doing it, but you can make a living. By the way, you're not supposed to be hanging out in here."

"Oh, okay. Sorry. Thank you!"

Their names were David Coronado and Jennifer McCarthy, and if

I see them again, I will buy them a pony, and if they like, I will gently kill and clean the pony and serve it to them in a lavish feast, with a potato dish of their choosing. Or, alternatively, we can ride the pony to a nice restaurant, where I will fete them with a hardy repast, including beverage service, dessert, coat check, and valet charge.

What I mean to say is that I'm in their debt. That momentary chat in the hallway of the Krannert Center for the Performing Arts, which was to become the foundry in which this young performer would forge his inconsistent and unwieldy steel and then begin to test its mettle, was possibly the biggest turning point in all my tender years.

It took some pretty sincere cajoling on my part, convincing Mom and Dad to let me audition for the program at the U of I. They had been incredibly supportive of my outlandish ideas up to this point in time, but this was truly frightening to them. It was as though I had come home and informed them that I wanted to study wizardry so that I might travel into alternate dimensions and commune with Lord Morpheus in his studies of the alchemy of sleep and, more importantly, of dreaming. Sweet dreaming.

Ultimately, my father told me that I always seemed to find a way to prosper at whatever it was I chose to pursue, so they would get behind this nonsense as well, BUT THAT I SHOULD MAKE SURE THAT I HAD SOMETHING TO FALL BACK ON.

Having never prepared a proper audition, I turned to my school librarian, Mrs. Kinsella, for help. She was a fan of plays and readily provided me with the two requisite "contrasting" monologues for which the audition called. I later learned a few key errors that we made in our preparations: that the term *monologue*, specifically the "mono" portion, refers to *one* person speaking a paragraph or more of text, and also that *contrasting* means, say, a comedy piece, like Neil Simon or Christopher Durang, paired with maybe a dramatic speech, like Ibsen or Chekhov. Shepard and Shakespeare. Molière and Mamet. Contrasting. If it was furniture it might be a Nakashima coffee table and a Queen Anne highboy. Nailed it! (Only figuratively—neither piece of furniture requires nails.)

What we *did* prepare was a speech from *The Elephant Man*, in truth an actual monologue, delivered by Dr. Treves to his colleagues, describing in some medical detail the deformities with which John Merrick was afflicted. Gripping stuff, eh? I have no idea why we thought that was a good idea, but it actually was nothing short of brilliant when held up to my other choice.

My second selection was a SCENE OF DIALOGUE between two characters from the 1970 Bruce Jay Friedman play *Steambath*, which opened in New York on June 30, just four days after my birth. The play depicts the afterlife as a steambath in which the attendant is God. The scene I chose was between God and an old-timer (played by Hector Elizondo and TV's Conrad Bain, respectively), and I simply turned my head from side to side to denote which character was speaking. Accompanied, of course, by some undoubtedly spot-on dialect work and physicality. Christ. I imagine it was one of the more interesting choices for a monologue they had witnessed, although I am equally certain that I was far from the only ignorant jackass plying his troth to the assembled theater faculty.

I also wrote an essay and underwent an interview, during which I described my self-admitted ignorance in the field, my work ethic, and my burning desire to become as effective a performer as really anyone on *The Dukes of Hazzard*. They could tell, I'm sure, that I had a hard time finding my ass with both hands theatrically, but also that I was very athletic and could use tools. Now, I don't know if you get to the theater much—chances are, you don't (you really should, it's worth it)—but a couple of times in every theater's yearly season, there will fall a couple of larger productions requiring a bigger cast of players and no small amount of pageantry of one sort or another. For example, directors love to see their leading ladies carried onto the stage lounging upon a sedan chair or palanquin borne by a couple of scantily clad brutes.

I am 100 percent sure that the theater faculty at the U of I weighed my "monologues," my essay, and my interview and thought, "Well, he looks like he could carry some shit." There is an operatic term for what we in the film biz call "extras" or "background players," or we in the theater call the "chorus," and that term is: *supernumeraries.* Those professors saw before them a prime cut of corn-fed supernumerary, and so they accepted me into the program for the fall of 1988! My gratitude continues to this day, because they were absolutely right in their assessment. When I began acting school, I was just plain terrible at acting.

Each yearly class held sixteen students, of which five to eight traditionally made it through the four intense years to graduation. So we began, sixteen hopeful young Anthony Hopkinses and Jessica Tandys and Gene Hackmans and Kate Hepburns (What's that you say? All white, yes) seated in a circle, getting to know one another on our first day. We went around the room, stating names and fun facts and counties of origin (there was even a girl from Kentucky!), and maybe a favorite role from high school. A lot of territory was quickly mapped in that first session.

I learned that, unlike yours truly, several of my classmates had a) heard of Shakespeare, and b) PERFORMED IT in the Chicagoland area. I clearly had some major catching up to do. I also was fascinated by Jeffrey Goodman, who was apparently Jewish. I had heard of these people but had never to my knowledge laid eyes on one before. Jeff was nice, but by the time he had explained the fraternity hazing he was undergoing, which included wearing lox in his underwear all day, I knew all I wanted to about this beleaguered group. I asked him what lox was, and he looked at me in disbelief.

"Salmon," he said.

"Oh, okay," I replied. "Like the fish?"

"Yeah. It comes on bagels?"

"Bagels?"

Another look of disbelief. "Yeah. It's like a donut, but made of bread. For breakfast?"

I still could not discern whether Jeff Goodman was having me on. He was very charming, and perhaps the fact that he was being made to wear what he claimed was breakfast fish in his Fruit of the Looms put me on my guard.

"Breakfast bread, eh? I believe they have that product already. It's called toast."

"No, no, bagels are amazing. With cream cheese. I'll get you some."

Before I could learn the truth of this Jew's less-than-credible claims, another chilling power overcame the room. We called her the Yellow Peril.

"Hi, my name is Monica, but everybody calls me Nika [*nee-ka*]."

The inward eyes of fifteen students involuntarily rolled. Monica was cute as shit with blond hair, but perhaps too cute by half. She immediately established herself as a person who had not been told no enough in her childhood. She was "from the suburbs" and she couldn't decide if her favorite role to date had been Ophelia or Juliet. Fifteen students swallowed groans and gnashed their inner teeth. The Yellow Peril had made her stinky mark.

Then we came around to Joe Foust, destined to become my bosom friend, but we hadn't learned that yet. Joe hailed from Monmouth, Illinois, a town so far west that it might as well have been IOWA, for fuck's sake, but for all that, it had a college. As I have learned again and again from our nation's finest towns, like Madison and Austin and Boone and Bellingham, a college lends a town excellent personality and panache. It brings David Lynch to an otherwise contentless channel. An established, funded center of learning lends an inquisitive air to the surroundings, attracting sources of imaginative wealth, like the art house movie theater, the craft-beer pub, and the art gallery. Touring music and comedy acts of worth will detour for hours to attend to the pool of thirsty minds in your college town.

Hence, Joe Foust knew shit. He also had a cool older sister and her friends supplying him with items of taste, from punk bands to Zappa and from Jim Jarmusch films to an interest in theater and even art. He knew so much cool shit! That first day he had on the well-distressed uniform of the 1988 punk rock enthusiast, including shredded jeans held together with dozens of safety pins, combat boots, a torn Monmouth College sweatshirt, and a Mohawk. "Who's the junkie?" I thought.

When he began speaking, it became quite clear that he was Sid Vicious in attire only and otherwise meant serious student-ly business. I was soon to learn that Joe had transferred over from the chemistry department, which he had gravitated toward after taking third place in an international high school science fair in Puerto Rico. Impressive, Joe. Most impressive. He was well-spoken, with a gentle nature that belied his intimidating appearance. "Hmm," I thought. "The junkie's all right."

Finally, it was my turn, at the end of the circle. As Joe later described, my (Sun-In) dappled hair and tan football player's physique filled him with loathing even before he learned that I was a born-again Christian. "Who's the square-ass corn-boy jock?" he thought. I introduced myself and leaned upon my aptitude for farmer politics by informing the group that we were all on the same page when it came to our feelings about the Yellow Peril.

"Hi, everybody, my name is Nicholas Offerman, but everybody calls me Olas." With one deft rejoinder, I had informed the assembled group that I was about as wise as a wiseacre was going to get and also that we needn't be taking any shit from the Yellow Peril.

Monica didn't last very long in our class. She discovered, along with several others, that despite the glowing reviews for their Lady Macbeths in the *Wilmette Herald*, they were in fact not cut out for a life in the theater. I hope that they are all happy now, with healthy families and rewarding vocations. Jeffrey Goodman also fell by the wayside, although I did grow very fond of him after corroborating his food yarns with another fellow named Abraham. To this day I cannot eat a bagel with lox (delicious) without thinking of Jeff Goodman's underwear.

As the year went on, the further I slowly extricated myself from Christianity, the closer I grew to Joe and the little tribe of weirdos we had formed. Our group of friends voraciously consumed content of which we had all been largely deprived for one reason or another in our hometowns. I had exponentially more catching up to do than the

others, but I was game. Like a young Midwesterner newly home from
the cultural desert, I slaked my thirst with Tom Waits and Talking Heads.
Laurie Anderson and Kurt Vonnegut and Elvis Costello. David Bowie.
They Might Be Giants. The Beatles! I had not been turned on to the Beatles. Mel Brooks. Woody Allen. Kurosawa. *On the Road. Siddhartha.* Jim
Thompson and Charles Bukowski, William Burroughs and our main
entrée, Robert Anton Wilson. We thrilled to his historical fiction about
the Illuminati and its progenitors, the Knights Templar, the Freemasons,
and the Rosicrucians. Striving to align our own newly formed cabal with
cloaked allegiance to a set of values that only we young artists could
countenance and comprehend, we devoured Wilson's books with the
fervor of, well, a young initiate to Freemasonry. We met on the level, and
by Christ, we parted on the square.

We watched *Twin Peaks* like it was the lunar landing. David Lynch
legitimately blew our minds with that delightfully masterful series,
rife with humor and terror in equal doses, not to mention just honest-
to-goodness weirdness. Witnessing such surrealism on a prime-time
television show was incredibly inspiring to our warren of baby artists, wondering what of our own issue the world was going to be
willing to swallow.

Twin Peaks House Rules:

No late seating, front door locked.
Blinds down. Lights OFF!
Peeing allowed only during commercials.
No talking.
No phone calls, obviously [meaning landline calls; this is
   long before the cell phone].

The episode would be recorded on our VCR and then immediately screened for a second viewing, same rules. The bong would be in operation only between showings.

Whoopsie, a bong, you say?! It would seem we have rolled into sophomore year, fully free from the constraints of the Lord and fully exploring the world of intoxicants with my tribe. Joe was very much my teacher and spirit guide, as well as my best buddy. We were inseparable; people often thought we were a couple because Joe cultivated an androgynous thing in those days. It worked for him. He saw a lot of action.

As we trudged through our years of theater tutelage, we learned a great many methods by which to stand and move and speak, but the most important transformation taking place was in our small platoon's growing adherence to a set of artistic principles. We were producing our own plays in a local free theater space and discovering that while our standards, or production values, were very high, our virtually nonexistent budgets caused those values to require a lot of elbow grease.

Outside of classes, shows for school, and part-time jobs, we were mounting our own productions of Brecht and Pinter and our own rock-and-roll renditions of Shakespeare. Weed was allowed. A rather ragtag collection of tea heads and beatniks, we saw that our work was sound, and this was noticed by the rest of the department as well. By the time we graduated, the Defiant Theatre had been largely assembled, like a group of stoned, hyperintelligent Super Friends, equipped with all the piss and vinegar necessary to take on the city of Chicago.

Don't Walk Alone

A chapter pertaining to the string of noble friends in my life whom I would call best. I am lucky enough to have counted several, and I'm still young, by gad. The adhesive joining us, always, has been a sense of confederacy. A penchant for mischief and irreverent humor. Us against Them. As long as we were together, we managed to have as much fun as possible, because really, otherwise, what's the fucking point? As *The Book of the SubGenius* (the main text of a hilarious faux religion based in Dallas—get *The Book of the SubGenius*) says, "Fuck 'em if they can't take a joke," right? Even if we were in church or somewhere even less fun than church, if such a place exists, like, I don't know, in the galley of a slave ship? A vegetarian restaurant? Limbaugh's colon? Sequestered there in church of a Sunday, we would be plotting and turning red with the knowledge of our various current jokes, which, perhaps nothing more than Mr. Dollinger farting again, was sufficient amelioration for us to withstand another dreary lecture. Marching through life with a confederate in mirth is one of the greatest pleasures that can befall a man, woman, or chipmunk.

I'm subtitling this chapter "Pilotus," inspired by a wonderful writer named William Least Heat-Moon, who has given us, among other excellent works, *Blue Highways*, a thoroughly edifying philosophical journaling of his circumnavigation of the United States and its people, undertaken in a simple van. What unfolds is a sojourn eschewing any major highways, sticking rather to the two-lane state and county roads, registered in blue on most maps, hence the title. A book I strongly recommend. Strongly.

Then, as if that wasn't enough, he completely bowled me over with another of his books, *River-Horse*. It's a similar undertaking to *Blue Highways*, at least on paper, but *River-Horse* details his journey from New York Harbor west to the Pacific Ocean, across these United States, BY BOAT. It's an intensely fascinating adventure undertaken in two different watercraft—one flat-bottomed motorized cruiser for the lion's share of the miles, especially necessary on the bigger water, and then a canoe for the more intimate streams where the motor would run afoul of the shallow bottom.

Traveling thus, he always needed a subsidiary team to be transporting whichever second boat he was not himself occupying at the moment to the next swap-out location by trailer and road, and whenever possible he also carried a passenger aboard with him, for company, safety, and the occasional assistance. No one friend could stay by his side for the entire journey, which lasted months, and so Heat-Moon took to referring to the string of them collectively as "Pilotus," simplifying the literary task of rendering all of these individual characters by combining them, symbolically, into one charismatic helpmeet. The compatriots in this chapter of mine have represented my own copilots, but, unlike that thankless bastard in the boat, I will use their names so that we may know them as separate people.

The first was my pally cousin Ryan Roberts, who was born six months after me. We ran much like brothers for the first sixteen or seventeen years of our lives, living some few miles apart. We grew up working on the family farm side by side, although I always envied his much heavier involvement, as he actually lived on the farm. To this day, Ryan is about as good as an American can get, as far as I can tell. He has a hilarious sense of humor, but only up to the point of indecency, where he draws the line (a line I would have also gladly drawn, were I not too busy sticking the chalk up my fanny). While I ran from Minooka as fast as I could, Ryan stuck around and became a paramedic, while still working on the family farm, firmly establishing him as one of my heroes.

Our age difference of a half year put him one grade behind me in school, otherwise we might well have burned the place down. Still, we managed to create enough havoc in the time we shared in band class and on sports teams to require a few trips to the disciplinary wing. For me, mostly, not Ryan. We developed a sort of secret language around a mispronunciation of *José Feliciano*, complete with weird facial expressions and little hand gestures, surrounded by an air of conspiracy, that has stayed with me throughout my life.

Ryan played the trumpet and I played the saxophone in school band, then marching band, then jazz band, and we were lucky enough to hold the "first chair" in those instruments, which meant we were afforded a little more respect by the rest of the kids. This allowed us to formulate a deadpan sense of leadership that we thought was goddamn hilarious. We always enjoyed giving each other a solemn nod, as though we were army officers keeping everyone calm in the midst of a gaggle of civilians. Even playing our solos in jazz band, we managed to try to insert grace notes in a way we each thought the other would find amusing. There was not a lot to do for fun, so we made our own fun whenever and wherever we could. It was around this time that we developed together what has remained one of my signature moves to this day. One of us would bleat out a sonorous ass-toot, and the other would respond by giving him a steely glare, like he had just received some catastrophic news, perhaps from Leslie Nielsen in a scene from *Airplane!* or *The Naked Gun*.

Comedy films of the day also played a big part in our matriculation, most notably John Hughes offerings. For some reason, the grandparents in *Sixteen Candles* cracked us up to the point of choking, and Paul Gleason's definitive portrayal of Principal Richard Vernon in *The Breakfast Club* ("Don't mess with the bull, young man. You'll get the horns") was likely the seed of what became the full blossom of the comedy fruits found in our facial expressions and mannerisms.

Leaving Ryan and my boyhood in Minooka (at least symbolically—I believe I still have a healthy portion of inner child in my pocket), I found my next Pilotus at theater school in a wise but puckish lad you may recall by the name of Joe Foust. Our illicit work commenced almost immediately, as we shared a mutual need to engage in some form of insubordination. We were excellent students, as our artistic passions drove us to work as hard as we could, and we excelled as a result, but our mischievous natures were not completely on board with this level of diligence.

It's important that I chronicle the fact that Joe taught me to smoke weed. He had patiently waited more than a year for me to excuse myself from the Bible study group and find my way to the party. Traditionally, a first-time pot user would claim to "feel nothing" and often threw in the towel before achieving a proper bake. To guarantee that I would have no such problems, Joe told me a bald-faced lie.

He had a favorite pipe which was, if I recall correctly, a zombie knight with fake rubies for eyes and a large, open mouth that was the bowl. His name was Sir Frop-a-Lot. Packing a good-size bowl with buds, Joe casually imparted that it normally would take seven or eight of these bowls to feel anything, so by the time we had actually hoovered in four or five such bowls, I began to cotton to the idea that Joe was full of shit, because I was completely wasted. I laughed my first long, teary stoner laugh then, giggling maniacally at my Pilotus's delightfully dirty trick with the straight face that has been the key ingredient to all of these friendships. Deadpan humor required.

As well as the plays of Harold Pinter, Eugène Ionesco, Sam Shepard, Charles Ludlam, Bertolt Brecht, and beyond, Joe and the rest of our weird tribe—Ragsdale, PeePee, Kimmel, Flanigan, Tatro, and Prescher—were deeply studying the Church of the Sub-Genius, and we were collectively invigorated by these sources of humor we were finding in the "grown-up" world. These signposts assured us that we too could find careers engaged in artistic pursuits that contained a subversive sense of humor.

One night while working in the costume shop, we decided to borrow a couple of wigs and head out on the town. We walked over to Green Street and, like most troublemakers, ended up at the video arcade. We were big fans of Kubrick, of course, and we aspired to be our own Alex-and-Dim kind of mischievous duo. We would stand next to a dude playing a game, we would give each other a nod, and as the guy was about to get a high score I would shoulder him to the floor and then we'd run. That was our big prank. Brilliantly crafted. We would run screaming back to the costume shop and laugh maniacally at our triumphant bout of grab-ass. If you're out there reading this book and I did this to you, I am very sorry. Sometimes we're assholes. We thought it was just so unbelievably funny then.

Joe and I sort of came into manhood together as artists, with

Joe's creative puberty prefacing my own. We formed part of the spine of the Defiant Theatre, where we were able to fully flex our creative muscles once we arrived in Chicago. The two of us continued to live together for our first year in Chicago and had what I would call a rich time, indeed. Working together in Champaign–Urbana at the U of I and also at the Station Theatre, a very high-quality local company in an old Urbana train station, we learned a lesson that we would later exploit to great pleasure in Chicago: If one was responsible and hardworking when the job required it, then one was free to fuck around as much as one wanted to when the work was over! People were comforted by our dependability, for they knew we would sweep up any mess we made, which gave us the freedom to be the finest class clowns working. The key resided in the first part—make sure you work hard and do the job right. Once that notion was implemented, the fun began and has really never ended.

As the director of our best Defiant plays, Joe was a great teacher to me. For years he had refused to give me the plum roles for which I thought I was perfect, because I wasn't yet a good enough actor. As you can imagine, I pulled him aside and said, "Look, maybe I still have some things to learn as an actor, but we're best friends. Cut a guy a break?" to which he replied, "Listen, you muscular fool. I am trying to make this production the best that it can possibly be, so I'm going to cast the best actors I can, even if they're strangers. You're getting better. Excruciatingly slowly, yes, but you ARE improving, and the day will come when you WILL get the part."

This was such a huge lesson for me (and it's also why nepotism doesn't accomplish as much as people might suspect in showbiz. Can it get you in the door? Sure, maybe, but you still have to exhibit "the goods" to get the job), and it only made me admire Joe all the more for the integrity of his vision. I realized that we're being paid nothing or very little for this work, at least in dollars. If we're not going to do this job as sublimely as possible, then what the hell are we doing?

One of my very favorite of Joe's many bedevilments over the years, and one that can well represent for you his charismatic combination of leadership and monkey business, occurred at the Abbie Hoffman Died for Our Sins Theatre Festival in 1997. Every year in August the Mary-Arrchie Theatre presents this festival to celebrate the anniversary of Woodstock in 1969. This splendid debauch was a nonstop, seventy-two-hour procession of everything from high-quality theater pieces, music, and monologues to absolute absurdism and nonsense. (I once, having had no time to prepare material, dressed as a clown and downed a fresh goblet of my own urine as my offering to the audience. They were moved, I'm guessing, at my talent?) Theater companies could sign up for a half-hour or an hour slot and do whatever they damn well pleased. Part of the charm of these proceedings was that between acts the previous group would quickly load out, and then the next players would hustle in their necessaries, props, minor scenery, and what have you. This was always a good time to nip down to the liquor store for a half-pint of Old Darling.

On the evening in question, we Defiants, some twelve hardy roustabouts or so, hustled in an entire kitchen and set it up upstage with other assorted mayhem including a six-foot penis tucked into the lighting grid, a lovely lass in a bumblebee costume, and a small hippie tuning a guitar. Downstage center was only an easy chair, a standing lamp (lit), and an occasional table upon which sat an old-fashioned telephone and a bowl of mints. After an impressively instantaneous load-in that would have given the Tasmanian Devil pause, we the crew disappeared, the dust settled, and our dear, lone thespian, our late, great champion and friend Will Schutz, sat in the chair without pomp, unfolded his newspaper, and began to read. As the silence lengthened and the audience was beginning to smirk, the phone began to ring. A good, old-school clanging telephone bell ringer. *Rrring. Rrring. Rrring.* The crowd's smiles grew. *Rrring. Rrring. Rrring.* Will Schutz inscrutably eyes the Business section. *Rrring. Rrring. Rrring. Rrring.* Titters. *Rrring.* More rings. Minutes of ringing. *Rrring.* Finally, Schutz makes as if to answer the phone but only gathers a mint instead and pops it into his gob. The audience was experiencing differing waves of reaction from loud laughter to mild bemusement to tedious unease to insouciance as when one man in the third row began to utter, "Hello? . . . Hello?" Still, the phone rang on. Really, a surprising amount of laughter. *Rrring. Rrring.* The laughter would die, then after a lull even more enjoyment. This experiment had an audacity that the audience was largely on board with. *Rrring.* For a time. *Rrring.* Then they began to turn. People shifted in their seats and some few got up and left. Finally, a young lady trepidatiously rose from her seat. As the audience shouted more and more encouragement, she more confidently strode into the lights onstage and picked up the handset from the ringing phone. The moment the handset cleared its cradle, clearly silencing the ringing as though a switch had been flipped, Joe bellowed, "STRIKE!!" and quick as we came, we silently hustled the props and scenery out of the theater and into the night leaving nothing but an empty, black stage mere moments after the ringing had ceased. The name of this evening's offering? "La Surprise Grand." That's my boy Joe Foust, folks.

My first "real" job in LA brought me out from Chicago for two weeks in 1996. Nickelodeon had a new show called *Kablam!*, which was a thirty-minute block of mostly animated shorts, with a little live action thrown in. One of these live-action shorts, "The Adventures of Patchhead," featured me as the young hero's nemesis, Colonel Kudzu. Four five-minute episodes. AFTRA-adjacent. Hey, they flew me out. It was super fun, although no one had told me that LA is not a proper city, like Chicago, where one can get within a block of ANYWHERE using mass transit.

I landed at the airport and found a bus that would take me downtown, which my map told me would be near Sunset Boulevard, which was the street I sought, upon which the studio resided. So I literally landed in Los Angeles and unwittingly took the bus to skid row. Anything approaching "hip" was several years away from occurring in the decrepit, forgotten streets of downtown LA. It was scary, but I had my crazy-man technique ready to fly, and so I shouldered my green army duffel and set off on foot to find Green Jelly Studios. (I'll be right back; I'm going to Google Maps the distance.) Six and a half miles I walked with my large duffel on my back in ninety-eight-degree California sun, so I was about ready for a goddamn soda pop when I walked into the soundstage, a greenhorn drenched in sweat.

The first person I saw was a tall, McQueen/Nolte–lookin' dude in a battered straw cowboy hat, painting the slats on a cartoony picket fence with wood grain and knots. Upon closer inspection, I saw that he had made the last set of knots read

"666," and the cowboy hat had a large Chewbacca button on the front. Enter Pat Roberts, genius clown artist. We were fast friends and were soon roommates and drinking buddies. (This guy is still the funniest, most confederate thinker I've ever come across. Whatever opinion anybody posits, doesn't matter who, Pat will playfully oppose it just to get a rise out of everyone and make them laugh. Which can grow irksome should you be in the habit of positing opinions.)

Gifted with a rascally talent for embroidering intelligent themes and guileless emotions into his paintings and collages, Pat eschewed conventional methods of applying color to canvas, instead using his fingers or whatever implement was handy. I learned of his stubbornness the hard way when I bought him some artist brushes for Christmas. He snapped them in half and painted with the broken handle ends. My adoration and admiration only swelled.

One of the secrets to maintaining my gassy artistic integrity over the years, I was to learn, was in allying myself with a like-minded miscreant whenever possible in order to protect and maintain my self-imposed "outsider" status. As two largely foot-loose and fancy-free (unemployed) artist types, Pat and I fit that bill to a T.

So long as one had an operable motor vehicle, Los Angeles could be a lot of fun when one was young, broke, and stoned to the gills. For example, Pat and I were once contracted to create some three hundred custom-painted hubcaps as a giveaway promotion for a band pleasantly called Suicide Machines. We had worked on the art department of a music video the band made centered around a demolition derby and shot in an enormous automobile graveyard deep in the San Fernando Valley. After sourcing and acquiring the hubcaps, we then painted each with splatters of black, white, and red, finally applying a decal with the band's name to the center.

This was the kind of work a man could perform whilst in an "elevated" mood, so to speak, with Johnny Cash accompanying our toils under the sun over a large blue tarp in the producer's yard. As we were waiting for the production gofer to pick up our masterpieces, and as nobody was home, we rooted around in the garage for some diversion. We found exactly that in a can of electric-blue PVC cement, the kind that gets a person "high" if he or she should catch a whiff of its vapors.

"Shit, let's take a crack at it," we remarked, and manfully huffed one single draft of the noxious devilry emanating from the can's orifice. Well, folks, I can assure you we got plenty high, as a kite, really, for a good forty-five seconds, before the dull roar became simply a splitting headache. "Well, that was stupid." "Yup. Ow." I clearly remember thinking that things must be going pretty not-so-great for me, standing unsteadily in someone's yard, squinting from the pain of a glue huffing. Pat picked up an overripe grapefruit off of the ground beneath the tree which had spawned it, and stated, "Watch how hard I can throw."

His six-foot-three-inch form wound up and delivered that pregnant globe of citrus to a cinder-block wall across the street like a veritable six-pound lead cannonball. Old Pat Roberts could put some mustard on it. The resultant explosion of pulp and bejeweled juice droplets, in an expanding aurora of dazzling refracted sunshine, made the discomfort recede handily. It was almost as though he had placed a soothing poultice over my eyes and brain. I looked at him, unsteadily statuesque there in the valley's heat signature, and knew in my pith that I had never beheld a finer man. Goddamn, we lived like kings.

If you were a shiftless wino in Hollywood and you did not frequent the auspices of Jumbo's Clown Room, well, sir, you were a fool. No fools we, Pat and I could be found with some regularity in the smoky environs of that hallowed dive, watching the incredibly varied collection of ladies disrobe and dance upon the runway. The nomenclature that Roberts bestowed upon the scantily clad members of this motley coterie established him as my favorite living brain, beyond the belch of a doubt. The pallid young lady who seemed to pretty clearly be using heroin on her breaks (as evidenced by the way she aimlessly wandered about the stage, pausing occasionally to pump her fists, eyes closed, as though willing herself to continue breathing) was dubbed Power Surge.

Next up, a rather lovely young blonde who seemed all too innocent for this entire neighborhood, let alone this room, wore her disappointment at her circumstances plainly on her crestfallen face as she politely two-stepped in a bustier plucked from a Betty Grable pinup. She bore the name Miss Nebraska. Now imagine a young Toni Braxton, with just a knockout Playboy Bunny's figure, exhibiting to the funky bass of "Brick House" that she had about as much rhythm as a crescent wrench. Heartbreakingly beautiful and 100 percent unattractive was Ebony and Irony.

Finally, our hands-down favorite, also gorgeous in all the right superficial physical departments, a perhaps forty-year-old athletic dancer who could have been an action heroine. She commanded the stage and pole with a warrior's confidence, working her magic to "Crazy Train" as she disrobed down to, oh, what are those? IRON CROSS PASTIES and a G-string. Heil that! As if that wasn't badass enough, she would then lose the thong and, on her knees, lean back, spread a bit of fuel, and LIGHT HER PUDENDA ON FIRE. I believe she was what David Mamet had in mind when he penned that "coffee is for closers." She was a goddamn closer, and Pat righteously branded her Clitler. Pat Roberts, ladies and gentlemen.

That was about as low as things got, I would say. Weathering squalor and then staying together once the grass has grown exponentially greener (420, bro) is a true test of friendship, one that ours has passed with high marks.

In my forty-two years of good fortune (and some scattered bad I suppose), several other stalwarts have ridden shotgun to my cockamamie schemes, and although I lack the space in this tome to detail all of their flatulent and heroic exploits, I would like to give a hearty lumberjack's shout-out to Mssrs. Rapcan, Mitchel, Olichwier, Karr, Decker, O'Brien, Hinshaw, Rusty, Kimmel, Flanigan, Hynes, Ragsdale, Garno, Wheeler, Leman, Tesen, Prescher, Primeaux, Clements, Loquist, Tatro, Kruse, Gerson, and Healy; my brother, Matt; Lee; Jimmy Diresta; and especially Rob Ek and Martin McClendon, two true brothers who have stood by me regardless of my weakness, to set an example for me and all of us in how to conduct oneself as a man of worth in this modern age.

8

Doing Time

In the midsize college town of Urbana, Illinois, along the former Big Four and Wabash railroad lines, there sits a picturesque little train station that served local passengers from 1923 until the line shut down in 1957. It's just as cute a little brick train station as you might imagine.

In 1972, an enterprising group of long-haired hopheads (Commies) took ownership of the building and established the Station Theatre. The combination of open-minded citizenry (freaks) and the students from the local University of Illinois theater department (younger freaks) has made for forty years of surprisingly high-end theater productions in the Station's modest black-box stage space. I am proud to have served my time as one of the enlisted weirdos at both the U of I and the Station Theatre. During my delightfully hedonistic college career, I enjoyed performing in and building scenery for several productions at the latter, and I made some very good friends there amongst the confederacy.

A word about live theater: A great many of you have likely never seen a production at your local small theater company. I urge you to correct that deficit, as live theater is loaded with a certain sense of altruism that cannot be found in any other art form. By engaging in the act of "putting on a show," a theater is holding up a mirror to our hilarious and tragic human foibles so that we, society, may see ourselves therein and thereby receive a dose of social medicine.

That "holding up a mirror" line is not mine, by the way, but I can't remember who said it first, Aristotle or Hamlet. Banding together with others to achieve a common pursuit cannot help but engender a strong feeling of community, whether you're baling hay or mounting *A Chorus Line* in a tiny theater space.

Thus, when you produce a play with friends, you feel very gratified to be contributing in some small way to the spiritual health of the community, especially nice since you never stand to make any actual money. Theater artists are paid in the coin of an audience's laughter and tears, a sentiment which sounds corny, but, let me assure you, is anything but. There is nothing so delicious to me as tickling a room full of people with a gesture or well-timed rejoinder. We thespians are doing our part to keep humanity on the road to decency, and also to take a pie in the face so that everybody can enjoy a chuckle. Let me take this opportunity to again cajole all thirty-seven of you who are still reading this drivel to get out and see some live theater, music, art shows, etc. Is a movie more convenient? Yes. More spectacular? Most often, yes, in a superficial way, but more prone to mediocrity.

There's a reason a night in the theater seems to take all night. It's not meant so much as a comfy diversion, like, say, watching an episode of *The New Yankee Workshop*, as it is an *event* in which to engage the hearts and minds of the audience. It's a bit more like church than your local multiplex, because the performers, the celebrants, are there with you, the audience, participating with complicity in a rite. When you see a play and consider that the artists are pulling this show off *every night*, it's impressive in a much more immediate way than seeing James Bond jump over a hedge.

Good theater is necessarily more viscerally engaging than other art forms, because you, the audience, are participants. Movie theaters and stadium concerts have their advantages, sure, their pyro and their Dolby sound, but I will always prefer the intimacy of small-theater plays and live music where I can see the details on the mandolin's pegboard. Seeing a performer's facial expression goes a long way toward experiencing his/her charisma. I can happily tell you from experience that watching Patty Griffin weave the spell of her songs in person spins an enchantment entirely superior to hearing her records, already amazing in their own right.

In addition, while movie theaters are traditionally a place to get romantic (although please note that anything more than hand work is crossing the line), seeing a musical or play with your date can be very stimulating to conversation and the stimulating cranial exploration necessary to further your relationship to the level of, well, stimulating. Theater, to me, is always a bigger turn-on than film. It's alive. Maybe if the play goes well you can then catch a movie next time and tug and twaddle each other to your heart's content. Do as you please. Now that you know how I feel about participating in live theater, you can more fully grasp the sense of camaraderie and loyalty that thrived amongst we young initiates back in Urbana.

It must have been 1990, after a summer performance of the Neil Simon classic *Biloxi Blues* at the Station Theatre, that the infamous Boneyard Bust occurred. Myself and two frequent compatriots, hardy lads Tatro and Craig (who was so skinny we had a contest to determine an appropriate nickname for him—after rejecting the likes of Wisp, Sliver, Wafer, and Spook, not to mention the generous estimation of T-Square, the winner was Line), were sitting upon the large, two-foot-diameter sewer pipe that spans the Boneyard

Creek behind the theater and acts as a footbridge of sorts for the not-so-faint of heart.

Aged twenty or twenty-one, we three lads spent our days together in the U of I acting studio class of '92, but our nights, especially over the summer break, were consigned to the Station Theatre. Like any self-respecting young, aspiring actors, we were seriously involved in the study of smoking cigarettes, and the pipe bridge was a favorite classroom of ours.

We settled comfortably upon the pipe and fired up our squares with élan and my Zippo, our surroundings ideal for a real artistic think-tank session, except for the annoying presence of someone using power tools across the creek somewhere in the darkness. This particular night, we were also sampling some of the illicit weed marijuana by means of a kick-ass new one-hitter and dugout box of teak with ebony and holly inlays that Tatro had purchased just that afternoon from Bogart's head shop. Puffing away, fulminating over the finer points of the new Dead Can Dance record, striking ne'er-do-well poses we thought worthy of a young Malkovich (John Malkovich, like Gene Hackman, remains a hero of my brand of actor, as he too matriculated in central Illinois), we were aglow in the torrents of a bohemian reverie seldom achieved by any of we three before or since.

Awash in the euphoria of Urbana's finest Mary Jane, we lost ourselves in the tinkling burble of the Boneyard's waters, echoed by the ghostly babble of water through the pipe beneath our bottoms, and the bobbing, faerielike lights along the bank upstream. It was a beautiful peace we had discovered there, as we lightly floated, buoyed upon an updraft of hallucination.

That was right about when Line whispered, "Hey, you guys?

Those are flashlights." We each reluctantly tugged our consciousness back from its field of dreams to focus in on the flashlights searching the area fifty yards upstream, across the creek. Yep, those were people. What could they . . .

"Cops!" Tatro hissed. "Shit. What tickles?"

"The Fuzz," I said. "Ditch the weed."

"Right," he replied.

We slowly and carefully gained our feet so as to tiptoe back to the safety of our benevolent train station, gripped in the paranoia of the young, inexperienced stoner. When the police shouted, "Stop! Hold it right there!" we, of course, took off running like shit-faced squirrels in a blind panic.

We scattered, and I'm not sure where my friends got to, but I made it around the theater and into the parking lot next door before being neatly tackled by a diminutive female officer, who popped to her feet, placed her boot on my head, then pointed her pistol at a spot slightly below her boot. What in the fucking what? Hang on, whoa, please and thank you.

This was all insanely wrong; what in the fuck was going on?! In my estimation, toking up on the Boneyard did not equate with a gun to the head, not remotely, so I calmed right down real quick-like.

"Um, okay . . . I don't think we did what you think we did," I sagely remarked.

"Save it, dipshit," she replied.

She was impossibly tiny and incredibly scary. As my heartbeat slowed from the tempo of a twin-prop seaplane to the cadence of a playing card in a bicycle wheel, I saw that my two fellow dipshits had been welcomed similarly across the lot. The three of us, confused and terrified, were hustled and herded into three police cars and hauled all of the five-odd blocks to the Urbana sheriff's station, where we were kept in separate areas so we couldn't get our stories straight. As I was being *deeply* patted down and then booked, I whispered a silent thanks that Tatro had had the good sense to lose the weed.

Thankfully, and due no doubt in part to the cornucopia of acting techniques we had all gleaned, spongelike, from that legendary tome *Acting One* by Robert Cohen, we all three managed to explain to the baffled police interrogators that we had just been hanging out, talking, and smoking. You know, tobacco. This elicited repeated utterings on their part of "Then why did you run?" to which they received an endless sequence of shrugs and unintelligible mutterings.

Once this unfortunate graveyard shift of Urbana's finest copped to the reality that we were, in fact, relatively innocent, they filled us in on the malfeasance behind the whole night's episode. Apparently those power tools we had heard across the creek (so obviously suspicious in hindsight; a Skilsaw at twelve thirty A.M.?) were the sound of a team of thieves quite loudly breaking into a restaurant where, it turns out, was stashed a ridiculous amount of cash. About $20,000, I seem to recall.

The robbers made off with the dough, and the police were notified, thanks to an alarm system and a more alert neighbor than we pipe dwellers. The police had arrived to investigate what must have been at least partially an inside job, and as they were scanning the surrounding area for evidence, suddenly there were three young men in eyeliner, fleeing in panic. Understandably, it seemed pretty obvious to them that we must be somehow attached to the caper, although we pointed out that if we were involved, it would have been pretty stupid to lurk about the scene of the crime once the money had been properly purloined, ha-ha. Ha. We all had a pretty good laugh by the time the ordeal had passed. Ahem.

We were released the next morning after a nerve-racking night in the hoosegow, just as the sun was coming up. Walking onto the front lawn of the police station, we laughed with relief that our freedom had survived the tests of the previous night. Comparing critiques of the prisoner's bathroom, Line and I were suddenly horrified to see Tatro reach into his crotch and produce his one-hitter box. He said, with the most righteous of indignation, "I just got this fucking thing yesterday. It was forty-five bucks; I'm not about to toss it into the Boneyard."

Once I finished up the warm and free release of urine into my own jeans, and it seemed clear that no one was going to sound an alarm or unceremoniously tackle us onto the pavement, we each fired up a hit, exhaled, and felt the warming sunlight on our young, relieved faces. We set off on foot to face the day and get a nap before the show that night. We had been—and we remained—men of the theater.

The moral of this story? Clearly, when the po-po give you a hassle, stand your ground and talk to them. Don't run. Just be cool.

One minor detail that may have further colored my character in the eyes of the officers that night, adding to our collective suspiciousness, was the fact that I had a record. That's right. A rap sheet. The Boneyard bust was not in fact my first dalliance with the Urbana sheriff's department. Let's rewind the tape to the previous autumn. ("Rewind the tape" is what we said in my youth when audiovisual content was recorded on media "tape," wound or rolled around "reels" in an actual "cassette." It was fucking crazy, kids. Like wiping your ass with a corn cob.) The previous autumn. So, 1989. As a sophomore in the theater-acting conservatory at the University of Illinois, I was newly eligible to be cast in feature productions (aka "fresh meat"). The department produced two main-stage and two studio plays per semester, for which the entire body of eligible actors, fifty or sixty strong, would audition at the beginning of each semester.

Each auditioning actor would perform two contrasting monologues for all four play directors at once. The directors would then hold "callbacks," and the actors they liked for each role would come back and read specific material, often with other actors, to get a look at chemistry and physical size matchups and what have you. Then the directors would go behind closed doors and engage in a sweaty round of horse trading, mother-fucking, and mollycoddling to try to land the best actors in their own shows.

According to apocryphal student legend, a staggering quantity of oral and manual pleasuring was exchanged between faculty in these negotiations. For example, rumor had it that scoring Michael Shapiro as your Jacques or your Sky Masterson cost two rim jobs and a finger blast. (He really was much sought after. It was his sublimely wry enunciation more than anything.)

Finally, a four-show casting list would be posted on the hallway bulletin board (again, youngsters, public announcements used to be made using paper hung in one physical location. Hilarious, right? You had to walk to the location to see the news!), with everyone's casting assignment for that half year. Can you imagine the drama that unfurled at this posting? Children and young adults, having dedicated their lives to embodying the tender renderings of history's most sensitive playwrights, publicly witnessing the joyful tidings of a whole semester's work, or else the devastating lack thereof.

Oh, there was wailing. Ho boy, there were tears. There was indeed gnashing of teeth. (PS: If you think you might end up gnashing your teeth in public, send a friend to read the casting and bring you the news in private. Looking at you, Greenberg.) Yes, there also leapt jubilation and at times deafening caterwauls of sheer elation shook the building to its roots.

But the real show was in the disappointments. For many young hopefuls, having chosen an admittedly dicey program of study to begin with, in regards to future chances of financial stability, on Mom and Dad's dime no less, the casting sheet could spell the doom of their entire life's dream.

If the theater department didn't see you as a Juliet or Lady Capulet, or even a lady-in-waiting, then the Actors Theatre of Louisville was goddamned unlikely to think so either. Let alone Chicago! "Goddamn it, honey. We tried it your way. We got you the colored contacts. We got you the LeBaron convertible. You won raves as Ado Annie at Glenbard South, and rightly so; you really were just magical. You really were. And I know, everyone says you look like a young Julie from *The Love Boat*. And you do. You could be her sister. Your mother and I bought into it, too. It was intoxicating; I mean, we were all three of us giddy with delight at your prospects. We were drunk, is what we were. On your talent. But you didn't get cast in *Romeo and Juliet*. In Champaign–Urbana. Nor did you get cast in *Three Sisters*, or *The House of Blue Leaves*, or *Kabuki Achilles*, whatever the hell that is. Forty-seven actors got parts. You did not, Monica. So, NOW you will, by god, get a degree in poli sci, like we always thought you should in the first place!"

You get the idea. I, myself, was very much a newborn baby in acting school, which is to say that I was not very good at acting, which, really, is to say I was bad at acting at this point in my training. So, as this was my own first time through the wringer, I didn't have high hopes to begin with. I did dream that I might just have a crack at the leading-man role in William Inge's American classic *Picnic*, just because there weren't a lot of manly types in the department. William Holden plays Hal in the movie version, a rough-and-tumble drifter in jeans and no shirt. Mumble, brood, mumble, smoke, flex, spit, kiss the girl. Right up my alley. We got into the callbacks, and lo and behold, the director had the same idea, so suddenly I was reading opposite lovely ladies in scenes for Hal and Madge. Everything was cool! A little too cool, turns out.

For right about then this new grad student showed up, a man named David. Nice fella. His main focus had been the ballet (a fact), but now he was leaning toward theater. He was hairless, he was slightly effeminate, and he was ripped. He was sweet as pie. The kind of guy who would never upset you unless he was cast instead of you to portray a virile, swaggering cowboy.

As we continued to pair off in the callback scenes, the director eventually had David try one with his shirt off, and I knew immediately that it was over. The director turned out to be the sort of chap who didn't necessarily cast the best actor for the part based on ability. He cast the best actor for the part based on tits. There are, sadly, *astonishingly* too many directors in this world who operate similarly, but such is life. Tits are nice; I get it. If I had succeeded in my life thanks to my sweet tits, I imagine I'd be singing a different tune. I'm certain that we've all suffered defeat at one time or another, at the hands of a lesser foe who just happened to be brandishing better tits. David was a fine actor, certainly my better in that regard, but he was simply miscast as a manly person in jeans and cowboy boots.

In any case, I was barely given time to foment my sour grapes, because unfortunately, there is more to the story. You see, this director also liked the cut of my particular jib, despite my medium tits, so he turned right around and started reading me in the scenes for Alan. Who is Alan, you ask? Oh, just the milquetoast college boy who is publicly emasculated when Hal poaches his girlfriend Madge and she chooses to acquiesce to her animal desires, succumbing to Hal even though he has trouble written all over him! For Hal is a man, my friends, and Alan is merely a boy. A cuckolded boy, no less. Alan the boy even has a crying scene, downstage center, lamenting the loss of his gal to this bohunk.

So now, not only am I pissed that David the dancer is going to handily unman me by playing Hal, but all the bookish, boyish actors who thought they had Alan sewn up are damning my eyes! Fortune presents gifts not according to the book, friends, a lesson I have learned too many times to mention. The casting was over. The list was mounted upon the hallway board. I was to play Alan. Very well.

I put my shoulder to the wheel and tried as hard as I could to accomplish some semblance of "good" scene work. Boy, howdy, did I try. I never came close that fall, or for a few years beyond it, because what I had to ultimately learn was that I needed to be "trying" less. I'll save the rest for my acting technique book (coming this never, from E. P. Dutton, an imprint of Penguin!).

The important thing was that I tried my best and I never gave up, and I could even discern that, although I had a lot farther to go in my journey, the audience at least understood the words I was speaking. I've always taken my small victories wherever I could find them. Now I'm forty-two, and I am happy to report that I still have even a lot farther to go. But goddamn, folks, I'm a good sight better now than I was during that *Picnic* autumn.

*   *   *

Anyway, we were talking about crime. Joe Foust was a year older than me, and he was also more mature in some very practical ways, which I admired. He was not so mature, however, that he wouldn't join me in our favorite running joke: shoplifting stupid items. It was hilarious. We'd try to outdo each other, with an item's useless-ness being the key value for scoring points toward an intangible vic-tory. A box of panty liners. Granny glasses. A book of Bible verses for dealing with fatal diseases. Hilarious, right? Being nineteen was amaz-ing. I was an unstoppable pilferer. We would exit the chosen establish-ment, barely containing our mirth until we could pull out whatever dumb trinket we had just heisted. Then we would laugh. Oh, how we would double over and cackle in the glow of the parking-lot lights. What could be more fun than pointless petty larceny? Fracking, maybe?

One day we went to the Kmart so Joe could purchase a micro-wave for his girlfriend for Christmas. I wandered innocuously about while he selected his oven and paid. Then, as we sauntered out, the security man said, "Excuse me, can I please talk to you?"

"Ulp. Yeah," I replied, thoroughly AMAZED that they had some-how detected my thievery. He asked to examine the front of my jeans, and, sure enough, there he found not four, not five, not even six, but *eight* Ronnie Milsap cassettes. EIGHT RONNIE MILSAP CASSETTES. Please pause in your reading to calm your exploding heart rate . . . All good? To resume. Eight Ronnie Milsap cassettes. Eight disparate Ronnie Milsap albums. On cassette. You have to ad-mit that was an amazing haul in terms of scoring points in our game. I had apparently shoved them into the front of my jeans standing di-rectly in front of a two-way mirrored security window.

The man took me back to his office to show me where he had been sitting whilst watching me commit my smooth misdemeanor.

His chair behind the mirror was about fourteen feet from the display of country greats on sale. I said that I felt pretty stupid, and that it was actually just a hilarious joke, and that I wasn't actually even familiar with Mr. Milsap's stylings.

He told me that if I could pay for the tapes right then, he'd let me go. I remember the total being about seventeen dollars and change. I did not have it. He said he was sorry, but he'd have to call the police in, then. I stoically said, "Welp. That's your call. But I fucking won, bro." So, puzzled at my bravado, he did. That Kmart bastard had the rectitude to call the fucking cops. Imagine hearing my end of that call: "Hey, Dale. It's Cleve. . . . Heh, it's hangin'. . . . I got one for you. . . . Nah, white boy. . . . You ready? Eight Ronnie Milsap tapes. . . . Ronnie Milsap. . . . Eight. . . . Nope, eight. . . . He says it's hilarious. All right, see ya." It suddenly dawned on me that this might be not so great, because in about five hours, I was supposed to appear in the opening-night performance of *Picnic*. Oh, my good Jesus.

A deputy came from the sheriff's office and arrested me and cuffed me and walked me out of the store in front of all the mothers pulling their children in close to them, and my friend Joe, who quickly communicated that he didn't think the Ronnie Milsap tapes were really that funny in this instance. He was just pissed because I had driven us there in my Subaru BRAT, and he couldn't drive a stick, so he was stranded. In an attempt to further diminish my ultimate victory, he pointed out that he had written a check, with our address on it, for the microwave, so it wasn't really the ideal setup for lifting humorously useless objects.

As he spoke, all I heard was, "You are the ultimate champion, forever, of our awesome game." The deputy said something like, "Okay, let's move along. Gird yourself—we're about to pass some Engelbert

Humperdinck cassettes." Then he shoved me past the candy bars and out the door. This whole pageant was meant to cow and shame me, and it worked. Like a charm. It was an intense wake-up call to suddenly be handcuffed in the back of a police car, heading "downtown" at about three o'clock in the afternoon.

My life as I knew it was about to come to a screeching halt, for this was the worst possible night I could have chosen to be unwillingly detained by the law. Visions of Sean Penn and Esai Morales from *Bad Boys* (1983) filled my mind's eye, and I expected, upon arriving "up the river," to soon find myself garnished with the hocked-up loogies of my new, jeering fellow inmates.

I was taken into the station and booked, straight up. The sheriff's deputies told me that, due to my tender years, they would go pretty easy on me. I'd be released that day if I posted bail, then I'd have to return to a sort of lightweight court for sentencing, which would probably be a fine or community service. I started to think I might just find my way clear of this bed I had just shat. Suck on that, Esai Morales. (I have always been such a fan of his that I used to dream of growing up to be called "the white Esai Morales.")

Shortly after I arrived in the Urbana joint, my friend Goliath, alerted by Joe Foust, showed up with my bail, which I think was about $250. Good man. Seems I was all set to get off easy. And it was here, right here, right at this goddamn point, that I made my second-biggest mistake of the afternoon. It was in the words that I spoke aloud to the fine officers processing me.

"Gentlemen. I want to say to you that I am truly sorry that I committed this grave error this afternoon, and I can assure you that I am and will remain sincerely repentant. I am a jackass of the first order; this is now clear to me. Jack. Ass. Totally. I mean, wow, guys, officers, I have learned a lesson here. A lesson and a half. Has been learned. And. Now, if you wouldn't mind, um, hustling my paperwork along, expediting it, as they say, for you see, I am a student. Of the theater . . . and tonight is actually the opening night of my play, *Picnic*, on the main stage over at the Krannert Center for the Performing Arts, so . . . it's pretty much a big deal, and it's my first show ever because I'm a sophomore, and they have a whole hierarchy/pecking order kind of thing, where they post the casting on the board, so, anyway, my call time is six thirty for an eight P.M. show . . . it's five o'clock now. So, thanks. For the hustle."

The officers looked kindly at one another and said to me, "Opening night? You don't say. That sounds important all right. Don't you worry, we'll take care of it. We love the arts around here." Amazing. I sighed my relief all over them, I made my gratitude very clear to the deputies, and I don't believe I cried.

I flashed back to my grandpa Ray telling me years earlier, "You made your bed. Now you have to sleep in it." I briefly hated that beloved man, now gone, for the painfully appropriate timbre of his aphorism. How close had I just come to bringing the curtain of justice down upon the closing night of my whole shebang? This was seriously, seriously bad. Missing the show for such a delinquent reason would certainly see me expelled from school, and so I would not have blamed myself for crying, but I believe I kept it together. I'm one hell of an optimist, is all it is. Such a sunny disposition can make a body powerfully stupid some of the time, but it's mostly worked out for me so far. "Blissful ignorance," I believe, is the operative phrase.

The officers had put me relatively at ease, and then they put me in the holding cell right there across from them. I could see them through a large window, but I couldn't hear. Five thirty P.M. Six P.M. Everyone seemed pretty calm. Immobile, really. Hold up. I didn't need to hear. My eyes were all the equipment I required to deduce that the men wearing the uniforms had not lifted a finger since putting me in the cell!

The clock was ticking. Six fifteen. Oh my lord. What? Fucking what, now? The bail had been posted; Goliath was waiting to drive me to the theater, a mere fifteen-minute trip or less; and all that remained was for these sons of bitches to punch my ticket and show me the door! Six thirty. Holy Jesus and Mary and Joseph. My misstep dawned on me slowly as I watched the two deputies look innocently at each other with the very slightest of smirks, then continue reading the newspaper. Feet up on the desk, the whole bit. Hoe. Lee. Shit. Seven o'clock. Mother. Fuck. Finally, the penny dropped. I cottoned to my precise dilemma *just* before I banged on the window to communicate that I was shitting little green apples in there. I saw their game, I comprehended the bit, and so I waited. They were fucking with me. They wanted the idiot in the headband, the one with the Ronnie Milsap tapes (oh, fuck, what if they were huge Milsap fans?!) and the opening night, to at least sweat a little bit. Right?

What a dipshit I must have sounded to them. What a dipshit I was, in fact. I most certainly obliged them, as I did readily sweat some bullets and also some Brazil nuts and a few lumps of rock salt as well. My time in the joint—my stint—had run up to literally *dozens* of minutes by now, plenty of time to think about where I'd go from here, a hardened criminal with a *record*. I supposed I'd go back to framing houses in Minooka, my hometown. My sweet parents would be so disappointed in me. The most decent people I had ever come across, about to be handed back this steaming pile of a son. Shit.

It was 7:38 when the fuzz finally roused themselves to emancipate your pudding-headed author. Man, they thought they were pretty goddamn funny. I did not have time to join them in their mirth, however. Goliath violated some speed limits, flagrantly, on the way down Green Street to the stage door of the theater and I sprinted into the dressing room with about seven or eight minutes to get it together. Slapped on some makeup and threw on my loafers and yellow cardigan. Alan, remember? Our assistant director, Mike Seagull, a friend, had gotten wind of my predicament and covered for me with some little white fabrication or other, and before I knew it, I was clumsily blubbering through my crying scene in act 2. Most definitely the best crying scene I've ever delivered. I was saved! Did I mention that I got lucky every now and again?

The final chapter saw me called in front of a "court" of kindly and august senior citizens, who, I daresay, saw me for what I was: a harmless dumbass. When one sweet grandmother complimented my work in *Picnic*, I knew I was sitting pretty. After sincerely communicating to them that I had learned my lesson, I was gratified to hear that my "sentence" would consist of a mere one hundred hours of community service. I was shown a list of departments to choose from, and I went with Animal Control. Easy. Did anyone ever choose Sanitation? With no exaggeration whatsoever, I can report that I spent some weekends helping sorority girls look at puppies at the Humane Society. It was not too hard to swallow, to be honest. Confirming my absolute reputation as an asswipe, I didn't even show up for the entirety of the hundred hours, and I never did hear from anybody about it. Yes, you are correct. I was a douche.

Now, friends, what can we take away from this cautionary tale? I do think it's important to behave rebelliously when leaving the nest and striking out on one's own, but I would suggest coming up just short of breaking the law. If you are going to burglarize a retail establishment, for Christ's sake, case the joint ahead of time. Also, don't ever underestimate the value of Ronnie Milsap.

Be Smart While
Getting Stupid

When the work is done, then we deserve to play. After ten sweaty hours in the woodshop, when I'm covered in sawdust, that first Corona tastes like the jizz of the Lord (which has to be the most magnificent beverage, right? The Libation of Glory?), and in my life, one of my greatest leisure-time pleasures has been smoking a bong in the living room before settling down with the new episode of *Twin Peaks*, or maybe a Jim Jarmusch film. *Dead Man?* Heaven. Or some animation or claymation. *Akira?* Wallace and Gromit? Sublime. Therefore, if I had to choose one god to serve, I would choose . . . Dionysus. The Greek god of wine, song, and theater. My Eucharist is found in entertaining people, receiving the bread and the wine of laughter and tears from the crowd, and being brought to catharsis by the work of others. When I take the stage, Dionysus (or Bacchus) sees and hears my ministry and he is muchly pleased. Or she. No reason to stick to the tired dogma of the patriarchy.

I like to engage in revelry. I like to celebrate the human experience through performance. I like to engender mirth. I like to abide pleasure with my body, and one way that we funny monkeys have learned to know delight is through the consumption of intoxicants. All splendid treats in the proper dosage, but, just like religion (the opiate of the masses), you can use them responsibly, and do good, or you can use them like an asshole and ruin it for the rest of us, who just want to get a little high and look at a maple leaf. Let's have a look at our choices, shall we?

1. **Wine, Beer.** The workhorses. You keep these expendables in stock, like paper towels and salt. And just like salt, you will enjoy them throughout your life, as long as you don't overdo it. Beer, in all its infinite varieties these days, is obviously one of the staples of life. For a pint of beer, you can never beat Guinness or Old Rasputin. In the life of the theater professional, three pints a night in the local public house is simply part of one's workday, and it's nice work, if you can get it. My leisure time was dominated by beer throughout my youth and into my twenties, because wine just didn't have much of a foothold in my part of the Midwest. Aunt Dee would drink white wine, but then she always was a bit fancy. I never understood what all the fuss was about until my wife bought a really nice bottle of Cabernet Sauvignon on New Year's Eve 2000. We were at a beautiful cabin in Santa Barbara, and we counted down the last hours of our first eight months together as we sipped this red wine that made my head and body feel like delicious candy. I'm not talking about shitty candy (which also has its place of honor), your Skittles, your Willy Wonka varietals, your PayDays. No, I'm talking about handmade, rich-people candy. This wine—fermented grape juice, mind you—tasted and felt like Edmund's description of Turkish delight in *The Lion, the Witch and the Wardrobe*, and, buddy, I signed up as, and I remain, a card-carrying member of the wine enthusiasts' club. For, lo, it is some good shit.

2. **Whisky and the Lesser Spirits.** Try to utilize the hard liquors with less frequency than you do beer. Did I spend a period of my youth chugging Jim Beam? Sure I did, as it provided a swift and complete oblivion, which is sometimes what we're looking for in life. That was a thankfully brief stint, when I was despairing of ever finding a lady who could stand me, and one whom I could tolerate in return. Once I got my head on straight, I learned that bourbons exist to rival even the qualities of Jim Beam! Furthermore, I discovered Irish and Scotch whiskys, to which I remain devoted. For a single-malt scotch, Lagavulin will never disappoint. It's practically furry. I'll be happy to further enumerate the admirable qualities of whisky consumption over a glass of the good stuff should you ever catch me out at the bar.

3. **Nitrous Oxide, N_2O, Laughing Gas, Whip-Its.** Ahhh, old friend. Not just at the dentist anymore. For those of you who have deprived yourselves of this brief delight, please hustle out to the store and pick up several cans of ready-to-squirt whipped cream, and let the fun begin. The cream remains in the can, fully wasted, as the propellant nitrous oxide enters your lungs, and thereby your circulatory system. You will experience a light-headed euphoria as well as auditory hallucinations, culminating in smiles of glee or laughter. If you want to consume this goodness without wasting all that yummy dairy product, go to the gourmet store and purchase a case or three of N_2O cartridges and a whipped cream charger! Or buy a little twist "cracker" at your local head shop and empty your cartridge into a pretty balloon! Load up a hit, put on "Echolalia" by Dead Can Dance, and drink deep, chum. Find a nice place to recline and listen to any good noises—a freight train, a subway, a waterfall, a Wilco show. Just sit where the po-po won't be hassling you. Good, clean fun. I've seen friends fall down and go boom whilst using this stuff, so maybe keep your seat.

4. Weed. Sweet, sweet lady. Marijuana is quite possibly the finest of intoxicants. It has been scientifically proven, for decades, to be much less harmful to the body than alcohol when used on a regular basis (Google "Science"). I applaud and support all of the legalization efforts perpetually under way in our country, but I kind of doubt it's going to make it all the way through the federal legal system until big tobacco wakes up and gets behind it. I'm calling you out, R.J.! Step right up to yo' face and dis you, Philly Morris! You continue to cling to the legality of your carcinogenic smoking product that has been *outlawed* in most public spaces in America, but do you not see the potential in Marlboro Green? Own it! Regulate it! Tobacco will be going away; you know it! You have seen that writing on the wall! Turn that acreage over to cannabis, my brothas! People are constantly committing crimes whilst under the influence of, or looking for funding for, every other intoxicant besides marijuana. I am a supersweet teddy bear, but when I drink tequila, I want to knife somebody. When a person injects heroin, I've read, they want to lie in bed and drool with pleasure, listening to Coltrane's *Giant Steps* until the fix wears off, then they want to go out and threaten to knife somebody, to get money for more heroin, so they can get back to drooling on their pillow. When I smoke pot, I want to look at nature and laugh about everything and eat some delicious things and then sleep. For Willie's sake, do the math.

5. Mushrooms. Yes indeed. The gentle brother of the hallucinogen family. All the giggles and visuals without the chemical jaw-grinding and speedy aftereffects of big brother LSD. I remember one beautiful day in the woods of Allerton Park near Monticello, Illinois, tripping on 'shrooms with my brother Falcon Smoker, looking at leaves and trees, swimming in the river, listening to the birds and frogs and wood nymphs' song, gulping in the sweet air and glory of living, then winding down to wait out the waves of sensory bliss so we could head home. Once we were somewhat straightened out, we set off for home, blasting Ennio Morricone's magnificent soundtrack to *The Mission*, particularly track twelve, called "River." And in the early dark on the highway, all the other taillights looked like X-wing fighters, which lent a comforting perception of nostalgia to the ride. Treat your intoxicants with respect, and they will do right by you.

6. Amyl Nitrate, or "Poppers." Not worth it. Small head rush, massive brain cell carnage, often followed by a splitting headache. Might as well huff glue.

7. Glue. I've tried some and gotten the most profound effects from that crazy blue PVC plumbing adhesive, but it's a very low-grade high. Your head feels dirty inside, probably from all the poison from the glue. Pass. Huffing vapors is the intoxicant of true desperation.

8. Chicharrón, Cracklins, Pork Rinds. Not technically an intoxicant, but you couldn't ever tell me that. My buddy Pat Roberts and I were hooked on those bubbly, crunchy skin chips, and we had it bad. The great thing about this snack food is that it's mostly protein and therefore much healthier than most of the garbage Frito-Lay is churning out. No offense, Frito-Lay, I love a bag of Doritos as much as the next Midwesterner, but I've read all of Michael Pollan's books, so let's just call it like it is. To place my pork-skin problem chronologically, let's just say it went real nice with Jim Beam and Virginia blister peanuts for dessert. Keep the peanut can for loose hardware, and you've done your part for Mother Earth today.

9

Born Again Again

During our last couple of years of high school both Lynette and I worked part-time at Minooka's video store, Mick's Flicks. This should serve to date the business just a bit for you: The video store also had two tanning beds in the back (Kool Rays Tanning). I was fifteen or sixteen at the time and my boss, Jeff, was about twenty-two. He had a BMW, which was just insane in Minooka. He might as well have been driving around a spaceship. He was a dashing, young, entrepreneurial guy, and his folks had helped set him up with this video store, which was doing very well. Turned out, people liked movies back then in 1980s Illinois.

Jeff and I took a shine to each other, despite his insistence on calling me "Tricky Nicky." I have found, in life, that the person signing the paychecks will tend to call you whatever the hell he/she pleases. A couple of other friends also worked there part-time, and the video store was, of course, in a strip mall, so we indulged in meals from the TeePee Hut, two doors down to the right, and sometimes we'd get beers from Minooka Liquors, one door down to the left. If we needed prophylactics or batteries or lube, we could nip next door to the right, to KODO Pharmacy. In other words, we wanted for nothing. As a responsible young chap, I was trusted to be on the receiving end of such dreamy tasks as delivering Jeff's BMW to him in Chicago and making sure the ladies in the tanning beds had all the beverages they required.

In the days when the VCR was king you can imagine what a big to-do would be made over films like *Aliens*, *Platoon*, and, yes, *Three Men and a Baby*. We practically had to open a new wing to accommodate all of the VHS copies and cardboard stand-ups of Tom Cruise for *Top Gun*. I enjoyed playing *Highlander* over and over on the in-house system in the hopes that the populace would come to know the pleasures of the Quickening. Little did I dream then that I would one day come to reside on those shelves myself. To date, I think my most popular title in Minooka is *Miss Congeniality 2: Armed and Fabulous*.

C ut to: our first semester down at the U of I, where Lynette and I were learning that our affiliation was by this juncture ill-fated. The writing on the wall plainly read that we should part ways, but we (I) weren't (wasn't) quite ready to give up my security blanket, by which I mean, of course, her vagina. I could hardly get to sleep at night without curling up in that cozy thicket. Reality continued to splash cold water on our situation, and Lynette finally put her foot down and sent me packing. I went into withdrawal, and although my new friends and my life in theater school made it a bit easier to go on, I just couldn't shake what turned out to be a bit of an obsession. We still spoke often, which of course helped matters very little in terms of my attempt to quit her cold turkey.

Interestingly, her sister had just won three plane tickets to Jamaica. So Lynette, her mom, and her sister were going to go to the beach for a week. By this point she had commenced with seeing other guys, which only sprinkled sweet gasoline on the flame I continued to fan. She told me about the Jamaica trip, and I very casually asked, "So, is anyone going with you?" No. Just the ladies. Splendid.

An idea was taking shape in the steel trap of my lust-riddled noggin. A goddamn great idea. Over the course of a few conversations, I took note of the pertinent details regarding their travel arrangements. I had seen pretty much every episode of *The A-Team*, so I knew how to hatch a goddamn plan. I knew (Mick's Flicks) Jeff's sister Kelly worked at Midway Airport in Chicago, which was from where Lynette and co. were to depart. So, after twenty-four-odd tallboys of Miller Genuine Draft had changed hands (wink), Kelly hooked me up with all the details and a standby ticket to Jamaica, the day before Lynette was to arrive. I would infiltrate the perimeter, perform some recon, get the lay of the land, and then just hunker down to wait.

I had once flown home from North Dakota, but this flight out of the country was major. Added to which, the whole "standby" thing was baffling. Then things suddenly turned from baffling to terrifying when I got the call that my flight was oversold, and I was to be bumped to the next day. TO HER FLIGHT.

There was only one flight a day, and this was a great many years before Expedia.com, not to mention I was a total babe in the woods when it came to airplane travel, but even so, Kelly told me that I really had no choice. It was either fly on the same flight as my target (I mean, the object of my affection), or bail on the plan. To this day, I can never tell if I'm ballsy or just stupid, but by god, I generally tend to go for it.

I went to the airport armed with some items I had borrowed from the costume shop at school. Ironically (in hindsight), I glued on a full moustache, which was very much like my adult moustache. I dabbed some gray into my hair, which was slicked with Brylcreem, and donned aviator glasses. Additionally, I wore a fat suit of two towels wrapped and bound around my middle, along with some of my dad's more conservative schoolteacher clothes. "Average middle-aged guy going to Jamaica" was the look to which I aspired, with a newspaper and a small duffel bag.

Ignorant of the ways of the boarding gate, I was utterly bewildered when told to stand next to the door whilst all of the ticketed passengers walked past! I held up my newspaper, real cool-like, and managed not to wet my dad's brown polyesters as Lynette and her party of three sauntered by, laughing.

Once the legit flyers were all aboard, then the standby crowd was assigned seats. So far, so good. I made my way onto the plane, and I'll be goddamned if I wasn't seated one seat behind her, one seat to the right. "Okay. Okay. Be cool. You got this, buddy." I could actually see the right side of her face through the gap between the seats. This was pretty goddamn hilarious so far! During the flight, Lynette got up to retrieve something from the compartment above her, and we actually nodded at each other. I thought, "Man, are you gonna crack up when I tell you about this later!" In my head, I was absolutely living out a fantasy as the cool protagonist in my very own John Cusack superromantic comedy, when in truth, I was 100 percent stalking this poor young dancer. Terrific!

We landed in Jamaica, and, having done the recon back stateside, I knew just where to go. I got in a cab and sped to the beachfront hotel where they were staying. It was all feeling pretty insane, what with the tropical climate, not to mention the big Rasta dude driving a jeep as a cab, blaring some kick-ass UB40. I went into the hotel men's room and donned my cutoff jean shorts, which were still a pretty ac-

007 DEADLY SINS

ceptable garment in the eighties. The moment of reckoning was drawing tantalizingly near!

As I had correctly surmised, within an hour of their arrival they were down on the beach, an incredibly long stretch of beautiful white sand, at the far end of which I sat reading, incongruously, a book of Thornton Wilder plays. Lynette was walking toward me in a bikini, thankfully with some distance between herself and her mom (who, it bears mentioning, had been a fan, at least up until this point). I walked up to her in my super-Swayze cutoff jeans and, just like I rehearsed, stated, "Hey, Lynette. How's it goin'?" Her jaw dropped, amazed. She was clearly feeling something powerful, like probably love, and she said, "I don't fucking BELIEVE you did this. YOU ASSHOLE!" (which means "motherfucker" in born-again speak), and she punched me in the chest.

"I came here to get away from you. This is my vacation from all the crap I have to figure out in my life."

"Holy shit. Um. I am so sorry. I meant for this to be awesome . . . but I have clearly just upset you. Sorry. You won't see me again."

Then, as though seeing them for the first time, she took a good long look at my jean shorts. Then she took in my book of plays by Thornton Wilder. Something shifted behind her eyes and beneath her intestines. Within an hour we were having rub-sex in the shallow water on the beach. I had had a positive feeling that she would appreciate my surprise, and she did. Eventually. But then, after a solid scrump-and-munch session, she said, "Okay, this was really nice, and now you have to leave. I seriously don't want to see you again, this is my week here. And when we get home, there's no more. For real." All right. Okay. All in all, things had gone pretty well up until this point. I wasn't trying to win her back; I think ultimately we were both just happy to make our final love-time a memorable one. I had happily suffered a chest punch in exchange for a rich, romantic coupling in the Caribbean surf. I couldn't help but clench an imaginary cigar in my teeth and utter to the B. A. Baracus in my head, "I love it when a plan comes together."

Unfortunately, that was the end of the successfully orchestrated part of my plan. I had been so focused on my big *Say Anything* moment that I hadn't given much thought to the postcoital accommodations. I mean, I was old buddies with these ladies, so I was sure they'd at least let me crash on the couch. No dice.

Not knowing what to do next, with all of $70 in my pocket, I went in to a pay phone and called Jeff back home.

"Well, Jeffrey, the eagle has landed, and the eagle has been kissed, but now the eagle is homeless and without much bread. I guess I'll fly home tomorrow. Pick me up?"

"Ah, Tricky Nicky! Ha-HAA! You got some major brass ones, my friend. You got it. I'll see you at Midway."

Great. Now what? I looked through the phone book and found a cheap place in the mountains. I called up, and the lady was very nice on the phone. She even sent their jeep to pick me up. Looking back, this was probably a pretty crappy hotel, but for a nineteen-year-old playing hooky from Illinois, it was a crazy paradise. I was completely enamored of the colonial style, situated as it was amongst the jungle foliage. When I arrived, the manager, Maria, with whom I had spoken on the phone, was just as nice in person. There was a big shindig under way with a live reggae band, and everyone was drinking daiquiris. I had never even heard of a daiquiri. Turns out, it was like, strawberry rum booze, all cold and shit. Fucking right on. Jamaica.

I commenced to dancing with the people and feeling like life was not too bad. I was thinking of calling Lynette, because we really enjoyed dancing together, and I thought she would love this music, but then again, this Maria was beginning to be ever more super nice. Long story short, I spent the night with her, and she packed me off to the airport the next morning in the blue and yellow dashiki she had been wearing.

Ultimately, this caper turned out to be a really fun way to wrap up a great teenage romance. When I tell this story, people often accuse me of behaving like a stalker, and even in those pre-9/11 halcyon days of travel, my subterfuge could definitely have been interpreted as creepy. But I hope that the story's resolution makes it plain that everyone involved came out of the fray with a satisfied smile. The only downside, really, was discovering that I was allergic to something, presumably strawberry daiquiris, judging from the painful red rash all around my crotchal area.

The Moustache Makes the Magick

First of all: Teddy Roosevelt. Pow! How's that for a punch in the teeth? Or moustache?

As a mere sprout, moustaches always represented, simply, manhood to me, as well as heroes, cowboys, and my uncles Don and Dan, who were already my idols and had moustaches that were flinty, bristly, completely virile, and tough as nails. When I was just a little pisser, I knew that I would only truly become a man upon the day that I could grow a moustache. I associated the notion of those noble whiskers mostly with my uncles, because they owned tractors, wore vise-grip pliers on their belts, and were out in the weather harvesting their incomes by way of cultivating crops in the soil. They were brave, admirable souls to me (they still are), much like Burt Reynolds and Tom Selleck were at the time.

A moustache carries with it a little bit of derring-do. You're the kind of guy who will come barreling up doing a power slide in your pickup truck and then give a girl a wink. You know your knots. You know what to do with beef tallow. Freddie Mercury was also a major idol of mine, and he had a badass moustache to perfectly complement his whole leather-guy Tom of Finland thing. When I eventually learned that he was gay, I didn't think less of him, I just thought that gay people must be pretty kick-ass, then, if he was one of them. Before I ever knew anything about sexuality I just thought he was a rough/pretty-looking dude who could sing his face off, and once I began to learn about the varying sexual orientations of we humans, *then* I thought he was a rough/pretty-looking dude who could sing his face off.

I recently had the extreme pleasure of showing my friend the seminal 1986 film *Highlander*, which is REQUIRED VIEWING (for young men, anyway), and I was blown away, yet again, by the amazing Queen songs that make up the film's soundtrack. Freddie Mercury brought manhood to the stage like few before him and damn fewer since.

A moustache tells folks that you're willing to take the bull by the horns. You have a certain amount of gravel in your craw, like many of Sean Connery's characters. Name me one actor since Connery to bring to life such a swaggering sense of manliness, with or without whiskers, but especially with. Can't do it? Neither can I. But by sporting a moustache, I can bring a hint of that staglike flavor to my own savory life. Later on, Sam Elliott took an awfully fine swing at that feeling with his incredibly aesthetic lip hedge in *The Big Lebowski*. Portraying the Stranger in that film, a man with such life experience, including enough notches on his belt to be able to give advice to THE DUDE, for Pete's sake, required a brambly thicket of absolute chaparral beneath his nose, and Sam brought that shit. Hard.

I also emulated a lot of sports figures in the eighties. We were *really* into sports in my house. Mike Ditka and Dick Butkus were the two most Rooseveltian members of the Chicago Bears organization, to my way of thinking. It was an amazing time to be loving sports teams around Chicago, because the Cubs were great (They're always great! Shut up, reality!) and the Bears had the best season in NFL history (suck my balls, Miami '72) in 1985. No question. Then Jordan's Bulls showed up. Phil Jackson. MUH.

STACHE. I was at "teen" age, a very formative time for me to indulge in revering these superhero-looking guys with moustaches, like Walter Payton, Mike Singletary, all the Bears' linebackers, Wilber Marshall, and Otis Wilson, plus William "the Refrigerator" Perry and Willie Gault. The Cubs were also great upper-lip role models, with Ron Cey, Billy Buckner, Dennis Eckersley, Fergie Jenkins, and Lee Smith all sporting cool-as-shit moustaches. Cy Young Award–winner Rollie Fingers of the Oakland A's must be included on any such list because he was a bewhiskered badass on the mound who brandished a full-on Snidely Whiplash handlebar moustache that was mighty intimidating to any poor sap facing him in the batter's box. Also, Goose Gossage, ladies and gentlemen.

Earlier moustached film heroes Errol Flynn and really anybody playing Zorro forever associated for me the gentlemanly pursuit of sword fighting with the moustache. Wyatt Earp brought his hirsute stache to the gunfight at the OK Corral and was justifiably pissed that he was mainly remembered for only that one heroic day when in truth, his whiskers saw him through careers as city policeman, county sheriff, teamster, buffalo hunter, bouncer, saloon keeper, gambler, brothel owner, pimp, miner, and boxing referee. Now, that was a moustache. In the same vein, Mark Twain had the kind of lip bracken to land him on the list of men I've always idolized. His sense of humor always sounded to me like if someone real smart came from my neck of the woods, and he said what he meant. I shouldn't be surprised if, in my later years, I try to emulate his technique even more than I already do, writing stories about mischief while riding the nation's rivers astride a steamboat.

In general, depending on style, your moustache can read as heroic and lend a granite quality to your visage, or if you go in a slightly different direction, your moustache can connote criminality in a character. I think it's funny that when I'm playing a sheriff, I think, "I am going to need a kick-ass moustache," but if I am playing a bank robber or cattle rustler or Irish thug, I think, "Oh, I had better grow a kick-ass moustache." The important thing is to *start* with the moustache. Everything else can be adjusted around it, forcing your truth to trumpet beneath it, be that truth good or bad, strong or weak, sexy or abhorrent. On the heroic side, astronauts rock a moustache if they know what they're about.

The straight dope is: If we're TRUE to our natures, then we grow a robust beard. That is what was intended by the ORDER OF THINGS. Society has put a spin on us, making a "clean-shaven" countenance the social "norm," which, from Ma Nature's point of view, is bullshit. But then, so are air-conditioning and Saran wrap and Cap'n Crunch and a bunch of other cool shit that allows us to "rise above" nature at times. A moustache is a socialized way to say, "Okay, look, I'll let you see most of my face, since that's what we're all doing right now, but if you would kindly direct your gaze to this thornbush above my mouth, you will be reminded that I am a fucking animal, and I'm ready to reproduce, or rip your throat out if called upon, because I come from nature." In this way the moustache can be considered a relief valve of sorts, for the buildup of animal preening that most people completely repress. That's what makes a man with a good stache so cool, calm, and collected.

It's funny to me that people ask me for tips on growing a moustache. I often reply, "I honestly don't know. I was born with this moustache. I just cut it periodically so that it doesn't go down my throat when I'm enjoying my soup." My whiskers grow without any provocation from me whatsoever.

I have about as much advice on growing a moustache as I do on growing fingernails or hemorrhoids. I'll tell you this much: My life is always more delicious when I have whiskers on my face, but that might just be because those whiskers tend to accumulate bacon crumbs and scotch, rendering them literally delicious all day long. In response to the query, "How do you grow that robust moustache for Ron Swanson?" I can walk you through the steps:

1. I don't shave my lip area.

2. After two weeks, I have a passable moustache, in the form of long, luxurious stubble.

3. I continue to eschew the razor.

4. After three to four weeks, my whiskers have developed to the point where I can play a sheriff who is so tough that he eats nails, but still not Swanson.

5. I refuse to shave.

6. After five weeks, the whiskers growing from just beneath my nostrils have extended down, wirelike, to reach my top lip, a distance of one full imperial inch. Now, and only now, may I don the pleated Dockers and thick, long-sleeved knits of Pawnee's director of Parks and Recreation with confidence and authority.

Finally, I just want to add that I am a character actor, which means that, unlike "good-looking" actors (your Will Smiths and your Daniel Craigs), who always play (with great aplomb) different versions of the same dreamboat, I, lacking their cheekbones, rely on versatility to color each of my roles with a different crayon or brush. My old pal Mother Nature has done me quite the solid by bestowing upon me a thick mane of hair and a rampant growth of whiskers, both excellent basic materials from which to sculpt wildly differing character details. I have deeply relished my opportunities to try disparate hairdos, from Mohawk to hippie, and the same goes for the facial bush, from Grizzly Adams beard to muttonchops to Swanson stache.

The peculiar thing is, people familiar with my television work now seem to expect me to wield the moustache at all times, when in reality, I will wear it seldom outside of the shooting season. Having enjoyed my life as an aspiring chameleon thus far, I look forward to many more years of it. *Parks and Recreation* films for seven months of the year, and when I add on the month of moustache growth to prepare for the season's launch, that's eight months, or two-thirds of my year, that I am locked into that look. Therefore, I take great pleasure in spending my off-months looking like anything but Ron Swanson. Sometimes I shave my head bald, and sometimes I grow a large shaggy beard, and either direction sees me happy as a clam.

For an actor, donning a character is a strange transaction. Ron Swanson, for example, does not belong to me, and so I cannot in good conscience "be" him when I am not at work with his cocreators, my boss and the writers of my show. It's like the Iron Man suit. As much as Robert Downey Jr. loves to play that particular iteration of Tony Stark, it would hardly be appropriate (though yes, it would be awesome) for him to wear that suit to the grocery

ACCEPTABLE

The Minimum

The Tracker

The Trucker

Mr. Natural

UNACCEPTABLE

Emasculator

The Douchebag

Bruce

Prison Pussy

The Nut Smudge

The Fop

Minus Balls

The Joke

FACIAL HAIR

store or the beach. It's no different than the uniform anyone wears at work. Wearing Ron Swanson in my "regular" civilian life would feel to me commensurate with a Best Buy employee putting on that blue shirt and proselytizing to strangers at the car wash on the virtues of high-def televisions. I will have to be satisfied with the amazing good fortune bestowed upon me, that it's what I get to wear whilst working at the greatest job anyone has ever had.

10

Wax On, Wax Off

Without teachers in our lives, we would be a bunch of sorry dullards, indeed. Dimwits and dunces. One of the many gratifying advantages of mammalian life is that the older generation tends to teach the youngsters the skills they need to thrive in these harsh elements. I can tell you nice folks as a flat fact that were it not for the teachers in my own experience, not only would I be unable to extricate the toilet paper from the roll, but I would not ever have even found my way to the john. My parents, naturally, have been my first and best teachers, along with their respective families, who shared in the chores.

Many hands make light work, and a little "handful of joy" like myself, not to mention my little brother, two sisters, and a bunch of cousins, provided a workload that was equal to an army of aunts, uncles, and grandparents. Dad first taught me to drive a clutch, followed by my uncles Don and Dan and grandpas Mike and Ray. Each threw in his two cents, instructing both me and my cousin Ryan so that by the time we were nine, after years of gentle lessons, I could engage the consarnit transmission without any crunching.

Grandpa Mike's teaching was especially efficacious. He was an old man who didn't have time for maneuvering, so he just went straight at us. I believe Ryan and I were six or seven when he asked us if we would like to sample a chaw of the Red Man chewing tobacco forever in a pouch in his hip pocket. You bet your ass we wanted to try it. Not only did the patriarch of our lives favor this masticating medium, but so did most of our favorite Chicago Cubs! The time had arrived for us to join the legion of men, moving mountains of hay and oceans of yellow corn about the county. Grandpa gave us each a portion and said, "Now, you just chew it, like chewing gum." We complied, champing away in a manner worthy of any swaggering jack down at the grain elevator, if I do say so myself, lasting all of ninety seconds before we both promptly vomited in the yard and lay down in the grass to die. Class complete. Grandpa Mike wasn't fucking around.

Later in my ongoing career as a student I was to win the teacher lottery not once but twice, at the Krannert Center for the Performing Arts in Champaign–Urbana. Permit me to "wax on" now, if you will, as I unfold the Ballad of Robin and Sato-sensei.

Robin McFarquhar was my "movement" teacher. In any given year, he shouldered a variety of classes, like Stage Combat, Circus Techniques, Deep-Tissue Massage, Mask Work, Intro to Your Spine, Tai Chi, and Guts. I also took an independent study in piss and vinegar with him. Every student in the department, both undergraduate and graduate, fell under his gentle British wing, and Robin did everything in his power to heap learning upon our virgin, spongelike spirits and bodies. McFarquhar, with his actions, illustrated to me a quality that I have really learned to look for in an instructor: that he/she be one who continues to indulge in a hungry course of learning for him/herself. When he wasn't laying some delicious tutelage upon us, which meant mainly during summer vacation, Robin was traveling the nation and the world, participating in workshops of all sorts, from Feldenkrais to Alexander Technique to stage combat to literally walking on coals. That might sound extreme to you, or at least a tad hocus-pocus, but let me assure you it was anything but, for he would dutifully return to his classroom every fall and do his utmost to inspire us to perform that very act in all of our work: walk on fire.

Robin's movement syllabus at the U of I theater school generally taught one to know and understand the instrument of one's body, along with its possibilities and limitations (imagine any time you have begun a new program of exercise, and some long-unused muscle group speaks up and says, "Hey! Whoa! You've paid us no attention whatsoever for these twenty-seven years, and now you want us to perform repeated sets of lat pull-downs? Take it easy, sailor."). We got acquainted with all of the disparate muscular work-teams in our own operations, especially those crews handling the spine, that finicky nerve center from whence all bodily motion springs. Once we had socialized with all of the labor divisions, we then put our company to work in tasks requiring both finesse (juggling, mime, courtsword) and brawn (backflips, broadsword, wrestling). As you might recall from your own school days, the divergent realms of theater nerds and athletes seldom experienced any crossover, and so Robin was teaching us merely to be athletes before we could begin to participate in his artistic decathlons.

As amazingly delivered as these disciplines were, they were mostly dealing with the vessel. If it was whisky school, these classes focused on the barrel, with its distinct cooperage, the tinctures in which the oak staves had previously bathed, the truing of the hoops, and the application of peat smoke in some exceptional cases. But, continuing this well-distilled analogy (cough), the real pedagogical treasures in Robin's classroom concerned the spirits contained within the cask. The man taught us guts, plain and simple. At the top of every session of circus class, the assembled troupe would recite:

> *"Come to the cliff," he said.*
> *They said, "We are afraid."*
> *"Come to the cliff," he said.*
> *They came, he pushed them*
> *and they flew.*

The sense of it is, come to the edge of the cliff, face the leap, and be afraid. Then acknowledge your fear, step forward once more, and then push yourself off the cliff. I was lucky, as I was already stupid, so I was ready to take any flying vault that people would watch, but for many of the softer students, ones who had enrolled in the program aspiring to become the next Molly Ringwald, the prospect of attempting a backflip was terrifying stuff.

Every one of us was gently coaxed toward overcoming his/her own insecurities and, as a result, flying like a motherfucking eagle. These classes took all of the good parts of self-help ideology and the religious mind set and employed them with the sole objective of instilling self-confidence and creativity in the participants. One of the greatest epiphanies a performer can take on board is the understanding that one must simply fly free. Your flight may be beautiful and sexy (hi there), or it might be awkward and labored. It might be hilariously encumbered by disheveled feathers and an ill-kept beak, or it might be workmanlike and steady, but, whatever your aeronautical style, your soaring has just that: STYLE! Whatever it is that makes you different, weird, unique from the others, it is *that*, if anything, which will see you prosper. When I managed to work that golden notion through my thick head, it was then that I knew I would be okay. Not everyone will like the cut of your jib (looking at you, Les Moonves; more on that later), but many others will. One simply needs to seek those others and then somehow trick them into buying tickets for your production of *Gangsta Rap Coriolanus*.

In 2012, Robin McFarquhar invited me to come back and speak to the current students of the department, twenty years after my own graduation. I leapt at the opportunity, remembering so clearly how we yearned back in my own student days for professionals working in "the business" to come and tell us how things stood in the big, bad world outside. I sat in front of the assembled department and told them, first and foremost, to be sure not to squander their time in this facility in which we sat, the Krannert Center, which contains four gorgeous better-than-professional-quality theaters with accompanying scene shop, costume shop, and light and sound departments, staffed by absolute superstars of their respective crafts.

"I have worked all over the country in theater, film, and television, and I have sincerely never come across a bounty of resources like those contained in this one benevolently be-bricked city block of artistic rectitude," I spoke to them.

"You talk weird," they replied.

"Silence!" I commanded.

I went on to discuss the pros and, sure, a few cons to working there as a lad, mentioning some faculty members and what have you, and then I came to speak of Robin, who was sitting off to the side, probably willing me to pick up the pace, as teachers are wont to do.

"Let me tell you about this guy . . . ," I began, but before I could get another word out, I promptly burst into tears.

"Oh, sorry. [*Sob*] I did not see this coming . . . ," I managed to utter, before openly sobbing for several minutes. No shit. Even typing this description of that scene has me welling up with gratitude for that man. Hard as it may be for you to believe, I didn't get to where I am today because I'm so cute. I'm sorry, gentle reader, I should have suggested you take a seat before I dropped that thermonuclear-shock nugget.

"Where I am today," by the way, is in class, a class of my own devising, based upon the generous teachings of men and women like Robin McFarquhar, to whom I would say, "I shall forever don my largest cap just so that I may doff it to your life's work."

As luck would have it, when I had finished crying like a baby in front of that assembly of twenty-year-olds and I had spoken my heartfelt piece about Robin and his auspicious curriculum, another of my teachers walked through the studio door. I said, "Oh, great, and then there's this guy . . . ," and promptly renewed my sobbing. That teacher was Shozo Sato. My sensei.

This is a cheap comparison, but it will go a long way toward elucidating for you the basis of my relationship with Sato-sensei. The original version of the film *The Karate Kid* (1984) features an absolutely enchanting performance by the great Pat Morita as Mr. Miyagi (if you have enjoyed the newer version with the winning Jaden Smith and Jackie Chan, then you should check out the old-school flavor). Shozo came into my life and immediately bewitched me and my future Defiant Theatre cronies with his Kabuki Theater class.

A traditional four-hundred-year-old Japanese theater form, Kabuki literally translates to: "sing [*ka*] dance [*bu*] skill [*ki*]," or "acting."

This very presentational style employs some of my favorite aesthetic tricks and techniques, such as the use of silken fabrics to represent elements like water and fire and blood (to great effect—a stabbing victim might erupt ribbons of red silk from his chest, eliciting gasps from the audience) or simply the employment of hugely broad mugging during "*mie*" poses (grandly expressive freeze-frames onstage describing moments of great emotion). At such moments in the execution of Japanese Kabuki productions, expert audience members will shout either the actor's last name, as a great compliment to the performer's skill, or even more flattering, the name of the actor's house, as well as the phrase "You are better than your father!" the pinnacle of praise. Next time you see me in a play, it would not hurt my feelings were you to shower me with such a pronouncement.

Another stroke of great fortune in my life was landing a role in Shozo's touring production of *Kabuki Achilles* in 1991. What started out as an enrollment in a reputedly cool class became a tour of Japan, complete with participation in an ancient theater festival in the small mountain village of Damine. In addition, three or four of my closest new buddies were in the show as well, so we were treated to quite a vacation. For most of the cast, it was our first-ever international travel, and Shozo and his wife, Alice, did an absolutely masterful job of parenting their brood of twenty students, who were incredibly fond of sake, it turned out.

That tour was so rich with beautiful experience and detail that it rather merits its own volume, but one chapter sticks out in my memory. Because Japanese farmers lavish an exceptional amount of attention on the cultivation of their fruits, especially melons, that particular fruit is considered the finest delicacy on the Japanese menu, bringing a price astonishingly more dear than the finest steak. In Tokyo, my dear Joe Foust and I were seeking breakfast one morning in the hotel restaurant when an old gentleman noticed us buying cigarettes from a vending machine. He was very friendly, trying to communicate something to us, the meaning of which we could not discern.

Gamely, we kept pointing at ourselves and stating, "Illinois Kabuki," whereupon he would grow excited and noddingly exclaim, "*Hai!* Kabuki. Kabuki!" He was awfully nice, buying us each a pack of smokes and continuing to energetically speak a stream of unintelligible Japanese. He even gave me an enthusiastic handshake at a certain point, which in Japan was apparently executed a little differently than I was used to. "Kabuki! Kabuki!"

It grew a bit strange, although this man was clearly a big fan of our show, which he must have seen at one of our tour stops. He brought us over to his nearby table for breakfast, it would seem, as he persistently pointed at the melon on the menu, the most premium item, so expensive, we were told, that it was often purchased as a gift, much like a bottle of fine champagne in the States. Eventually we thanked him as best we could and called our friend Tatro over, explaining that the gentleman wanted to buy him some cantaloupe. Joe and I withdrew to our people, and as we explained the odd scene to the group, Shozo began to laugh very loudly. He reminded us that the word *Kabuki*, besides representing a revered national art form, was also slang for "prostitute," since the style had been initially developed by traveling bands of whores visiting the camps of warring shoguns. Well, I guess that explained the ticklish handshake. Everyone had a good laugh until we remembered Tatro. Running to his rescue, we were surprised to see him sitting with the old man having a good chuckle, finishing up a beautiful serving of melon. "Best damn cantaloupe I ever tasted," he said. "This guy is a hoot!" We never did tell him the rest.

Because of my ability to carry heavy objects, Sato-sensei made me a bit of a teacher's pet. Pulling weeds in his garden one day, he casually dropped this bomb: "The act of pulling weeds has the very same impetus that causes war. We're killing these bad shoots so the ones we favor can receive all the sunlight, nutrients, and water. That's all war is: killing weeds." That was the first but certainly not the last time I was floored by my sensei's wisdom.

Over the years, he continued to call upon me for my mulish abilities, at one point hiring my classmate Mike Flanigan (another Pilotus) and myself to move him and Alice to their new home in beautiful Mendocino, California. We drove the moving truck whilst Shozo and Alice drove their minivan. Filling a truck with scenery, a false world, and driving it to a new place to re-create that world anew was an act I was quite familiar with, but the notion of making that transition in real life was still quite an adventure to my way of thinking. Shozo had a real sense of the swashbuckler about him, albeit a relatively small, graceful version. A published master of several Zen disciplines, such as Kabuki theater and dance, ikebana (flower arrangement), *sumi-e* (black ink painting), Zen meditation, and the tea ceremony, Shozo had spent the year of 1981 touring the American Southwest in a van, painting the landscapes for his *sumi-e* book. Pretty badass. By the time I was twenty-three, he had taken me to Japan, Hungary, Cyprus, London, and California and had gotten me paid for most of it!

Foust, Flanigan, and I were never the leads in his shows, as there were more beautiful actors who were better dancers, but we were dependable, so he kept us around the most. We would be called upon for comic relief. In between long, elegiac sequences of shifting light and undulating, colorful dances in museum-quality traditional costumes of Shozo's design, we would run onto the stage, fall down, then run off. There's room for everyone.

My favorite rule from Sensei was "Always maintain the attitude of a student." When a person thinks they have finished learning, that is when bitterness and disappointment can set in, as that person will wake up every day wondering when someone is going to throw a parade in their honor for being so smart. As human beings, we, by the definition of our very natures, can never be perfect. This means that as long as we are alive and kicking, we can be improving ourselves. No matter our age, if we always have a project to which we can apply ourselves, then we will wake up every day with an objective, something productive to get done. This allows us to go to bed at night in the peaceful knowledge that we have done some good, gained some achievement, however small. Having ears for this lesson has been one of the luckiest pieces of listening I've done, because it has led to my woodworking discipline, one of the greatest joys of my life.

There were less refined lessons in Shozo's textbook as well. Visiting Cyprus with a professional tour of *Kabuki Achilles*, we young men were housed at one point in an ancient monastery in the mountain village of Kalopanayiotis. After a week or so, Shozo looked in on us and noticed that the bathroom was in a state of dishevelment much as one might have expected from six young drunk men sharing one bathroom. We were thoroughly humiliated when our sensei came fuming out of the facilities, severely admonishing us for our slobbery. "And not just here!" he said, lecturing us. "Any bathroom you ever use, if there is a mess, it does not even matter if you made the mess. The next person to use the room will *think* you made the mess. What if your mother was coming to use this bathroom?" Heavy, heavy, deep shit, and true. I have never been in a messy restroom since without thinking of that day. His mentality then further ties me directly to the Wendell Berry of it all, for if we think of others in our fastidiousness or lack thereof around the toilet, how can we not extrapolate that notion into how we are leaving the rest of the world for the others who will come to use it after us?

His most all-encompassing bit of erudition is perhaps found in the Zen koan "The way of the arts is the way of the Buddha." According to Sato-sensei, Buddhist teachings tell us that we must strive to return to the purity of the day we were born. In the performing arts, the visual arts, as well as the martial arts, when you are completely focused on your art, you are in that pure state. Therefore "the passage"; "the way of creating art" is the same as "the way of the Buddha." I love the focus that this sensibility places on the importance of one's art in regards to a person's inner journey as opposed to all of the attention paid today to the exterior effects of artistic performance.

Like Robin McFarquhar, Shozo Sato–sensei continues to be an important influence in my life, so it seems like they're getting the pretty short end of the stick: I took their classes, I graduated, and now they have to continue to teach me? Whatever the case, they seem to persevere without complaint, which is, I suppose, the teacher's lot. When Megan and I were married in our backyard, Shozo performed a tea ceremony for us as part of the proceedings, a rite which felt profoundly more sacred than the recitation of any corresponding Western religious dogma. Our marriage is ten years strong as of this writing, so I guess that hearty bowl of green tea was a pretty good batch.

I have been lucky enough to see and do a great deal in my forty-two years of life, but I have not discovered a greater treasure than a good teacher. My only hope is that I can begin to repay them by passing their lessons along to anybody with their ears on right.

Make a Goddamn Gift

This chapter hopes to serve as a gentle reminder to myself and all the rest of us to make our gift-giving opportunities in life count. To my way of thinking, the tradition of giving and receiving gifts has been all but ruined by the general prosperity and largesse that we enjoy in America and much of the world today, in effect devaluing the very value and meaning of gifts themselves. The circumstance that makes us so soft as a society is to be found in our complete achievement of personal comfort. The vast majority of our nation's people can buy pretty much anything they need. Not anything they want, necessarily, but anything they *need* to achieve a satisfactory degree of creature comfort. Clothing, water, shoes, shelter, food. Beer, throwing stars, charcoal, Doritos, diapers, iPhone apps. The staples.

We're all complicit here, holding hands, or linking arms, rather, so we can look at Twitter whilst huddled together in our handbasket, barreling straight to hell. To wit: If you had the sand to suggest to me that I lower the window of my vehicle by the method of the downright cardiovascular exercise of pumping a window crank lever around in circles, literally moving the window with my mechanical exertions, I'd pitch a fit that you could hear for a country mile. Holy good Christ, we have made things so goddamn easy for ourselves! Finding our schedules relieved of so many of the tedious household tasks that wore our parents' fingerprints off, we find ourselves with a surplus of spare time on our fleshy hands. One might proffer the suggestion that we exploit that bonus time to do something like build a canoe, or at least haul one to the creek and paddle it, reveling in the birdsong and whitetail deer that come right down on the creek banks to eat gummy bears straight from our hands. But then, one might easily argue that such an activity would require some energy, some gumption, or, god forfend, some work! Wouldn't it be easier, one might continue, to remain inside upon our pillowy duffs, lollygagging in regal comfort? It's a short fall from making that choice to finding oneself online. Shopping. And hey, buying things is fun!

We love to buy presents for our children, our friends, and our neighbors. In America, there really is a lot of time to kill with all kinds of noble pastimes like shopping, and, when you get right down to it, perhaps there is a recipient even more deserving of treats than those aforementioned beneficiaries. I do believe that, as a group, we have determined that we most prefer buying gifts for *ourselves*. Objects are just so easy to come by. Michael Pollan puts out a new book? Boom, preordered it on Amazon. We can buy ourselves gifts before the ink is even dry on the pages there in the book machine. Once upon a time for me, something commensurate with a Michael Pollan book or a new Tom Waits record would have been the prize of my year, were I to find it waiting under my Christmas tree or unwrap it upon my birthday. I also used to thrill at receiving necessary items as presents, like simple socks or work gloves. Nowadays I have too many gloves. Because I have purchased leather gloves online that appeared to be a good deal, or just because I liked their look. Their nice cut. Well-shaped fingers. Add to Shopping Cart. Click to Complete Order. Here they come.

Prosperity is a good thing, right? Having too many gloves is a state of affairs preferable to working one's hands raw, yes? Abso-

lutely it is. No question. But for me, "too many gloves" is symp-
tomatic of a larger deficit that I don't feel good about. Because I
find that the greater the ease with which such bounty is purchased, at least in my case, the less the significance the giving of
it contains. This is why I try harder at gifts.

My first line of offense against this sort of apathy is simply
understanding the impact of a little time spent. Even merely writing out a thoughtful/funny card goes a lot further toward signaling your affection than a "cute top" purchased from that popular
garment-shopping website. Not only is it apparent that you took
the time to select your words and commit them to cardstock, but
by gifting a poem or a joke or a few verses of your own, you
force the reader to pause in his/her rhythm and consider what
you were trying to accomplish when you scribbled those words.
That transaction between the two of you is the gift. In it resides a
ceremony rife with tradition that outstrips in my estimation a great
many retail goods. Short on words? Draw a flower. Draw a frog.
Draw some tits (always hilarious). Add a triangular bush below
them for a bona-fide slam-dunk. PS: Cards don't have to be your
conventional folded thin cardboard or paper. Unlikely objects
add a flavor of whimsy that scores a lot of points. A two-by-four.
A pair of underwear. A piece of fabric or leather. Go nuts.

When people admonish me for making Megan a card, I say
to them, "You make a goddamn card for your significant other!
Go to your printer. There's paper in there. Locate it and pull out a
few sheets (in case of mistakes). Fold one in half and draw a heart
on the front. Open it up and write *I LOVE YOU* on the inside. Sign
your name. You will get kissed—big time. You want the bonus
round? Go outside and find a tiny piece of nature, a twig, a leaf,

a pebble, a shell. A chrysalis if you're really gifted. Adhere your artifact inside the heart and then get stretched out, because you're going for a ride to the realm of coitus."

Once you've mastered the card, take it up a notch to hand-made gifts. Ho-ho! You think you like the card-fueled oral pleasurings you're receiving now? Just wait until he/she gets a load of the scarf you have knit for him/her! That won't be the only load exchanged that night. Making gifts is also a great way to perpetuate a hobby in a productive way, and a solid hobby can keep you out of the hair of your significant other. What do you know? That's another gift!

Don't have the time/budget/inclination to take up woodworking or chandlery or glassblowing? No sweat. Step up to some tasty papier-mâché. I have used this childhood art-class technique more times than I can count (well, actually, no, probably just seventeen times) in my theater work, and it is super fun EVERY TIME. You make just enough of a mess to know that you've achieved something, and you could potentially end up with a sculpted masterpiece. Something I love to do as a character actor is to craft my own facial prosthetics for the stage, which is a fancy way of saying that I like to make funny noses. If you cast your face in plaster and then sculpt your new features in clay upon that plaster version of your face, then your noses or chins or devil horns will fit you perfectly, providing countless hours of hijinks!

Other fun objects to immortalize in paper and glue are the breasts and the penis. If/when you replicate your virile member, or really any body part, it is key to coat the area with petroleum jelly to prevent an intensely painful (hair) removal once the papier-mâché is dry. In the case of a penis casting, one obviously needs to maintain an erection until the glue sets up, which can take several minutes (I've read), so be prepared to sustain an atmosphere of arousal for the necessary duration. Once you have achieved crafting a successful facsimile, you can also elongate the shaft of said manhood by sculpting an extra couple of inches in clay, then adding more papier-mâché to the extra length (I've also read). When you are happy with your product, you might wonder what the hell you're supposed to do with a papier-mâché version of your rig. Well, I'll tell you. Create a waterproof seal on the inside of the paper dick with epoxy or spar varnish. Glue the base of the shaft to a flat rock or piece of wood to create a strong, heavy foundation. Gently cut in a urethra (pee hole) with a sharp knife and paint to taste. Fill partway with water, insert a nice daisy or tea rose, and you have a darling bud vase!

No matter how you decide to spend a little more time on your gestures of giving, the point is just quite simply that you do. You don't have to give a person a papier-mâché penis vase to get a reaction, but you won't be sorry if you do.

11

Kabuki Farmboy
Takes Chicago

As is only proper, my years in college saw me undergo a drastic personal transformation, as well as participate in a larger group consummation with those several champions who were to form the Defiant Theatre. Our sage Robin McFarquhar has since asserted that, in the twenty years since our matriculation, he has never seen another band of students with such an unquenchable work ethic, willing to stay up all night regularly to fulfill our artistic missions of mischief and beauty. I am very grateful to hear that I, once again, was in the right place and time to be valued by these peers, despite my relative inexperience onstage. Joe Foust and Christopher Johnson, destined to become Defiant's first artistic director, spearheaded production teams to create pageants of theater both challenging and hilarious.

A ragtag team of puckish miscreants coalesced, membership in which required only an adherence to our collective taste and the willingness to work one's fingers to the bone. The original gangsters were Johnson and Foust, Darren Critz, Chris Kantowicz, Jen Cotteleer, Rich Norwood, Kara Loquist, Richard Ragsdale, and myself, soon to be joined by Michelle "PeePee" Primeaux, Tatro, Emil Boulos, Andrew Leman, Linda Gillum, Rob Kimmel, Lisa Rothschiller, Jim Slonina,

Sean Sinitski, Will Schutz, Barb and Chris Thometz, and many others as the years rolled past. We capering fools were drawn inexorably together to weave shows of intelligence and silliness in a way that thrilled us and fed us completely. Joe's was my favorite brain, wickedly clever and funny for days. A naturally magnanimous leader, he had such a great sensibility for utilizing old-school theatrical conventions in a completely fresh way to incite mirth in any audience. He also wielded a fresh perspective that made him a wonderful and sensitive leader, which I have since learned is exactly the type of person in whose service I thrive.

Late one stormy night, properly buzzed, we all convened on our Nevada Street porch, festooned with fairy lights, incense, and candles, to draw up the first charter of our artistic collective, with plans to move our efforts to Chicago and thereby take over the known universe. The swollen sky hinted at great portent. We signed our names to the magnificent parchment in fire, jam, and absinthe. Lightning crashed, the four winds howled, shrieked, and yee-hawed, neighborhood mothers shuddered in their sleep, and the frilly little gillyflowers in the south meadows wilted and shed their pretty petals. The Defiant Theatre was born.

As daunting as this transition seemed, we had found pockets of encouragement when we had previously visited the city of big shoulders—we'd taken group trips to see plays at the Goodman Theatre, which had been very inspiring. It was there I first witnessed a great Chicago character actor named Steve Pickering, who was a big, thick Juggernaut sort of a guy. I saw him assay some unlikely roles for a guy built like a small tractor, such as Mercutio in *Romeo and Juliet* and Puck in *A Midsummer Night's Dream*. In the opening moments of this particular production, Steve/Puck rappelled in from the lighting grid above in commando gear. There was a park bench center stage, which he examined, and then, brandishing a can of spray paint, administered the word *fuck* onto the bench. He furtively glanced about for passersby, and then he turned around and transformed the *F* into a *P*. Puck. This was my kind of guy! After years of being surrounded by more classically thin and frail theater gents, I was very exhilarated to see a guy who was a little more stout (like myself) getting cast in these plum roles. Having had some trouble getting cast thus far, I was reassured by Steve's success that Chicago might just have some goodness in store for me.

Fortunately, just as we moved up to the city in the fall of 1993, Wisdom Bridge Theatre, where my sensei, Shozo, had produced earlier award-winning Kabuki shows over many years, like *Kabuki Othello*, was doing a revival of one of his biggest previous hits, *Kabuki Medea*, starring a couple of Chicago theater luminaries, Henry Godinez and Barbara Robertson, as Jason and Medea. Lo and behold, we three or four Defiant youngsters were just moving to town with more recent Kabuki training than anyone in the city of Chicago, if not the nation (not a lot of Kabuki training going on outside of Shozo's classroom). Thus, as if his training and generosity to date weren't enough, Shozo then handed us our first paychecks in our professional lives as well. Now that's a teacher.

A select portion of our Defiant number had already been fortunate enough to participate in a couple of productions of *Kabuki Achilles*, having toured Japan, Hungary, and Cyprus, as well as performing it professionally outside of Philadelphia at the estimable People's Light & Theatre Company for several months. Shozo's bread and butter was adapting Greek and Shakespearean tragedies into the traditional Kabuki style. The epic story lines and larger-than-life emotional arcs lend themselves perfectly to the spectacularly presentational style of Kabuki, which we studied diligently for years under our sensei. Imagine Hector and Achilles in samurai armor, fighting it out with *katana* (samurai swords). Amazing.

Amongst the Defiant tribe, this experience resulted in a communal company reverence for the tried-and-true conventions of Kabuki theater, which we did not hesitate to later exploit in our own plays. Conventions like the *koken*, who are basically stagehands, technically visible but clad in full black robes and sheer black hoods that render them "invisible" to the audience. *Koken* will scurry across the stage in a sort of ducklike squat-walk to assist the actors in some sort of action. For example, if the character of Medea is getting ready to, say, transform into a demon and kill her children, the *koken* will come zipping out and trick her wig and kimono, whereupon they will turn into flames as if by magic. They'll simultaneously slash some streaks of red and black makeup onto her face while handing her a dagger, so that in a moment's time she is transformed from a beautiful woman into a hideous, bloodthirsty she-monster. Because of their all-black garb, the *koken* disappear into the black stage, so that the transformation appears to be happening as if by magic. These tricks were developed three hundred years ago, incorporating no technology beyond string and paint. Liking that price point, we immediately borrowed the *koken*, as well as a general sensibility of grandeur, from Kabuki and inserted them into our own Defiant productions. We created a tonal goulash kind of like a Shakespearean tragedy as writ by Tex Avery and Mel Brooks.

My good fortune kept on rolling. The stage manager of *Kabuki Medea* was doing *Richard II* next at the Goodman and they needed a fight captain, so, knowing that I had a penchant for the stage combat, she

fortuitously hooked me into that gig. The fight captain is a member of
the cast who is in charge of maintaining the choreography throughout the run of the show and helping to train the actors who need help
with their technique. If they had been looking for anything like a good
actor, I would not have gotten the nod, but they fortunately just
needed a guy handy with the slapstick. To my delight, the former
P(f)uck Steve Pickering was also cast in *Richard II*, as one of the main
combatants, so we got to work together almost as soon as I had landed
in Chicago. The cherry on top of this excellent pastry was that Robin
McFarquhar had been hired up from Champaign to choreograph the
fights! Christ, could I have gotten any luckier? My first two pro gigs in
Chicago were with my two greatest teachers, Shozo and Robin!

Pickering took a bit of a shine to me and enlisted me to work on
The Old Man and the Sea with him at the Next Theatre, in a nifty adaptation of Hemingway's classic story with four dancers and some
puppets, which were my department. I did the man-of-war bird and
the marlin as articulated puppets that could flap and fly for their moments in the spotlight. The four dancers, with masks and a small
boat, performed movements that accompanied the words of the
piece, describing the action and the sea and other elements with their
beautifully effective progressions. I also choreographed quarterstaff
fights between the old man and the marlin, then the sharks. This was
awesome, at least at first. I had immediately hooked up with my hero,
Pickering, and he rewarded me with a fine lesson: Nobody could do
what the Defiant Theatre did. Working with Steve was mostly fun,
but he was a self-proclaimed benign dictator. Since gigs like these
paid little to nothing, there was no apparent reason to continue a
collaboration that was not nearly as satisfying as that with my own
company. I am terribly grateful for the time I got to spend with Pick-

ering, and for the lessons I took away from his example, but from then on, I would focus my free work upon the Defiant stage.

Speaking of, we established our company quickly and we found a great little niche audience. Everyone in the company was making a meager income by whatever means we could scare up, but we were all very satisfied to have the opportunity to make some great theater. I could afford cigarettes, coffee, burritos, beer, and weed. I wanted for nothing, and I was making theater sixteen hours a day.

I was lucky that my day job was also working in theaters as a carpenter, especially compared to many of the company members who had temp jobs in offices or other equally depressing grinds. There was one slow winter, however, that saw a few of us reduced to this quasi-telemarketing job set up by another charismatic Kabuki alumnus named Goldberg (our actual Achilles). The job was to sit in a cubicle and call cardiologists on the phone to ask them to review a new perfusion catheter that they had been utilizing. Adding to the bizarre flavor of the experience was the fact that the company had located its offices directly over the Fulton Street fish market, so this "cool" brick warehouse office absolutely reeked of fish. Anyway, a perfusion catheter is a tiny balloon that is threaded into blood vessels around the heart. If memory serves, they would insert it down in the thigh, I suppose utilizing the femoral artery, and snake this catheter up into blocked regions around the actual heart, whereupon the balloon would be inflated, effectively opening up the blockage. How crazy is that shit? And how bizarre for a bunch of barely employed actors to sit around discussing it over the phone with these surgeons who utilized the technology every day.

The upshot of that tedious gig was that we fired up a fun competition going amongst a few of us wage slaves. One chap would go into the bathroom, right there at the side of the room, and commit the sin of Onan (beat off), then, upon exiting, he would strike the glass light sconce on the wall next to the bathroom door with the eraser end of his pencil, which would cause it to ring like the bell at a boxing match, signifying a tally of exactly one successfully blown load. We would all keep score, each adding to his/her total at every possible opportunity throughout the day, until at the end of an eight-hour shift, the winner would be feted with beers by the other participants. One of my cronies, whom we'll call Richard Krishna, and I were usually vying for the title, and I believe my record for sconce-dings in a day of work was no less than nine. You see, no matter how dreary your job, ways can be found of passing the time productively.

At Defiant, we prided ourselves on building our sets and props for next to no budget, often from scraps we would collect in the fruitful alleyways of Chicago. I was the technical director, or "TD," which simply means I had all the tools. We depended heavily upon each company member to come out and help with each build, but there were a few core stalwarts who brought most of the magic home. Joe Foust could literally make anything out of gaffer's tape, a condition born of necessity, but I was to learn later how valuable our poverty actually was to our creativity. Bigger theaters with a healthy budget could do things like drive a motorcycle onto the stage or build an entire two-story house set, whereas we would have to make our motorcycle or our two-story house out of refrigerator boxes and egg cartons. The amazing thing I learned was that audiences enjoyed ours more. If a crowd witnessed an actual motorcycle rev and roll onstage, that's a neat spectacle, which then immediately fades, as in, "Oh. Wow.

A real motorcycle," and then it's over, the exceptional but momentary delight of seeing an unexpected but recognizable quantity. But when an audience has to buy into whatever illusion you've created, say, a motorcycle made out of two people with some mailing tubes and two umbrellas, then they experience the delight of creating the object together *with* the performers, in the imagination. That's more fun and abiding for them, because they are part of the transaction, as opposed to just sitting and coldly observing. An audience loves to have a hand in making the magic real, which is what I think should be connoted by the term an "engaging" piece of theater. Our shows were just plain really fun and, in one way, the greatest work of my life. The group of artists and the freedom that we had at the time allowed us to create and perform pieces unhindered by obligations, financial or otherwise. An artist cannot do his/her best work unless he/she feels the necessary freedom to do so. For me, this freedom culminated in Defiant's third season, particularly in our production of *Ubu Raw*.

What is considered by history to be the first absurdist play, *Ubu Roi*, or *Ubu the King*, was written in France in the late nineteenth century by a gassy guy named Alfred Jarry. Our original translation, penned by Foust and Ragsdale, was called *Kabuki Ubu Raw*. In both cases, it's a sort of filthy *Macbeth* story. Jarry initially wrote it as a puppet show making fun of his science teacher. When first produced in Paris, Pa Ubu entered and proclaimed his first line, *"Merde!"* ("Shit!"). The theater rioted at the profanity and they shut the show down. There's a lot of innuendo, like, "By my green candle!" which, considered nothing short of pornographic at the time, is now completely tame. But more on *Ubu Raw* later.

*   *   *

We few core company members, our lives were fueled almost entirely by the ambition of youth. None of us ever had quite enough to eat, but we would work late into the wee hours of the night just the same. In a play called *The Quarantine*, I was acting in the show, so I'd rehearse the show from six until ten, then I'd go backstage to my tools and work on a life-size dummy of me, complete with a life-cast foam latex head, for, what else, the disemboweling scene. I remember driving a three-inch screw into my own knee (on the dummy) and actually thinking, "This is awesome and also kinda weird." I'd think, "It's opening night tomorrow night, or I guess tonight. It's three in the morning. I'm going to maybe get about three hours of sleep from maybe five to eight A.M. This is the greatest fucking life."

Exhaustion would occasionally catch up with me. There's a scene in *Ubu Raw* in which a six-foot ladder with a two-dimensional boulder attached to its front is placed center stage, and I could, as the titular Pa Ubu, "stand" astride the boulder by climbing up the ladder and straddling the top. On the night of our final preview performance, I climbed up, struck a pose, then passed out and fell forward onto my head. After laughing for a while, Joe realized something was wrong when I got to my feet and began whispering my lines. He came out to stop the show and I said insistently, "No, no, I'm okay," like a goddamn five-year-old. I was about to commence a broadsword fight with the character BuggerAss, but Joe took away my broadsword. We collected ourselves and then finished the show, minus the fights.

When I first moved to Chicago I lived with Joe and Ragsdale and Tatro in an awesomely crappy apartment at Chicago and Ashland in a pretty bad neighborhood. It was an old storefront that had been converted into a living space, which meant a kitchenette and bathroom had been installed, but no other rooms, so we built our own! Short on materials (to say the least), we just built four bedrooms with eight-foot-high walls (the length of a sheet of plywood), leaving a couple of feet of open air above the walls. Not exactly the most ideal situation when it came to privacy, but we were like family by this point anyway.

One night I was walking home to this hovel from the El train with my friend Rob Ek, who, while sweet as pie, was a very intimidating, manly guy in our tribe of troublemakers. (He was the one everybody thought of as macho, not me. Nobody in those days ever inquired of me, "How did you become so manly?" because I was usually standing next to Rob Ek.) So, we were walking home from the train one night, having taken some pints on board, when we had an unexpected social interaction with a few young men, teenagers really, who had appeared suddenly. I must have been juking about in a silly way, obliviously lost in my buzz, which they mistook for crazy. The main guy was spooked by my strangeness, and he quickly said to us, "Yeah, you better run!" and they all took off. Rob grabbed me and said, "Holy shit! Did you see that?" I said, "No, what?" Unbeknownst to me in my stupor, the guy was showing us a silver pistol in his waistband, telling us to give him our money. The depth of my intoxication revealed itself as Rob walked me through the details of what I had just missed. I went about as white as a sheet, and we realized that the perpetrators must have thought I was crazy. It worked that time well enough, so I took the ball and ran. I began cultivating this scary look, as I realized that being perceived as insane was a great defense late at night in the big city. I wore muttonchops and a brown cowboy hat that looked like something out of *High Plains Drifter*, and under a brown overcoat I favored this black classic motorcycle jacket with an airbrushed image of a skull on the back and the words *Watch Me Burn* beneath it.

The phrase had a number of meanings. I've always enjoyed these

BECOME A BADASS

triple-layered entendres. No one ever knew what the fuck I meant, but I thought I was being incredibly clever and hilariously rebellious. Part of the inspiration came from the summer after my sophomore year in college, when I was really trying to distance myself from my bucolic, wholesome upbringing. I was also coming down off a born-again Christian trip, so there's that. I was working for these born-again Christian house builders for the summer in Minooka; it was incredible, and I worked like an ox. We were framing houses and I was carrying four-by-eight-foot sheets of plywood up an extension ladder to the second- and third-story roofs. Looking back on it, it was an act of stamina that makes me long for the strength of my younger self. I'm still strong and have a great constitution, but you have to be eighteen or nineteen and a little stupid to haul plywood like that. At that age, nobody's terribly impressed that you can haul a sheet up, so you haul two of them. "Yeah, you guys didn't notice? I did two. No big." Even as a brute laborer, I needed to perform for anyone who would give me the time of day.

We had a lot of fun, my tool belt and I, as I learned all the different aspects of house framing. At one point my job was to burn all of the trash from the construction site out in the yard. I had this big mound of trash, lumber, and other dross. Probably a ten-foot-high fire pile. And I had a smaller brush pile already going, maybe fifteen or twenty feet away. I was standing on the larger, unlit trash pile, splashing about gasoline from a five-gallon can, because that's how it was done. We were building two houses next to each other, and the two brothers who owned the company were shingling the roofs and racing each other, one on each roof. I would add that they liked me because, as usual, I was a clown, but only just enough of one. I worked hard and cracked wise in acceptable proportion, until this particular occurrence. Screaming at them, "Watch me burn, boys! I'm going to do it!" like I was going to light the pile under me, I was laughing my ass off. Then, suddenly I saw that the vapors from the splashing gas had caught the brush pile flames and the fire jumped onto me and the unlit pile beneath my work boots. The gas can exploded and blew me cleanly off the pile and onto the ground, rolling. When the smoke cleared, I had lost a lot of my eyebrows and singed my facial hair, but, luckily, that was about it. I wasn't personally on fire, and I hadn't been injured in the fall, but that's how the phrase ended up on my jacket. The brothers not only fired me, but they had the stones to charge me for a new gas can, too. At the time I was riding a 1979 Yamaha XS1100, a big, fat, brown road motorcycle, and I envisioned *Watch Me Burn* on my jacket on that motorcycle. It meant "Watch me haul ass out of here," but at the same time it meant "Hey, everybody, just wanted to let you know I'm cool. I smoke weed now." An act of public service, really, because before I had the jacket painted, I don't think people were aware of just how goddamn cool I was.

Toward the top of 1995 I found this warehouse space on North Avenue. Rick, the landlord, didn't quite know what to make of me, but I think he liked having a clown around. He rented this big room to me—it was probably twenty feet by fifty feet—and that was the whole of my domicile. In addition, there were a couple of larger warehouse areas where I built a lot of scenery and I had my first real shop. At this point I had finally amassed the full set of tools for a scenery shop, and for a couple of years it became my own tiny "factory" in the Warholian sense. It was right around the corner from Steppenwolf, where I had been working in some plays, so my warehouse became a safe haven for actors to smoke bongs, basically. Suffice it to say that, as far as parties go, there were some pretty good humdingers at the warehouse. Besides the more excellent aspects of warehouse living, there were also some minor downsides, like the five-minute walk from my space in the very back of the building to the bathroom in the front office, especially late at night, especially in the winter. I found it much more convenient to tinkle off of the roof out my back fire escape door, mainly into the snowdrift on a subroof a few feet below me. This arrangement was perfectly agreeable and downright convenient until the drift melted in the spring and three months' worth of pee sat in a warm and pungent puddle beneath the windows I needed to keep open because of the uncomfortable heat. I knew, thanks to a popular proverb, what to do when life gave me lemons, but in this case, when handed lemonade to begin with, I was at a loss. I did some dumping of bleach and water and I burned a lot of incense.

My time working at Steppenwolf, arguably the best theater company in the country, was incredibly educational. No longer the wild and woolly young Turks who had put Chicago theater on the map (along with David Mamet's gang), they'd since become a more august, respected company. They'd grown up. Working with a budget in the millions, including some substantial corporate patronage, they had to brush themselves off and sit up a little straighter now. But not too straight—after all, my first show there was *A Clockwork Orange*. Once again, my beloved Robin McFarquhar was the fight choreographer and I was his fight captain. Rob Ek was in that show as well, so there were two of us representing our tribal circle. As fond as I am of the respective jib cuts of Rob and myself, it was really through our association with Robin that we got cast, because everyone in town wanted to be in *A Clockwork Orange*.

We started rehearsals and I have to say it was a little eye-opening,

THIS LIFE IS RICH

because Steppenwolf, in our minds, had been this kick-ass, rock-and-roll, irreverent theater company. But by the time I reached them they had graduated from their time as dangerous young upstarts, having become a company in early middle age with a big, beautiful new theater building that they had constructed with a great many American dollars, partially provided by United Airlines and other generous patrons. I was still yearning for rebellion at every turn, but in hindsight, I am more understanding of their position, and I now certainly think that it was ballsy of them to even attempt mounting an adaptation of a challenging novel like *A Clockwork Orange* in the first place. Regardless of my immature craving for insubordination, the one thing I can tell you for certain is that I was damn lucky to be there.

Although I ended up working there on six or seven shows over a couple of years with some of the best artists in the country, I never had the chance to shine in a major role. Instead, I performed in more workmanlike ways, filling supporting roles, choreographing fights, making masks, and even once working as a makeup artist.

I was twenty-five and the Steppenwolf founders were all in their midthirties, so they were naturally becoming a little more sedate, while still mounting some of the best plays around. My thirst for experimentation and risk was slaked by other, smaller theater companies, where the work could become quite explosive. One such company besides my own was A Red Orchid Theatre, whose membership included my pal Mike Shannon. I did a play there with him called *The Questioning of Nick*, which is a twenty-minute play that Arthur Kopit wrote—I believe to get into Harvard. It's a three-character play we did with Chicago theater hero Guy Van Swearingen, who was the artistic director of Red Orchid at the time. We did the play three times in a row, rotating the parts we played with each retelling.

The audience, simply seeing the three interpretations, found it fascinating, much in the spirit of *Rashomon*. Simply by changing our personal interpretations of each role, we altered the audience's point of view, as well, with each iteration. It was incredibly fun to do and it was a really fascinating little study in storytelling. To this day I've never worked with someone onstage with a presence quite like Mike. I'm forty-two and he's probably thirty-eight, so he was a kid of nineteen when I met him. He has such a captivating physical quality about him. In one version of the play he would wrap his dinner-plate hands around my head, as he was a police sergeant and I was a teenage suspect, in the story of a high school basketball star being questioned by a police sergeant and his assistant about allegedly throwing basketball games for payoffs. So when he was the sergeant he would take my entire head in his hands and speak to me very softly. I couldn't move. I was simultaneously terrified and in love. I have never had a more womblike experience whilst literally embraced by another actor.

I did a production of *The Crucible* at Steppenwolf for a high school series they produced on their main stage. I was cast as John Proctor, the lead, which was I believe the last time I was cast as an actual "leading man." It's such a great piece of literature to work on, and if you haven't read it, I highly recommend you do so now. This riveting memoir chapter will be here when you return. . . .

Okay, back? Pretty gripping, right? Arthur Miller was not too shabby with the typewriter and the dialogue and the drama and such. How about that Giles Corey, huh? Good shit. The gifted young lady who played Abigail in our production was named Cecilia, and she originally hailed from Mexico. You generally don't want new inter-cast relationships springing up in your play. They should be generally discouraged as they can tend to rock the boat. However, if there exists the remotest possibility of romance between the actors playing John Proctor and Abigail in your production of *The Crucible*, then you might as well throw in the towel, because you're doomed. The whole play is rife with an intense, forbidden sexuality between the two characters. So, naturally, Cecilia and I started dating.

The Defiant Theatre was this fun, weirdo, little 1920s-Vienna-wannabe theater art club that was quite an exciting bacchanal, by and large. Ultimately the pinnacle of my Chicago experience was living on North Avenue in my warehouse and building the set for *Ubu Raw*. We had always wanted to try this Greek scenery trick called *periaktoi*, which is a set of three-sided pillars, two feet wide by twelve feet tall, maybe twelve or sixteen of them, side by side, so all the front, or downstage, faces together make one enormous picture, as the upstage wall. The whole set of pillars was rigged to spin together so we could rotate between different scenes. It's also a modern billboard technique, but to execute it writ large like that was so fun and really cheap for the considerable amount of "bang" it carried. So we had these huge expansive cycloramas that we were all painting together in the warehouse and then rigging into the three-sided pillars. One of them had a trick door in it for a surprise entrance because we loved our scenery tricks. Magical theater scenery, like secret doors, revolving turntable stages, or trapdoors in the floor, are something I love to see properly used, as they still can make me feel the magic I felt as a child. It's like a ride at Disneyland with a more comfortable seat and better writing.

Ubu Raw was, in a way, the superhero movie I've always wanted to make but never had the opportunity to do so. I was at an age then and in the sort of physical condition that playing Aquaman, or, let's be honest, Ben Grimm from *The Fantastic Four*, might require. As Pa Ubu, I was in a fat suit with this huge, round belly, all in white with a big red target on the belly, and my mask was an old bike helmet with a huge latex mask built over it. The main *Ubu* masks were made by our incredible artist friend Stephanie Nelson, based on a drawing of the character by Alfred Jarry, who wrote the original *Ubu Roi*. Her mask for Pa Ubu was this huge head that came to a white point at the top, which folded over to the side like an old-timey nightcap, with these weird walrus eyes and a big moustache, so all you could see of my actual face was my lower lip and chin.

Joe's staging upon an absurd circus of a set designed by Emil Boulos was a joyful romp into the ridiculous. I made my first entrance on steps that were made by slaves who were holding planks—they would walk in formation and turn the planks into steps, which I would pound up and down. As advertised, much of the movement and line delivery was very Kabuki-inspired. In addition, there were vast broadsword and quarterstaff fights, which were incredibly demanding physically. At intermission it was all I could do to lurch into the alley and smoke two cigarettes and pound two beers. I'd just peel out of my fat suit, squat against the wall, and catch my breath, just in time for round two.

I'm so very grateful that I had that moment to revel in what turned out to be the greatest strength of my youth, even though I didn't realize it at the time. Even by age twenty-eight or thirty we all began to realize what a key ingredient youth had been in the rigorous performances at our Defiant Theatre company. As young ne'er-do-wells, we were able to give ourselves over to the lifestyle so wholly that we sacrificed so many necessary and practical (i.e., grown-up) parts of our lives. Like, I exclusively drove vehicles with no insurance or registration (because those things cost money), which really could have ended badly when I totaled my motorcycle on the freeway on the way to a performance of *A Clockwork Orange*, and because it wasn't registered to me and had no plates, I just left it on the side of the highway. So, with youth, apparently, came a certain amount of assholery, at least on my part.

I had been engaged, the day after the motorcycle crash, to drive my friend Todd's moving truck to Los Angeles, but I had three ribs out of place and all the blood vessels in my eyes had been broken. Todd, his wife, and I finally determined that I could see plenty well enough to truck their entire life's possessions a mere couple of thousand miles. In deference to my injured state, we did take a slight detour through the mystical town of Sedona, Arizona, where they had a friend named Mindy who practiced white witchcraft. She laid a poultice on my ribs and cleaned up my energies and whatnot, and it smelled real good in her room, so I was pretty down with a witching, all things considered. We rolled into Los Angeles the next day, and I just looked like a serial killer. At the time I was cultivating this "style" consisting of a porkpie hat, the completely bloodred eyes, a thick dog chain around my neck, old leather combat boots, and these weird sort of Swiss paratrooper red camouflage pants with matching cloth suspenders. I met any intimidation that Hollywood created within me in a full-on *Mad Max* mode, which is really the way to attack any frightening new terrain. I discovered that there was really not too much to be scared of in LA, beyond a lot of assholes and maybe some venereal diseases.

My final chapter in Chicago was centered around the venerated, unassuming Irish whisky bar across the street from

Steppenwolf by the name of O'Rourke's (now sadly gone). For some reason the magnanimous proprietor, Jay, took a shine to me and hired me part-time as a bartender. Not only was I a twenty-six-year-old drunk, but he added, "You can give your friends the first pint free." I thought, "You're insane. You effectively just told me to hand out a couple hundred bucks a week to my pals."

We had the greatest time at O'Rourke's, the most idyllic of what you might imagine as a smoky, dark pub filled with show folk laughing and dancing, or sometimes railing with all seriousness about the state of affairs surrounding the price of tea in China and so forth. Jay was a very benevolent avuncular figure who really supported the theater community, which, in turn, supported his business. He had Tom Waits and Jacques Brel and Nina Simone on the jukebox, one of the best lineups I've ever seen. The pub, after all, is where so much of theater life takes place. Romances are consummated and then torn asunder, theater seasons are planned, plays are cast, and chuckles are plentifully expended. While studying there, I served Albert Finney and Laurie Metcalf, Malkovich, and Jessica Lange, and I drank with Keanu. It was the place where I first began to rub elbows with hotshots from the world of film who came to perform in or just see plays at Steppenwolf, which has easily the most knockout ensemble of acting talent assembled this side of the Royal Shakespeare Company. I worked on *Buried Child* with Gary Sinise and Ethan Hawke, and Sam Shepard came to do some rewrites. Sam slipped me $40 and sent me out for a bottle of Maker's Mark one night, and it took a long time after that for anything in my life to eclipse that instance as the most exciting thing that had ever happened. I guess I still had a lot to learn, about bourbon whisky and about being starstruck, which I'm glad I got out of the way in the shadows of O'Rourke's, before I ever even heard of the blinding lights of a red carpet.

I know I have deep gratitude for this time in my life, because whenever I would later think things like "I missed the prime years of my acting life building fucking scenery! Jesus-goddamn, John Cusack had done two dozen films by this point!" I know I wouldn't trade anything for the time I had with the Defiant Theatre and Chicago theater in general, easily the most fecund and exciting theater community in the country.

What with savory stage roles in *The Ugly Man*, *The Kentucky Cycle*, *Golden Boy*, *The Questioning of Nick*, and *Ubu Raw*, I had such a string of good fortune in 1996 that I felt like I might never top this banner year. This, combined with my film work, led me to consider a move to New York or LA for the first time. Coming into my late twenties also made me realize that I would eventually want to make a little more of a living wage than my Defiant salary ($0/year) was providing. New York had a lot to recommend it, but ultimately all signs were pointing west.

In my Chicago circle at that time, moving to LA was called "pulling the Schwimmer," because David Schwimmer had left his great theater company (which is still one of the greatest—the Lookingglass from Northwestern). Shortly thereafter he won his life-changing role on *Friends* (this was completely unfair, of course, as David has always remained a loyal and valuable contributing member of Lookingglass, but you know how people are. Shitty).

So that was the flavor of the moment—that we thespians must disdain sitcoms. But I eventually came to realize that Chicago actors make a habit of bad-mouthing both New York and LA for many reasons, as a defensive mechanism to assuage their own fears about having to move to one of the coasts and give it a shot. One night at O'Rourke's, when we were both two sheets to the wind, my old pal Pickering pinned me against the wall with his finger and derisively said, "Hey, Nicky, I hear you're thinkin' you're gonna go pull the Schwimmer."

If my mind hadn't been made up by that point, that would have certainly done the trick. I owe Steve a debt of gratitude for spinning me a 238-pound cautionary tale, standing it unsteadily upon two feet, and poking its finger into my chest.

Carry a Handkerchief

My wife and paragon of comeliness, a lady of immense talent with pretty sublime taste who goes by the name of Megan Mullally, likes to tell the story of the first night we ever went to dinner together. We had been rehearsing our play, *The Berlin Circle*, at the Evidence Room theater in Los Angeles. We had known each other for only a few weeks but had become fast friends, with some seed of romance brewing in the fecund incubator that is the backstage area of a live theater. I had been living in the raw basement of some fellow troll-like company members and working piecemeal as a handyman, carpenter, and actor, and so one might accurately have described my circumstance as somewhat "down on my luck."

I had also been helping to build our new Evidence Room theater space in a warehouse, as well as the stage set for our show, so I'd been working all day in overalls, rehearsing in them, and then, in this instance, wearing them to a nice dinner. I would point out to the ladies and gentlemen of the fashion jury that at this juncture I did possess the wherewithal to change into a clean T-shirt. These were a fine pair of Carhartt canvas overalls, but, regardless of their durable quality, Megan seemed to think that they were not appropriate fine-dining attire. Especially abhorrent to her, for some reason, were the phone numbers which I had inked in Sharpie all over the thighs of said britches (when you're twenty feet up an A-frame ladder hanging lights, you often need to jot down information on the nearest handily available surface).

I suppose I didn't help matters any when I pulled up to the ta-

ble and tucked my napkin into the bib of the overalls. Her aver-
sion to my genteel show of elegance completely baffled me,
because I was positive I had seen Jed Clampett execute the exact
same nicety on *The Beverly Hillbillies*, but apparently I was somehow well over the line into the realm of faux pas. With such an
auspicious beginning, I am fully astonished and grateful to this
day that Megan ever took a chance on me.

She has since straightened out my closet considerably, as she
has a talent and a taste for choosing things like garments, poodles, houses, art, and novels. Really, anything but overalls. I hast-
ily learned to dummy up and wear the shirts she put on me, and
I'll tell you what: If I don't get a compliment on every shirt she's
ever upholstered me in, well, I'll eat my hat. Naturally, I retain my
Carhartts and other work wear for the woodshop and such, but
when I go anyplace that I might be expected to look "decent,"
"civil," or "not homeless," I reach for one of her choices, and
welcome the world's inevitable refrain: "Wow, nice shirt!"

That said, I do have some strong feelings about the world of
fashion. In order to chase the brass ring of "prosperity," I feel that
a jackass (like your author) must eschew fashion as much as possible. Definitely allow your significant other to choose your shirt,
but leave it there. Jobs that require a suit upset me. They displease
me much, as our world is rife with such superficial conformity. As
a member of a race of animals who are blithely burning through
the natural resources of their beautiful planet, laughing their faces
off like beer commercial models as they career across the water
on their Jet Skis, I am pretty well put off by the amount of attention
we monkeys can bestow upon things like bang length and pleated
fronts and skirt size and shawl collars. I can comprehend why I

need brown shoes and belt for some suits and black for others. I comprehend it, but that doesn't mean I have to like it.

In a grander sense, I'm quite peeved by the customs that we have allowed, even encouraged, to flourish around our collective appearance and hygiene. First of all, at some point we allowed ourselves to become stinky to one another. Animals, mammals in particular, seem to love the musk of their brothers and sisters, a scent so potent that they can actually communicate with one another through the odors they are giving off. We "people" gave that up centuries ago, and now our natural odor is counterintuitively offensive. This is a failure, people. It's the fallacious part of our human egos that informs us we're "better" than nature, which keeps us from enjoying the sniffing of one another's crotchal areas. I'm not preaching here, I'm one of us just as much as you are, but I'm always at the ready to try getting more stinky.

Additionally, we have somehow determined that men need to shave their faces every day, and now apparently their torsos require denuding as well? How far have we fallen? A hairy chest used to be the actual measure by which a man's virility was determined, and now we are requiring of our "men" a nubile, naked set of pecs, like some prepubescent teenager? If indeed a shot of rotgut "puts hair on your chest," why then you'll be required by modern fashion to have it waxed! Whiskers grow as designed by nature, so how can that be bad? They come standard on every model! They're like the weeds of the face, and as we all know, there are some very charismatic weeds in the world of flora, like asparagus. Also, "weed" is a weed with a pretty solid fan following. Perhaps, as our modern civilization slowly learns to accept the inevitable goodness of ganja, we can also return to the custom of honoring flocculent men. Look, you can shave all you want. Do as you please, I say, but if some of us want to look a little more woolly, then I would also ask you to let us be. I want to forevermore take "unkempt" as a compliment.

Speaking of the pudenda neighborhood, for glory's sake, everybody, what about all this waxing going on down south?! Of all the lovingly crafted details sported by Mother Nature's masterpiece, the human form, the pubic bush is easily the cherry on the, well, the pie, I suppose. That curly forest acts as a flag, signaling to the weary traveler, "Here is a feathery love-tick upon which you may rest your weary pikestaff or love-clutch." Caressing a mink-like crotch epaulette is one of the most comforting stages in any self-respecting seven-step foreplay strategy. Not to mention, the pubes act as an effective catcher to keep crumbs out of the more sensitive areas when consuming one's postcoital Scotch egg. For the love of Mike, bring back the bush.

Speaking of—ladies. Ah, beautiful ladies. In order to comply with the implied social regulations, women are required to submit to a much more rigorous program of hygiene than the gents. They shave their legs and armpits and wear meticulously applied paints and powders on their faces in order to appear more "attractive." It's a racket. When I see a person without makeup, I think she appears real, like nature made her, which to me is purely beautiful. When a person has applied, even expertly, a full face of makeup, then she appears to me to resemble someone on the cover of a magazine or something manufactured, like a doll. Therein lies the rub, methinks, that we as a people have been made to believe that we need to look like these "foxy" people on billboards and bus posters in order to appear "beautiful" and thereby find happiness. I am saddened to inform you that this sickness has penetrated our psyches so nefariously that some of the afflicted have taken to BLEACHING THEIR ASSHOLES. If you are worried about what your visitors will think of the window dressing around the orifice where ordure exits your body, then I'm going to go ahead and suggest you turn around. The stuff you want to pay attention to is on the front side. Men and women alike, if you think that altering the tip of your nose with surgery will make you happier, I would suggest you alter something much more malleable than your flesh, like your priorities, or your friends. Quit looking in the mirror so much. My two cents.

I know this is a clodlike "guy" opinion—I mean, look at me— but by and large, fashion seems like a huge waste of time and money. A good pair of jeans should last for several years. I don't really give a shit how they hang. They should not pass from favor because their shade of blue is no longer acceptable at the mall, or they don't hug your buns as tightly as they are required to by the cover shots of *Caboose* magazine.

Here is all a jackass like you or me needs to get by, fashion-wise:

Underwear is a great idea. Nothing is *required*, but the clever thing about drawers is that they can act as a repository for accidental (or on-purpose) discharges from the body, and the subsequent stains, without ruining the outer pantslike garment.

A pantslike garment. Jeans, shorts, overalls, dungarees. Pockets are a must, for the storing of your necessaries. Knife, money, tobacco, frogs, string, marbles, bullets. Read your Twain for suggested pocket wares. Pants keep the chiggers from your shins. Pants cloak the stained underdrawers from the world's prying glance.

Obviously, carry a **handkerchief**.

Work boots.

A good **hat**.

12

Subaru Leavings

In my life, I have left my parents' home in Minooka, Illinois, twice, following that grand old American tradition on both occasions, by taking my leave in shitty used Subarus, once for college and once to move from Illinois to California. In 1988 I purchased a used Subaru BRAT from my friend Joe Stachula, who was in *Oklahoma!* with me at Minooka High School, for $350. I test-drove it in a field near his house, where we did a lot of donuts and drove through the creek. Kick-ass action? Check. The BRAT is a tiny pickup truck that has four-wheel drive and a roll bar. There are two seats in the tiny bed behind the cab, facing the rear, that have airplane controller/joysticklike handles for the passengers to hold on to when traversing terrain like, well, the creek. It's built for fun, the BRAT, but it's also practical. A person can fit a full four-by-eight-foot sheet of plywood in the bed (by simply cutting it into eight conveniently sized smaller pieces).

During my freshman year we once drove it from Champaign to the nearby town of Decatur, Illinois, where Millikin University sits, to see some friends in a production of "the Scottish Play" (*Macbeth*). We had two guys in the front in the tiny little two-seater cab and two guys riding in the back action seats. On the highway, apparently bored, we began to execute a rotation—everybody moved one seat counterclockwise, with one guy coming in the passenger window, one guy going out by way of the driver's window, etc.—just for fun. At seventy miles per hour on the freeway, it was pretty big goddamn fun.

The BRAT was a constant location of tomfoolery. In one of Robin McFarquhar's classes we'd do an exercise where we'd split into pairs with one person blindfolded and the other guiding him/her around campus. It was called a trust exercise, for obvious reasons. Connected at the hip by this point, Joe Foust and I dutifully tottered to the BRAT, whereupon I drove around the quad blindfolded based on Joe's instruction. We got an A in that class.

That rusty and fantastic Subaru BRAT ended up being very instrumental in the mischief that Joe Foust and I would wreak among the polite communities of Champaign and Urbana. Sometimes Joe and I would just drive up alongside some pedestrians and shower them with Silly String or water balloons, and then drive away, leaving the slightly inconvenienced strangers puzzled at the identities of these hilarious (in their own minds) street clowns.

The BRAT was the final tool in the kit this young man needed to set off into the big, wide world on his own. I'll never forget my mom's reaction to my exit, standing in the driveway. As much as my dad is a heroic, Atticus Finch–type figure of the Minooka countryside and my life in general, my mom is his equal lady-Atticus counterpart. They're very Ma and Pa Ingalls, raising a family and a garden while maintaining and beautifying a household. She was quietly sweet as honey, and she was the more nurturing or "mothering" of the two, as mothers often are. She heroically made some of our clothes from scratch while producing meals with such frugality and acumen in the kitchen. For a few dollars a week she would feed all six of us like kings, all with an air of gentleness and competence. I've never met anyone nicer than my mom, and I've met Donny and Marie.

It's because her own family, the Roberts clan, is so affable, and they all share that same sense of competence. By mastering the implements in their immediate surroundings with determination and humor, they have created a dependability within themselves that then provides us all with the room to breathe and laugh. My mom's mother, Eloise Roberts—or "Grandma El," or best of all, on the CB radio, "the Gambler"—had a lot to do with my own mom turning out to be such a champion of life and family rearing. With a bit of misbehavior in her own childhood, Grandma El let me know that she generally appreciated a wiseass, encouraging a lot of the silliness that thrived in her grandchildren. Growing up amongst these rock-solid Americans was more valuable to my development and my disposition than any school into which I could have set my muddy boot.

My mom, as a result, has such a great sense of humor. I may be romanticizing, but I feel like this vein of humor that has traveled down the years via her farming forebears is a product of the Depression, wherein one could watch an entire year's profits be wiped out with one heavy rainfall. In such an instance, you have the option of either blowing your brains out or making a wisecrack. This family was always looking for the light, for any jape they could find in any unpleasant circumstance, and that sensibility really helped me develop my own sense of humor. I (eventually) learned that one doesn't want to jack around too much, as you are then regarded as a hindrance (also known as a "jack-around") to getting the work done. Bring just enough wit to any given situation to lighten the load with a grin.

Our family's humor made the emotional moments that much more poignant then, as I remember my mom in the driveway, crying at seeing one of her little ones go traipsing off to a school two hours south. Mom and Dad had already gone through this with my sister Laurie, a year my senior, but I think that Laurie would agree that since I got so much attention (because I demanded so much attention), and because I was the oldest male child, it would leave a different sort of a hole in the household (although she would argue that it was actually the "hole" who was leaving). Although Laurie could still beat the snot out of me, I was the strongest of the kids in areas like pushing the lawn mower and carrying luggage, not to mention my possessing the most obnoxious voice at the dinner table. Whether one was a fan of my stylings or no, there was no question that family meals would be conducted henceforth in greater silence. It was a very emotional parting for all of us, but my portion was pairing my grief with an excitement at my impending adventure far from the cozy nest. I knew very powerfully then that I needed to set off into the world and try to puzzle out how to become a man.

That particular departure took place in the fall of 1988. Some years later, after I had graduated from the U of I and subsequently served my years in the graduate program of Chicago storefront theater, it was time for a strikingly similar leaving on a blustery Christmas Day in 1996. Having planned for some months to move to Los Angeles, I had found in the newspaper a used 1990 Subaru station wagon for about $750. Rusted out and originally maroon, just like the BRAT had been, it was jammed with my worldly goods, which consisted of some boots, some jeans, a shitload of cassette tapes, and my tool kit. That was my dowry, I guess, should I ever find a willing rancher to take me to his marriage bed. Traveling with a good set of tools is a great comfort to the carpenter, because he/she knows that no matter where the wind blows him/her, somebody's going to need a gazebo, and that means he/she can purchase a sandwich and a pair of Levi's.

I had a large burrito-pack of goods tied down on top of the wagon as well, wrapped up in ratty old scenic canvas with a papier-mâché boar's head from *Ubu Raw* strapped on the front. With the portion of gumption I had been served by my mom and dad, I, like so many fools before me, simply thought, "Well, I reckon I'm driving this thing to California. What the hell. Let's do this."

When I had first gone away to college, I knew that the ultimate pinnacle of my career would be to arrive in Chicago and get paid American dollars to act in a play. That seemed, at the time, the equivalent of climbing Mount Everest. Even in Chicago, having summited that particular peak of making a living as a theater professional, during the first three years or so I had no thoughts of ever leaving. At Defiant, we had heard legends of people transplanting a play to LA or New York, but such a quest had not been undertaken by anyone in my immediate circle of acquaintance. Eventually, however, a certain wanderlust had crept into my psyche, and I wondered if a jackass like myself might investigate the treasures of the nation's coastal cities.

I knew that New York was a town to which an aspiring theater lad might emigrate, but I think I would have been equally as lost in New York as anyplace else, if not more so. Meanwhile, Los Angeles had been batting her eyelashes at me more and more during my last couple of years in Chicago, like a late-night lady in a bar, seeming more and more attractive with every beer I drank. The harsh difference between New York and Hollywood, in hindsight, was that no one moves to LA to get work in the theater.

During my last year in Chicago I did *Ubu Raw*, *The Kentucky Cycle*, and *The Questioning of Nick*, some of the best play productions I've

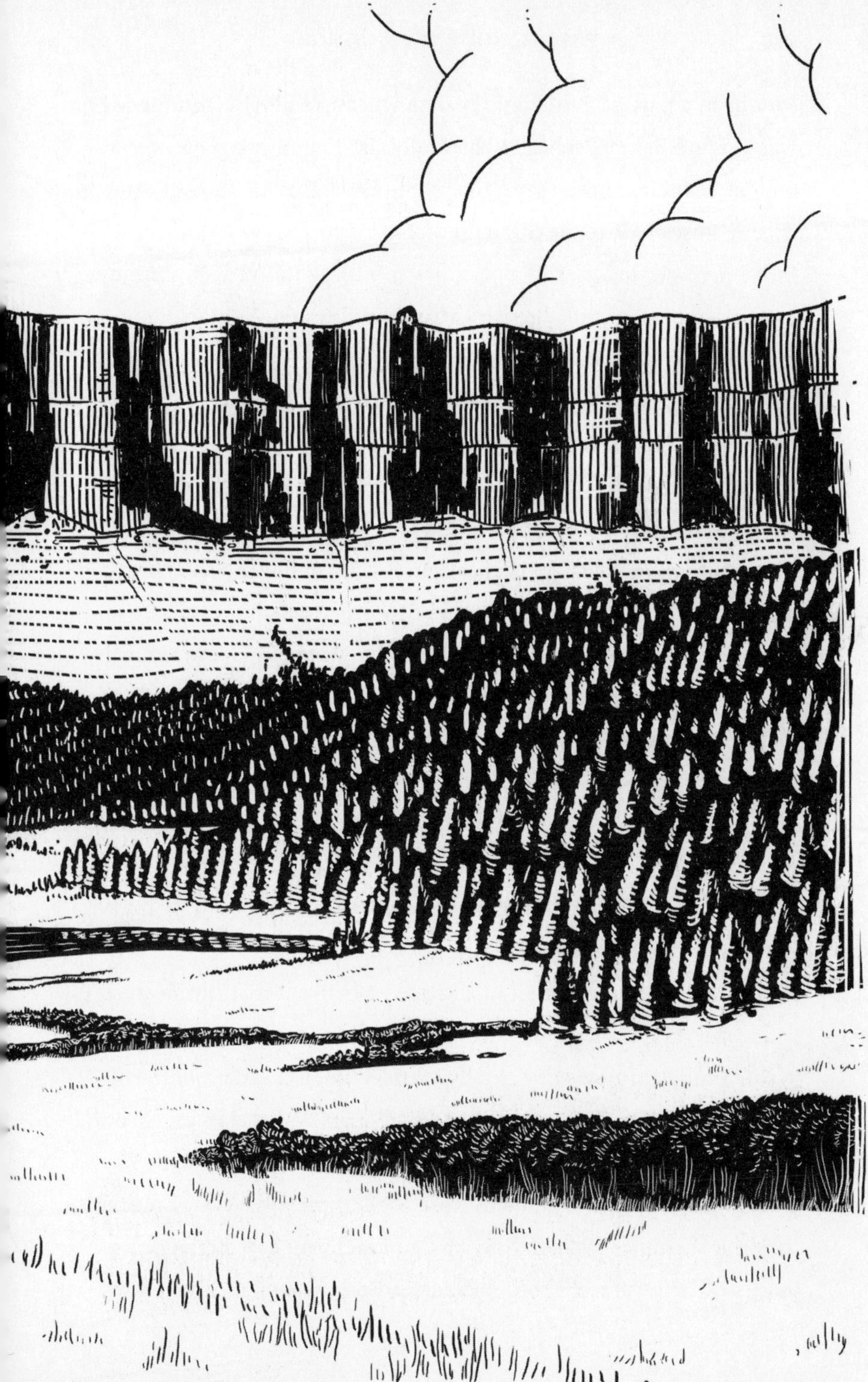

ever been a part of. Little did I realize what a wealthy community I was leaving behind, where I habitually did five or six plays a year, built sets for eight others, and choreographed fights for another three or four. I used to love making a list on New Year's Eve of all the shows I'd worked on that year. If a person was willing to live on a slim income, that person could be rich as Croesus in terms of satisfying theater jobs. Only by leaving that time of financial poverty behind me did I realize just how wealthy I had been artistically.

I'd also logged my first couple of legit film jobs in my final year. In one of them, a Morgan Freeman/Keanu film called *Chain Reaction*, directed by Andy Davis, I was cast in two scenes as Keanu's building super, but I never even got to meet Mr. Freeman. It was batshit crazy to me at the time—I was suddenly in a movie, for real! I was going to be on the screen at the movie theater! My education continued as I later learned from the film's premiere that both of my scenes were totally cut out, which is but one of the many harsh lessons we show folk are constantly dealt in this business. I still got my SAG card out of the job, which is a seemingly elusive necessity to finding further opportunities in the film business.

I got paid what was then two months of carpenter's wages, for two days of acting work. Literally. It wasn't an avenue I was actively pursuing, film work, but all of a sudden I realized that this avenue had some very attractive features to it. Shortly thereafter, I was cast in this Sundance movie directed by Mark Pellington and produced by Tom Gorai called *Going All the Way*, from Dan Wakefield's excellent novel of the same name, with some youngsters like Ben Affleck, Rachel Weisz, Jeremy Davies, and Rose McGowan, all of whom were babies at the time. Toddlers, anyway. At lunch one day, to give you a sense of where we were chronologically, Ben was talking about how he and a buddy had a "script that might get made" (which turned out to be *Good Will Hunting*). In *Going All the Way*, I played "Wilks" Wilkerson, an antagonistic high school buddy of Ben's character with a big mouth. There were more lessons in store for me: Out of my seven scenes, maybe four or five were cut from the final film, mainly because Ben had a prosthetic beard in most of the scenes that ended up not looking quite right, so they cut the whole beard story. Yet another class in the school of hard knocks, which I continue to attend even now.

The film was shot in Indianapolis, and all of the leads had been cast in LA, but fortunately my part was small enough to cast out of Chicago. I drove with another "day player" to Indianapolis for our few days of filming. This other fellow, Jeff, had done a couple of commercials on location before this, so he taught me about per diem shortly before he cottoned me to what filet mignon was all about, a blessed calling indeed. Wherever you are today, Jeff, I offer you my reverential thanks.

This was the first time I had ever heard about, let alone received, a per diem and I just thought, "Are you fucking kidding me? I get this great job acting in scenes with amazing actors for this crazily cool director for a very healthy salary, and you also give me extra money? You're worried about if I'm going to eat?" I don't recall what the amount was on that film, but the current MINIMUM amounts for a SAG union shoot on location are: breakfast, $12; lunch, $18; and dinner, $30!!! Some generous productions have just made a clean job of it by giving us $100 a day. Many times on location I have simply been handed a stack of Ben Franklins upon landing in town. In 1998 I did a movie in New Orleans, and it was early enough in my career that I was pleasantly surprised when they gave me a rental car. I showed up and they said, "Here's your car, and here's a stack of hundred-dollar bills. Your per diem is one hundred dollars per working day and you're here for three weeks, so here's $2,100 in CASH." Jazz Fest was in town, and . . . oh, it was New Orleans. They tell me I had a very good time. Nice work if you can get it.

The Keanu movie was amazing in its own right; I was walking amongst the giant playground of a big-budget action film set around downtown Chicago (although I was "local hire," so no per diem). Seeing how a movie was shot, through the fresh eyes of a new employee of said film, went a long way toward making me think about that side of the business. These thoughts were further bolstered on *Going All the Way*, where everybody was super friendly and very encouraging. "You should totally move to LA," they said, "you have a great mug. You'll work like crazy." In California, months later, struggling to find my ass with both hands, I was fortunate enough, at least, to find those same people, remind them of their goddamn encouragement, and then shake them down for a sandwich or a couple of tacos, to which they really had no choice but to "generously" acquiesce.

All of these factors played an important part in my calculations as I pondered the notion of leaving the womb of my Chicago theater family and illogically leaping into the mysterious void of either New York or Los Angeles. In truth, a major source of persuasion was a lower molar I was sporting, which boasted a hole so large I could fit a peppercorn into it. Yes, that was handy on long hikes, but not the healthiest place to stash extra spices. This made the promise of dental insurance through SAG a tasty-looking carrot indeed, leading me West. Another substantial factor at the time was my pretty serious relationship with a young lady from Tampico, Mexico.

My girlfriend, Cecilia, said, and I quote, "Motherfucker, I'm a

skinny Mexican girl. I'm not moving where it snows. We're goin'
where it's sunny." After weighing all of the pros and cons and applying logic as carefully as possible, I guess that settled it. It's truly
amazing what a woman can accomplish when she's chilly. I put what
small wheels I had access to in motion and set everything up. I had
lined up a couple of minor jobs in LA and laid some groundwork for
places to live. All very tenuous plans, but the beginnings of a new
life nonetheless.

It was about this time that Cecilia fully flipped out about the serious
reality of our moving to another city together. A pretty big step that, as it
turned out, she was not ready to take. All of a sudden, she disappeared.
Cecilia sort of dropped out of my life, then vanished farther from the
entire city. None of her friends knew where she had evaporated to until
she turned up back in Mexico, where I believe she has gone on to become
a Mexican movie star. Based on my eventual ability (or lack thereof) to
provide or even just contribute to our domestic comfort in Los Angeles,
I think she and I would agree that she made the right call.

By now, I've driven between LA and Chicago so many times that
I could start a courier business. The cheapest way to do it back
in the day was a service called "drive-away cars." Please heed this
warning, and don't ever use a service like this. "Why not?" you might
ask. "It's much more reasonably priced than having my car shipped."
Here's why: You'll get a fucking stoned asshole like me driving your
car across the country. They give your car to me or any asswipe with
a license, and all I have to do is put gas in it and leave a deposit of
about $150 (in the nineties). I actually totaled somebody's car once. I
was driving from Chicago to LA, on one of maybe six such trips in a

"drive-away," and I was hauling ass through Colorado in the winter. I was driving through the Rockies at about three A.M., I was cranking the music, and, of course, I was baked. Now, let me make something clear. The Offermans and the Robertses, as a rule, are great drivers. A lot of our livelihoods have revolved around driving domestic and industrial vehicles. No exception, I spent years calmly learning to back up a truck loaded with tons of asphalt, or a tractor with a wagonload of corn, and so I am a very dependable driver.

Having established this, however, sleep deprivation, a preponderance of marijuana, and its being three in the morning may have slightly hampered my dependability, resulting in my hitting some ice on a mountain highway and slowly spinning out of control. I turned down *Bone Machine* and thought, "Okay, friend, we've had a fine run. We've done some good shit, and now it's over." Fortunately for this idiot, instead of one of the cliff-top drop-offs that much of this mountainous route rides alongside, there was a huge, sheer concrete wall rising up on the right shoulder. I gently slammed into it and slid abrasively along it for maybe one hundred yards. I slowed to a sparky halt, checked my drawers for effluvia, and realized the car was still running. "Great," I thought, but when I got out to survey the damage, the entire passenger side of the car was, well, gone. It was just rubbed off, to put it simply. I thought, "Well, all right."

I completed the drive to Los Angeles and turned the car in to the drive-away company. I was pretty nervous, naturally, because I had never really read the shit that I signed when I picked up the car. Was I on the hook for this fucking thing? I managed to keep my cool when I learned that no, they were covered. They kept my $150, but that was it. I walked out of their front door and just played it real smooth until I got a couple of blocks away, whereupon I sat on a bus bench and wept for relief. This seems like a good juncture at which to reiterate, DO NOT ENTRUST YOUR CAR TO A DRIVE-AWAY SERVICE.

This exodus at the end of 1996 was about eight years after the original collegiate Subaru leaving. I'd spent four years in Chicago, so rich and full that it felt like a decade. When my parents first came to see my plays down at school, they really enjoyed them, despite my own usually underwhelming casting. I think they were just relieved that I was allowed onstage in the first place. They would generally come away terribly impressed with the production values, which were of a quality that was indeed quite professional. They were always very supportive, which was never lost on me, because there was no small amount of faith involved. When I got to Chicago and they saw me working at actual professional theaters they said, "Wow, okay. You're making nine thousand dollars a year, and that's tough, but you're resilient, you're doing okay, and we support you," which meant more to me than they knew. Then my dad would slip me $80, which I'm sure he didn't have to spare. Those are the types of people whose level I'm trying to live just halfway up to every day.

They saw everything I did in Chicago, which was a pretty intense calendar to maintain from Minooka, and they were close enough to Chicago that I was always able to bring friends home for dinner, which was like vacationing from Gotham to an episode of *The Andy Griffith Show*. By that time I had a couple of tattoos and had become very hedonistic. I was very interested in flexing my artistic muscles and letting everyone in Minooka know that I was an artist and I was different. That I was a nonconformist. They didn't particularly give a shit. It was more like peacocking that I needed to do for myself, to sort of cut myself loose from the security of my family and town. By the time I decided to move to Los Angeles I don't think anybody was too surprised. I had been traveling up this slight incline of better and better gigs, at bigger and bigger theaters, so making the admittedly daunting move to a coast was only natural.

It wasn't the nicest thing to do, looking back, driving two thousand miles directly away from my family on Christmas, but I had always had a flair for the dramatic, and I wanted to lend to the occasion a sense of the vital impending sea change I sensed occurring in me. Given the time of year, it was certainly a chilly leaving. Same driveway as 1988, same Mom and Dad. My dad's funny—he's one of those classic guys who keep their emotions tucked deep inside, although he's improved leaps and bounds over my lifetime. He'll now end a phone call with, "We love you," but he won't say, "I love you." He doesn't have to say shit; I know he loves me. For Christ's sake, he and my mom have made their lives nothing if not a graceful demonstration of their love for their four kids. He's always been very humorously taciturn, but now I'm tickled to report that he hugs me in moments where we used to shake hands.

My mom handled that leaving with a teary stoicism, and I'll always remember the gratitude I felt toward her and Dad as I drove west across Illinois's wide, rolling river valleys, the darkness dotted with sporadic farms that had been properly bedecked with Christmas lights. Parents have to weather a lot of fear throughout the normal rearing of a child, and I can't imagine the guts it took for my folks to stand on the chilly front porch and watch me putter away down Osceola Street in a rusty Subaru with a mightily be-tusked boar's face at the prow, collecting snowflakes like a Dada figurehead, pointing toward St. Louis and an even greater unknown beyond.

Discern Your Ass
from a Hole in the Ground

My dad is a map guy. While I was growing up we as a family drove the twelve or so hours to our fishing cabin every year in Minnesota, and every year we took a different route through Northern Illinois, Wisconsin, and Minnesota, sometimes veering into Iowa, Michigan's Upper Peninsula, or the Dakotas on side trips. He loved getting out his collection of maps and, scrutinizing them, he would say to me, "Well, Jasper, let's go this way, through Verndale, Bluegrass, and Hubbard, and we'll miss the speed trap north of Wadena." Using methods like this, we discovered treasures over the years that became tradition, like stopping at Grandma Schmercker's restaurant for her excellent pie.

I loved the power that those maps, and my dad's mastery of them, gave us. "Going south we can stay in LaCrosse, we'll pick up some cheese curds, and the next day we'll try to make it home without traveling on an interstate or through a town of more than one thousand people. We almost made it last year, but I got caught driving into Somanauk when your mom nodded off, and I lost my navigator. A five-and-a-half-hour ride happily took us ten hours."

To me this ability is akin to the tying of a knot, the building of a fire, or the changing of a tire. Maps are easily as valuable as any other tool, but in this day and age I've been very disturbed to see people neglect their maps and instead completely depend upon their GPS units. When Global Positioning Systems began to become prevalent in cars, what with the talking instructions and video-game-like street scroll, I grew disturbed. Now we have GPS and maps on our phones, with all kinds of extra information like traffic conditions and the location of the nearest Pinkberry.

Now, hold up. These developments are great, no question. I mean, I can ask my phone device to tell me where the barbecue joints are, as well as what people think of the brisket at each of them! NOTHING WRONG WITH THAT.

What does unnerve me, however, is the technique with which I employ this information. I often use the handy "maps" function on my phone, but I still do it like my dad, meaning I suss out the route and situation before I go. What I cannot allow myself to do is acquiesce to being led by the nose to my destination by a computer. I'll decide where to turn, thanks. Surely you all have been through the experience at least once of your computer giving you completely asinine directions because it simply looks for the biggest arteries for driving through an area, giving no consideration to context or mitigating circumstances. Even if it did, I just can't shake the feeling that the more we people depend, infantlike, upon such coddling, the weaker we grow in character.

Once we begin to depend on the sugar teat of the GPS to change our diapers and drop us off at whatever destination we require, then we might as well just climb back into the stroller and caterwaul until Mommy brings us a cookie. The day will come when your phone is broken or dead and you're stranded in a remote, desolate location, like Schaumburg, and you're going to have no idea where you are and how to get out of there. You will find yourself a day late, yeah, and a dollar short, because you lost the use of your map.

I don't want to be caught in that predicament. I read an article recently that said a new kind of robot car is coming on the market soon that literally drives itself. BUT I DON'T WANT ANY HELP DRIVING. Driving well in concert with all of the other people driving well, or at least trying to, feels good. It feels like we're participating in society. We're present in the moment as we share the road with one another, passing on the left, waving for one another to go ahead and pull out of that driveway, giving one another a spirited middle-finger salute. . . .

When will it end? I found the infantile grown-ups in the great film *WALL-E* to be poignantly frightening. Fat, mewling adult larvae, floating about in cradle-chairs, being fed their daily pap in the form of only blended shakes. Orwell predicted that shit, and it scares me to death. Here's my trip: Our cool, new technologies provide us with a surplus of convenience, and it seems to me that an overabundance of convenience leaves us with a surplus of leisure time. Our technologies then provide us with a panoply of choices of ways in which to fill that time, like video games, social networking, vapid television and film content, etc. We thereby end up spending money and time upon "their" diversions, when we could have been just performing all of the simple acts that our technologies are saving us from in the first place. Driving our vehicles. Looking at our maps. Fishing. Walking in the woods. Doing the dishes. Splitting firewood. That's living, plain and simple, and I feel like a crotchety old man saying this, but there is a great satisfaction in a drying rack full of dishes that cannot be found on Twitter or Scrambley Town. By all means, we should use these wonderful new tools in all the wonderful ways that we can, but we should also be wary that they don't begin to consume us, devouring our time and money that could be better spent on a mouthwatering stack of quarter-sawn oak planks.

The weather seems to be getting more severe all over the world. Global warming is a clear and present issue, perhaps even an imminent danger. The human race is always a potential powder keg, requiring merely one single crackpot firebrand anywhere in the world to instigate a full-on shit-fight. So, just in case some shit goes down, I will feel better knowing that I have the use of a map and a shovel and an axe.

My mom and dad are much more than parents and grandparents. They are, between them, gardener, tailor, woodworker, cook, baker, labor and delivery nurse, schoolteacher, and much more. My dad taught me to read a map and to take full advantage of the knowledge it conveys. The happiness and productivity I have seen amassed by them in their lives is all the proof I need that GPS is for the birds.

13

Resurrection

I had blown through LA and back a few times before moving my tool kit permanently to the City of Dreams, so in my Chicago circle of fools, I was the expert on Hollywood. A sad state of affairs, considering how incredibly ignorant I was about the place. Leaving the Defiant Theatre behind seemed impossible at the time, but it didn't look like I would have to: One of our next productions was to be *Action Movie: The Play*, conceived, of course, by Joe Foust and Ragsdale, and it was one of the funniest high-octane romps you could ever hope to see on a stage that didn't also include Bugs Bunny and GWAR. The plan was for the show to be produced in Chicago, then travel to Los Angeles, where it would be such a smash hit (who better to flock to a theatrical send-up of action films than the people who make action films?!) that we would certainly be moved to the Hollywood Pantages Theatre, and then probably to Broadway, on our way to the West End, which is a part of London where the best theater in the world occurs, according to some white folks. It was an amazing plan, and flawless, really, except for the fucking goddamn flaws in it.

When my theater-company mates told me they would be traveling our show to California, they didn't take into account the simple truth that they did not, in fact, want to go to California. Oops. It was an honest mistake on their parts, by which I mean I don't think they knew their true hearts in the matter until push came to shove. Some of them wanted to bow out of the business altogether, some thought the idea of a tour imprudent (which it most certainly was, but then, wasn't the whole megillah?), and a couple were just chicken. I'm certain it was smart of them to "walk on by" the LA tour, but doing things the smart way was not what had made us an exciting young Chicago company. We were not going to get to the West End by being smart! What I loved about these men and women, these gorgeous rascals, was precisely that we did *not* do things the smart way. Idiots. Whatever the case, the damage was done. Defiant Theatre was staying home in Chicago. I was alone in Los Angeles.

At least I had some friends in town, some of whom had small jobs for me to do, like acting on a minor Nickelodeon show, or carpentry projects, or art department or PA (production assistant) work. But I was without a stage upon which to ply my troth. Many people recommended shows for me to see, claiming that this theater company or that was really a lot like Defiant, and so I would go running all over town to see production after production, some mediocre, some godawful, but nothing remotely like the Defiant flavor I craved. I began to drink to (even greater) excess. I would go to a bar and think, "Aha! Who's smart now, motherfuckers?!" before vomiting into an empty pint glass.

"But enough about theater, you crybaby! How about 'THE BIZ'? Huh, bro? You didn't come here to do some Kabuki bullshit, you came here to get on *Baywatch* and shit! Kowabunga, dude!!!"

My subconscious, which had been very into *The Simpsons*, was speaking to me in such a derisive tone, but my subconscious was flat wrong. Like an absolute dullard, I *had* come to LA to do theater, at least among other things. One way or another, theater was just about all I could do. What I had failed to learn through my zero piles of research was that LA effectively had no theater community. Sure, there are theaters in LA, but compared to Chicago's big-shouldered strength, they are pretty weak tea. Foolishly I had assumed that the largest concentration of acting and writing talent in the country would have a healthy theater scene, but that is sadly not the case. It's a vicious circle, in which there is not a large theatergoing audience, so nobody does theater, so nobody goes, etc. I am being slightly unfair. Of course there are talented people putting up plays in LA. I can't fairly make such sweeping generalizations, because I have never seen all of it. Nobody has. LA is so spread out that you would need to make viewing theater a full-time job in order to canvass the entire area from Venice and Santa Monica to Pasadena, and from the deep Valley or even Ventura down to Orange County. The point is, it was as bleak to me when I landed here as it could possibly have been. I saw more plays that were written by a person trying to get a job writing for *Friends*, "plays" that seemed just like a seventy-minute episode of a sitcom onstage, than I care to say. It turned out that moving to LA to work in theater was the logical equivalent of moving to Chicago to work in television.

As usual, I had more than my share of dumb luck to buoy me. While I'd been in Chicago, a great casting director named Tracy Kaplan had gone to bat for me aplenty, and then she sent me to LA with a list of contacts with whom I could get in touch. She was vouching for me. From her list, I landed at a small but very nice agency, Progressive Artists. Bernie and Belle. I also scored a manager named Eve Brandstein, who taught me a lot about the business before going back to her first calling as a casting director. I'm very grateful to all these folks for getting me off to a running start. They hooked me up with meetings at networks and studios, and I promptly repaid them by falling flat on my fat face. The executives in these meetings generally had no interest in nor ability to comprehend a theater résumé. They'd look at my very nice theater résumé like it was written in Greek. "Oh, Steppenwolf!" they'd say. Or, "Oh, wow. Shakespeare." Those were the two words they knew. It was really frustrating. We'd just look at each other, mutually puzzled by my presence in their offices.

I learned later that in these moments I was expected to be cute, or winning, or electric. I was supposed to turn up my X-factor and come across all "fuckable," which I am afraid I did not do. I had always done just fine by working on plays in which people would see me, and then on occasion some of those people would put me in their next play. "We need a big dumb guy who falls down good. What about this guy? We'll put him in our play." Like that, pretty much. That system wasn't going to work in LA, apparently, so I quickly found myself beating my head against the wall.

As is well known, the business can be really shitty, especially when a person is just starting out. This did not take me completely by surprise, and I was not so naïve that I thought I would cakewalk into a successful career without eating some shit. More surprising was the ugliness that arose in my social life. All my friends and acquaintances from Chicago would get together for drinks at watering holes specifically peopled by ex-Chicago actors who wanted to commiserate about how hard the business was. The status of our auditioning lives and our "callbacks" became our conversational commodity. When we would see our friends, that's what they would ask about, rather than health or family or anything else. It would be, "Hey, man, what's up? Are you going out?" Which means, "Are you getting any auditions?" They couldn't wait to come to the bar if they had any such information to share, and then they'd play it really cool. "Yeah, I'm going in to read for *ER*, no big," and if they got a callback for a second reading, maybe for the producers, that was exponentially more valuable. One's true friends would be thrilled about any such achievement, whilst the majority of the Chicago "pals" would seethe with envy. Schadenfreude was easily the most popular cocktail served in those establishments.

This circumstance quickly became really unpalatable to me. I began to eschew the scene, opting for smaller gatherings with friends, at which we'd cook inexpensive meals and bemoan our collective lots to more sympathetic ears. In my desperation, I actually designed the set and puppets for a Defiant show in Chicago, built most of them in Hollywood with a couple of pals, then hauled them all with my tool kit to Chicago in, you guessed it! A "drive-away" pickup truck!

Some of my LA gang generously tried to hook me up with a couple of dates with cute ladies, dates that could only be described as laughably terrible. I remember one specifically with this cute actress named Elizabeth. I took her to dinner at Lola's, and I'm sure I looked like I was fresh off the construction site to begin with. She said, "What do you do?" which is LA-speak for "What can you do for me and how can you help me get a leg up on everybody else?"

I said to her, "Well, I don't do much—I just moved from Chicago, where I've got a theater company, and we're actually doing this Caryl Churchill play called *The Skriker* that I'm designing the set for, and heading up a team that's building twenty-five puppets and a bunch of masks . . . ," by which point she was out the door.

Things weren't going great.

*   *   *

Fortunately, my main squeeze Pat Roberts was in a similar boat as an artist feeling underappreciated and underutilized. He too had no interest in playing the commercial-art game and chasing the girls. I mean, don't mistake me, we were definitely interested in the chasing of the girls. It's just that the girls we were meeting were not of the most appetizing variety. Once in a while we'd meet an amazing woman, and, as if by a rule, she would be married or gay. So, wisely, we began to stay home and drink a lot of bourbon.

At a certain point I realized that I was not cut out for the self-promotional part of this industry. An unbelievable amount of money changes hands every day in Hollywood, forked over by hopeful performers with a dream, desperate for any slight inch of advantage they can beg, borrow, or steal to put themselves nearer the top of somebody's list. These monies are greedily received by countless photographers, "acting coaches," and shyster agents and managers, who promise the secret to gaining such inches. It was immediately clear to me that I didn't want to succeed at anything by "buying an inch," or by convincing an executive in his/her office that I was cool, so I made up my mind to ignore the business.

I got work fabricating stuff for people, like building an editing bay and some props for this small animation company I was friendly with. Thanks to my minor connections, I started getting sporadic acting jobs here and there. Every few months I'd score a guest-star job on a TV show or a little part in a movie, and these tidbits were just enough artistic food to sustain me. I began to describe my career as a very slowly—ponderously slowly—rolling snowball. Like all aspirants, besides my "theatrical" agent (film and TV), I had a commercial agent, for advertising jobs. I was giving it the old college try while maintaining my uniqueness. I loved driving straight to an audition from a job site, covered in sawdust and sweaty, because I knew that I was guaranteed to stand out from all of the adorably coiffed "cute guys."

One of the pearls of wisdom the agents would gift a body, if one was trying to break in as an actor in LA, was "Record a videotape of every show that's on TV. Be sure to watch one episode of every show, so that when you go to audition for that show you'll know what they want, what style they're looking for." My response came quite easily—I said, "Tell you what, I'm not going to do that. I'm not going to watch any fucking shows. I'm not taping *Angel* and *Buffy* to formulate how I can better play a demon when I audition for them. That way you'll have a hundred guys doing what they think the producers want, but you'll have at least this one guy doing something original." That was my technique. I stand by it. Did I ever get a job as a demon on *Angel*? I did not, and after some time went by, I learned that many initial rejections should eventually be taken as compliments. A lucky actor learns that the projects one says no to end up being much more important than the jobs one takes.

O utside of TV and film auditions, my time was spent traipsing to commercial auditions and working as a carpenter. Invariably I'd be working on the east side of LA and the commercial audition would be far to the west in Santa Monica, which can often mean an hour of travel. One commercial reading could be a three- or four-hour commitment—an ordeal of at least half a day, sometimes more, if one would (hopefully) be asked to "stick around so the director can see you." It didn't take me long to begin adding up these hours for which I was not getting paid as a carpenter. Even though I did shoot a couple of minor commercials, the total profits did not eclipse the amount of carpentry income I was missing to attend the auditions. This was just foolish. The only point of chasing commercials was to garner a paycheck, but if the whole process was losing me money in the end, what was the point?

Understandably, I started to find the commercial auditions really depressing. At least at an acting audition you have the possibility of your talent or your training getting you the job. "Hey, this guy's really good at acting, naturalistically portraying the story. He's funny." Or he's really scary, or really clumsy, or whatever was right. They could look at your résumé and see that you were a trained professional, meaning there was a good chance you'd be more dependable on a fourteen-hour shoot day. But in commercial auditions you're in a room with a hundred fucking yahoos, and basically whoever could make the right funny face got the job. The only qualification necessary to get into this audition was that one look like he enjoys beer, or tits, or Doritos. It didn't take me long to ken that any joker could get the job.

I began to comprehend that I was different from all of these guys, simply because I could earn money with my tools. Their ineptitude in finding any other gainful employment filled the waiting rooms with an atmosphere of desperation. They were led there, Pied Piper–like, bewitched by so many stories, like "Loren got a Chevy campaign last year and he ended up making six hundred grand. He bought a condo and a boat and . . ." etc. The foyers of commercial casting offices are festooned with visions of sugarplums dancing. I had been briefly beguiled by these pipe dreams as well, but I was beginning to get wise. I began to limit myself to national (as opposed to regional) commercial auditions that promised a big payday, like the ones for banks, beer, or automobiles.

I had been in town for about a year when I found myself auditioning for a Budweiser spot. I hauled my ass out to Santa Monica—
the same old waiting room, full of maybe sixty guys. It's a big square
room, and each wall has a bench along it—so it's a big square of
guys, mostly beer-loving, baseball-fan-looking guys (so, fat guys).
The shtick was, you're in the bleachers looking down at the outfield,
holding two huge beers, at a baseball game, and you hear the sound
of a home run crack off the bat. The crowd noise builds, and you're
watching the home run. It's coming straight toward you. You look
at your two beers, and you don't want to set either down, because
Budweiser is so delicious (or because ballpark beers are so expensive?), so the home run hits you on the forehead and you make a
hilarious face and then fall over. So the salient question was, "Who
makes the funny face of getting hit on the head with a home-run
ball the best?"

The Bud spot also contained the role of a little old peanut vendor. So there was a motley throng of hedonist-looking guys, the
beer drinkers, together with a bunch of assorted little old men. I
was looking around, calculating the carpenter wages I was not
earning, and I realized that sitting next to me was Donald Gibb,
who played the Ogre in *Revenge of the Nerds*. I was the appropriate
age for *Revenge of the Nerds* to have been a hugely beloved movie for
me. He was also in the movie *Bloodsport*, for mercy's sake. This guy
was a hero to me and every other teenager in the eighties, and now
he was sitting next to me at this commercial audition? I thought,

"Good god, you can be this minor movie star and do a ton of TV roles and then, ten years later, you're sitting next to me at a fucking Budweiser spot."

I was truly reeling, and so I got up and walked around the room to clear my head. Across the room I passed another guy whose face rang a bell, and I looked back, and I'll be goddamned if it wasn't fucking Carmine from *Laverne & Shirley*. I surreptitiously looked at the head-shot in his hand, and at the bottom it read, *Eddie "Carmine" Mekka*. I was dumbstruck, thinking, "You've got to be fucking kidding me." It might as well have been John Schneider from *The Dukes of Hazzard* or Burt Reynolds. You can be fucking Carmine and now you're at this Bud-weiser spot? Just then Carmine started up a conversation with the little old man next to him: "Hey, you're Joey such-and-such, you were in *Guys and Dolls* and *Singin' in the Rain* . . ." Joey was apparently an old song-and-dance man with whom Carmine was very impressed. In a grinning reply, the man said, "Come on, Eddie, you saw that shit? For-get about it." Fate, that fickle bitch, was grabbing me oh-so-firmly by the short hairs and sending me a very clear message.

I ran out to a pay phone, called my commercial agent, and said, "Thank you kindly, but I'm not doing this anymore. This is not the life for me." There was no shame in these commercial auditions, I just knew that I would rather be making a solid $20 an hour than making zero money to sit and wait for a lottery ticket that could pay off big. I understood in that moment what Robert Mitchum had meant when he said, "Acting is no job for a man." Years later, I got to work with Eddie Mekka on an episode of *Childrens Hospital*, and he was a dream-boat. Between takes, he would sing standards and Sinatra tunes, and he was an absolute peach. Now, if I could only shake hands with the Ogre, I could bring my Budweiser trauma to a neat resolution.

*   *   *

Okay. I had quit doing commercials, but I was still incredibly depressed and drinking a lot. Baby steps. Pat and I were having a lot of fun being young drunks in LA, but we realized with each passing day that we weren't really getting to utilize any of the talents we had. We did things for fun like watch *Dawson's Creek* ironically. We'd run around the house saying excitedly, "Oh my god, it's Tuesday night!" We'd sing, "I don't want to wait . . . for my life to be over . . . ," and get all giggly. Of course *without* irony, we loved the American institution *The Simpsons*. Pretty much my entire circle of artistic friends couldn't help but be profoundly influenced by the genius of *The Simpsons*'s writers and animators. *South Park*, as well, but *The Simpsons* was, and still is, like an encyclopedia of comedy. By now, there is literally no joke they haven't done three ways, and so we often turn to that venerated cartoon when we need a reference for any bit.

Every two or three months, something really exciting would come my way, which would usually end in disappointment. To wit: In 1998 I was up for the lead in a movie entitled *The Tao of Steve*. In fact, the director led me on for a couple of weeks that I had won the part when she had me in to read with other actors, but then they found out they could get Donal Logue, a great actor who had some buzz around him. I believe she sincerely thought I was going to be her choice, but the communication was left in a bit of a gray area, because, as was often the case with me, they found me to be an "adequate" choice but were still hoping they could get someone who was more exciting at the time. So, when they actually did find a more exciting actor, she had to sit me down and give me a talk. She was trying to save face in an unfortunate situation but didn't do terribly well when she handed me the lamest line ever: "You're more Gary Cooper and he's more Montgomery Clift, which is more what this story needs," as though I would think, "Oh, well, I *was* crushed, but since you compared me to Gary Cooper, no hard feelings!" I wonder if Donal knows what a powerful Monty Clift vibe he has going on, because he might be able to parlay that into at least a biopic at some point, right? The character was supposed to be really overweight and schlumpy, and Donal Logue did have a few pounds over me at the time, which didn't help my case either.

Unfortunately, thinking I was going to be making this film, I had begun to happily gain weight, putting on twenty pounds over three or four weeks, with Pat's gleeful assistance. In fact, you might say that he made me his project. I ate so much fucking ice cream and so many cheeseburgers that I thought I would clog my circulatory system right into an early grave. We had just seen an episode of *The Simpsons* in which Homer found out that if he weighed three hundred pounds he could go on disability. So he started wearing muumuus around the house, and there was this great joke that your food's caloric level wasn't high enough unless you could rub it against a piece of paper and have the grease turn the paper clear. Homer says to Bart at one point, "Every second I'm out of bed I'm burning precious calories." It was as though my very own guide for weight gain had been personally delivered via the genius of *The Simpsons*! So, obviously, I started wearing a muumuu (purchased down the hill at the Rite Aid!) and packing on weight just like Homer. I started quoting the lines from *The Simpsons* to our oblivious neighbors and the mailman. Getting fat was the greatest!

Then suddenly I wasn't getting the job and I had become overweight, and so that, of course, just made me even more depressed. Rather than take the weight right back off again, I chose to shrug and continue trudging through the hard-won life lessons of a young man, now "husky," in Hollywood.

Meanwhile, I was starting to more consistently land dependable character-actor gigs. I won a role on *ER*, which was very exciting, as it was the highest-profile drama on television at the time. It was to be the first live episode of *ER*, and so they wanted theater actors, because the show would be shot more like a live play than a film. Since it was live, we couldn't stop and do it again if a mistake was made, so they wanted a cast who could hopefully avoid mistakes. It was an incredibly exciting event of which to be a part. A year or two later I was on the fifth episode of *The West Wing*. This was quite bolstering, the opportunity to work on these shows that had some prestige. Even winning a little guest-star part says to a fellow, "You have worth. Stick around—maybe next time you'll do three episodes." I kept getting these invaluable little signals from the business that said, "Stick it out, kid, just keep plugging away. Something good will happen." Casting people would say things like that to me, too. One benevolent lady told me, "Look, you're going to do great when you come into your sheriff years. Grow a moustache and you're going to work like crazy." I wish I could see her now and shake her hand.

I was about due for some good news when suddenly I got some. A great theater company from Chicago called Roadworks, out of Northwestern University, was coming to town with a production of Mike Leigh's *Ecstasy*. They needed to replace a naked drunk guy in the show, and someone said, "Hey, Offerman's in LA. Perfect." So we staged this play at the Odyssey Theatre, which I found to be an excellent and dependable (still is today) Los Angeles institution, and let me tell you, that work put a powerful healing on me. Casting directors came to see us because the company had a great reputation, and I was able to ride on their coattails. Mali Finn, a generous and sublime casting director, sadly no longer with us, showed up, as did a few other great casting directors. Thank my lucky stars, some of these ladies saw something unique in me and began to champion me. For years they would bring me in on auditions and try to get me some really nice jobs. It took a long time, but I began to see more and more fruit from their efforts.

The best thing that happened immediately was that two casting directors—the same ones from *The Tao of Steve*, Nicole Arbusto and Joy Dickson, two of my greatest champions whom I love to death— were casting this film called *Treasure Island*, written and directed by a genius guy named Scott King. It was a delightfully peculiar script, written more like a theater piece than a film, so they were leaning toward some theater actors.

They ended up casting me and one of the lead actors from our production of *Ecstasy* (the heroic Lance Baker) as the leads of the movie, and then they cast the lead actress from the play (a winsome Rachel Singer) in a supporting role. I suddenly had a lead role in a movie, a hilarious, weird, and smart movie, and I was in heaven. The filmmakers were "old-timey people"—a sort of revival movement. Fifteen years ago in LA, there was this sect of hipsterish people who would dress in old-timey fashions, like from the big band era. Double-breasted suits and fedoras and poodle skirts and such. Every Friday night at the Brown Derby there would be big band music and swing dancing. They would use pomade in their hair and have DA haircuts and the whole nine yards.

Scott King was sort of an adjunct to this crowd but he held himself apart from it, and therefore above it. He had come into some money, so he whimsically fashioned himself as an old-time studio head with his company King Pictures. He had a 1932 BMW convertible that he drove around, and he was very generous with all of us working in his company. We had a lot of fun, both shooting the film and socializing outside of it. I had finally found an artistic circle in which I could hang my hat and a benevolent leader whom I could serve with ardor in Scott, a good friend of mine to this day.

We shot in a studio in Silver Lake, on a period camera called a Mitchell. The movie was set in 1943 and a Mitchell was the actual camera one would have used in the forties. Scott ran a very civilized set, insisting that we only shoot eight-hour days. I loved working with him and the producers. *Treasure Island* was also where I first met my good friend Austin filmmaker Bob Byington, who was the script supervisor on the film. Speaking of Bob, I ended up making a couple of prosthetic penises for the movie, because they didn't have anyone else who could, and I had made a lot of stuff like that for theater in the past. We also shot a week up in San Francisco, including some amazing locations in the city and in front of the Bay Bridge.

It was such an incredible feeling to finally have the lead in a movie that reminded me of the Defiant Theatre in its combined irreverence and intelligence. These people valued me as an actor but also as a dependable contributor; I consulted on acting scenes, drove the art truck, rigged lights, and more, which did my self-worth a world of good. The movie went to Sundance in 1999, and it really got us a lot of nice attention. We were awarded a special jury prize for "Distinctive Vision." I finally felt like things were beginning to sputter to life for me in Los Angeles. The snowball began to pick up speed, almost imperceptibly, but still, that was a good sight better than slowing down and melting.

*   *   *

Not long after this small triumph, planted in front of *Dawson's Creek* one night with our preferred dinners—a can of Virginia blister peanuts and a mason jar full of Jim Beam, water, and ice—Pat and I were undoubtedly feeling romantic after seeing what those rascals Pacey and Dawson were up to. We observed, "Okay. This is pathetic. There's gotta be some high-quality women in this town looking for us. We've met a lot of ladies, we've seen how this town works now. We're smart, after a manner of speaking, and we know that we have unique, weird talents and personalities. There are definitely ladies of refined taste looking for us. We just gotta find 'em."

Well. I'll be goddamned if that speechifying didn't work, as though we had uttered some sort of necromantic, romantic incantation. Isn't that *The Secret*? You just say what you want out loud, and it comes to you? Had some arcane kabbalah from a random episode of *Oprah* infiltrated our psyches? Whatever the case, *Secret* or no, within two weeks of saying it Pat met his future wife, Courtenay Valenti, who is a magnificent, beautiful, tasteful woman who also happens to be a brilliant film executive at Warner Bros. and classy as all get-out. It had happened exactly like we wished in our Secret! THANK YOU, DAWSON!!! PEACE, PACEY!!!

Through the cloud of smoke and patina of Silver Lake dirt, she was able to see the best version of Pat, in effect saying, "You are a brilliant, good-looking guy. Your artwork is somehow simultaneously hilarious and acutely intelligent, and I am laying claim to you." (And she was right. They have two amazing kids now, and Pat is a champion dad and husband, even as he continues to crank out uproarious, thought-provoking art.) Before we knew it, they were an item.

*   *   *

Shortly after Pat and Courtenay started dating, maybe a couple of months later, I was telling my friends, "Guys, ladies, I'm losing my mind. I have to do a play. That's my mother's milk. It's the only thing that can save my life." Once again, my heroic casting directors Nicole and Joy, who had put me in *Treasure Island*, hooked me up with an audition for a play at a new company called the Evidence Room, which had just purchased a building in the Echo Park area. They needed to build a theater in this old warehouse and they also needed to build a set for the show. There was a character in the play who was an East German soldier who had a monologue at one point comparing his anus to his phallus. I said to them upon our meeting, "You don't know it yet, but you are looking for me."

It turned out that an actress named Megan Mullally, who was one of the stars of a popular television comedy entitled *Will & Grace*, was cast in the lead of the play. This fact was dangled as an incentive when I was meeting the directors of the company, but I said, "Hey, I'm a man of the theatre"—real theatre folk (nerds) spell it with the old-school -*re*—"so I'm not that crazy about working with a TV lady, but I'm going to audition *despite* the fact that you're planning to include her."

Regardless of that jackassery, I got the job. And it, and indeed she, saved my life.

The show was *The Berlin Circle* by Chuck Mee. He takes Bertolt Brecht's *Caucasian Chalk Circle* and sets it at the Berlin Wall coming down. During the first read-through, the cast of twenty-four people was sitting in a large circle of chairs in this empty warehouse when Megan came walking in, all turned out and wearing very cute clothing and what I used to call her "fashion shoes." She was beautiful, okay, sure, and I thought, "All right, let's see what you got, hotshot."

We read through the script, and my attitude and, well, everything changed. She was so funny and so masterful, such a total pro, that she immediately went from seeming like some sort of TV actor with my own imagined inadequacies to clearly existing as a living, breathing, gorgeous pack of talent. Adroitly extinguishing my misplaced snobbery was the discovery that she had done two Broadway shows by that point. To my embarrassment, I was to learn that she had cut her teeth in the exact same Chicago theater community as my own snotty ass, just some years before me. Beyond that, she was simply hilarious. I am still so besotted by her talent that thirteen years into our relationship, I am amazed that I am the partner to such a bright and shining powerhouse of entertainment. In the play, I was doing a sort of cheap Colonel Klink (from *Hogan's Heroes*) German dialect, which, thankfully, she found funny. After the read-through I went up to her, thinking, "Of course, you fool—they have good people on TV, too." My first words to my future bride were, "Hey, I'm Nick. You're hilarious and I think this is going to be really fun." Little did I realize how effective this opening salvo would prove.

As it turned out, literally no one else spoke to her that day because they were all freaked out by loving her on TV. So my humble greeting turned out to be a huge windfall, unwittingly.

We had a lot of factors working against our becoming a couple. A rule I believe I've mentioned: One doesn't date another actor in one's play. Of course, we all end up breaking that rule, obviously, at some point, but everybody knows better. If you have your shit together and you're an adult, but you are feeling randy toward a castmate, you might make your urgings known to each other, but you simply wait until the play is over to seal the deal. Otherwise, chances are you're just signing up for little more than an afternoon delight (which can also be a pleasing option). I guess my point is that if you feel strongly enough about your fellow actor that you want to try to make a go at something lasting, then your amour has a better chance of surviving if you cultivate it outside of the theater, ideally after the play closes.

Beyond that rule of thumb, we were also both staunchly single. Despite the matchmaking glamour that Pat and I had conjured together a few weeks before, I was still being protective of myself because LA and her cute, superficial women had been very painful to me thus far. Megan was extra self-protective because she was on a popular TV show, and I'm sure she had prospecting gold diggers at every available turn. She had been dating guys who were slightly more rock-and-roll style, leather-pants wearing, skinny sort of guys. So we were sort of blindsided when we mutually snuck up on each other.

Because of our similar theater careers, we became really good friends pretty immediately. Plus, we were the two outsiders in the cast. The Evidence Room was an existing company with a couple of shows under its belt moving to this new home, and we were the two hired guns. This arrangement saw us banding together during rehearsal, during which we discovered that we also shared a filthy, irreverent sense of humor. It didn't take long, probably a couple of weeks into rehearsals, for us both to realize, "Oh, hang on. Holy crap. I'm really attracted to you." I can certainly say that for myself, at any rate. Megan's thoughts might have run with just a modicum of increased elegance.

I made the first overtures, although we were both sending pretty clear signals. My first hurdle, strangely enough, was a feeling of insecurity at being so outclassed by Megan. I saw her as a "fancy lady" who couldn't possibly have an eye for a working jack like myself. She wore "fashion shoes," for fuck's sake. In a way, my perceived class difference probably helped matters progress, as I felt like I could grow safely close to Megan without any danger of romantic feelings, because of my "low station." That dastardly Cupid snuck right up in my shadow and filled me full of arrows. Eventually the penny dropped, and I was understandably in some disbelief. To myself, I thought, "What?! No. No way is this happening. Who do you think you are? Is this *Beauty and the Beast*? She be a lady, the finest of ladies, and you be but a pagan laborer," but it was too late. Far, far too late.

Almost nightly, I was saying to Pat Roberts, "This is crazy. I think we like each other." I would call him constantly to say, "Jesus. Check out what Megan just said," because she said just the funniest shit. I couldn't believe that a woman that beautiful and sophisticated would say something so wonderfully pornographic about my balls.

Things started falling into place, and finally, we were becoming really winky and flirtatious with each other. One day, as she was leaving the theater in her Range Rover, I ran out and stopped her. I knocked on the window and climbed in the passenger seat and looked her in the eye as I said, "This is going on, right? I'm not that smart, but I'm also no dummy. This is happening."

She was very old-fashioned and businesslike about it. She said, "Okay. There might be something happening down the road, but I can guarantee you nothing is going to happen before the end of our play. But yeah, I think you're all right." Then we drove to Los Feliz (which means "The Happy") where we proceeded to park and make out for two hours. Beck's *Midnite Vultures* album had just come out, which included the song "Beautiful Way," and we played that song on repeat thirty-eight times. Seems like it was go time. We kept it a secret for a while but got busted opening night. The sound designer spotted us kissing out on the deck (that I had built).

Man, brother, I'll tell you, I was head over heels. I was solid gone, baby, but Megan was extremely old-fangled in her courting allowances. It didn't take long before I had moved out of the unfinished basement I was living in and moved in with her, but she stepped us through the process in small increments. I got to take her home and make out on the couch, but then I had to leave. Then I was allowed to start spending the night, but I had to sleep on the couch. Eventually, when I finally got to sleep in the bed I had to face the wall and behave myself. She did it for real, because she wanted to be sure that I was for real. It took veritable calendar months before she, as she puts it, "gave up the puss."

I had a job at the time hanging lights for Disney Imagineering. I was driving the forty minutes up Highway 5 to Valencia one morning when it hit me—I remember exactly where I was—that I was going to marry Megan. And I have to say, I was quite pissed off because I hadn't been consulted. Life just dropped it in my lap—"You're getting married." She's eleven years older than me, so it wasn't the most likely pairing for that reason and more. Didn't matter. I was hers. I thought, "Okay, I'm done." I was incredibly happy at this realization, but I was a little angry, as a man, that I hadn't been given the opportunity to weigh the options. I guess I got over it, but not for a solid thirty seconds or so.

Looking back on that period, I have to laud Megan and Courtenay for their ability to see any goodness in Pat and me. Don't get me wrong, I'm a big fan of both myself and Pat, but in all fairness to us, we were looking like a pretty dubious wager at that point, when our noble wives had the guts to hold their horses, reach down from their regal coaches into the muddy road, haul us to our feet, clean us off, and make men of us. As I'd suspected it would, doing that play with Megan in 2000 really did save my life, in so many more ways than I ever could have fathomed.

I guess the moral of the story would have to be: Read *The Secret*!

Measure Twice, Cut Once

When I encourage people to pick up a chisel and begin wood-working, I have to remember that I had a pretty solid twelve or so years of tool training before I ever sharpened a chisel myself. But I don't think that should be daunting to anyone who is brand-new to the practice. My education was probably accelerated by my existing shop skills, but basic woodworking comes pretty easily whether or not you've been running a table saw for years.

I had spent some time framing houses before learning to build scenery and props and then becoming a full-time scenic carpenter in Chicago. I have always loved building scenery. It holds a magical quality for me, the fabrication of some illusion upon which to place the action of a play or musical to best facilitate the imagination of the audience. Compared to, say, cladding the rafters of a roof in sheets of plywood, building scenic elements can be a lot more fun, containing a playful or whimsical quality that regular construction lacks. Building houses, both in the fram-ing and the finish work, not to mention the cabinetry, is also mightily satisfying, in that one is creating a solidly comfortable dwelling in which people can make their lives, but, having be-come soundly ensnared in theater's web, I thrived best spending my formative years in the scene shop. That is, until I moved to LA.

Lacking the bountiful theater community of Chicago, Los An-geles did not provide me the opportunity to make much of a living building scenery. Sure, there are a multitude of scenery shops for television and film, but the best ones are all run by a union to which I did not claim membership, and I couldn't find a position at the nonunion shops I investigated. My problem was that I was too honest with them. I told them up front that I was an actor, and so I would need to be able to go to auditions and then likely miss work if and when I booked a job. No shop foreman wants to begin a relationship like that, nor should they. My strategy should have entailed a little more smoke screen, as I could have gotten a job, then asked about auditions later, once they were crazy about me. I guess I knew better than to depend upon my ability to charm a bunch of carpenters.

Whatever the case, I had to revert to basic construction carpentry, picking up work wherever I could. I built some mediocre editing-suite tables and shelf units for a friend from plywood and construction lumber. I did some custom built-in work at a sports bar, a couple of closet built-ins for another pal, etc. Then a plum assignment came my way. Kara, an old Defiant pal, was living in a Hollywood Hills apartment building. The landlord, Chuck, wanted a really nice deck built on the hillside below the building. I drew up some ideas and got him to green-light one of them that had a Frank Lloyd Wright feeling to the railing details. I enlisted another old Defiant pal, Marty McClendon, who had designed a lot of our more incredible sets in Chicago, to help me out, as we had always had a great time building together.

We first dug six large holes and poured cylindrical concrete piers deep in the ground, upon which to anchor our structure. Next we built the legs, beams, joists, and cross-bracing of Douglas fir, treated for termite resistance, finally cladding the actual deck in redwood, which is naturally impervious to rot and the elements. It felt fantastic to be outside working, earning some recompense with our brains and muscles, instead of sitting around wondering when our agents were going to call with an audition. The railings were last, and they were comprised of six panel sections with an interior geometric pattern of rectangles reminiscent of a Wright stained-glass window. I designed these patterns by simply messing around with different combinations drawn to scale with a ruler on some graph paper until I found the iteration that was most pleasing to mine eye.

This was a big moment for me, looking back, as it was the first time that I was filling the role of designer. I had always enjoyed working alongside great designers in the theater, taking their plans and engineering the best method by which to accomplish their desired results, but now I was wielding the pencil! Once I had perfected my railing design, I then had to deduce the best way to build it, which led Marty and me to our first use of a common woodworking joint known as the shiplap joint. We cut them primarily on the table saw, a tool we had known and loved for many years but had never utilized for cutting joinery. This was a major development that was soon to provide further inspiration.

Soon after I had begun courting Megan, a well-heeled acquaintance of hers wanted a really nifty folly built on his property. His exceptionally nice, new house in the hills had an extra acre of what was basically park land tacked onto the backyard. Out in this "park" he wanted a cabin where he could go and have a glass of wine with his guests before dinner. Marty and I jumped and took on this project as well, hiring a couple more helpers, and once again we were thrilled to be working on such a substantial structure. We'd begin each day's work at seven A.M., and drinking our coffee as the morning sun burned off the mist in the trees made us feel like we could have been in the

STEP 2: BUILD CHAIR

middle of nowhere instead of smack-dab in the center of Los Angeles, creating such a satisfying sense of escape from the shitty, superficial grind of "the business." Our design was built around a post-and-beam structure, with some of our first attempts at beefy joinery connecting the six-by-six-inch posts. With a hexagonal deck off the front corner, there was plenty of floor space to clad with reclaimed Douglas fir two-by-fours that we had salvaged from a one-hundred-year-old house in Santa Monica, igniting our desire to reuse as much of the valuable timber that goes to waste every day as we could. If we as a society properly reclaimed all of the construction lumber heading to the landfill and the bonfire every day, we wouldn't need to cut down another tree for twenty years, if ever.

After we finished that cabin, another friend wanted a yoga studio built in her yard in west LA. By this point, I'd discovered, mainly in Pasadena, the architecture of Greene and Greene, who were contemporaries of Frank Lloyd Wright in the early twentieth century, and I became completely besotted with their style, which adds some sexy Asian curves to the Craftsman or Mission aesthetic. My design for the "Yoga Hutch" emulated their designs, as near as I could afford, anyway, and Marty and I were really enjoying our education as we continued to challenge each other to execute more complex designs and joinery.

One day, as I was chopping out a humongous mortise with a framing chisel, I realized that this huge mortise-and-tenon joint that I was creating to join the posts and beams together was also one of the bedrock joints used in antique furniture. I thought, "Hey, if we can build this structure, then surely we can build a table, which is just a smaller-scale version of a post-and-beam cabin." Another harbinger of the impending change in my carpentry style was instigated by a film job that I got during the construction of the Yoga Hutch. I had to leave my job site for a few months while I worked on the film, which was nothing short of an asshole move. I left this mostly finished building under construction in the backyard of these nice people while I traipsed around shooting a film. Not the coolest move. I promised myself from there on out, I would only build pieces in a workshop, where I could give a client a safe "lead time," so that I could complete their commissions when I was able to, without leaving a mess lying around their property.

I started driving Megan crazy because everywhere we went I would be on the floor, underneath the old tables, looking at the joinery. I was obsessed with the tricks employed by furniture makers over the years to ensure a structure's solidity. A contractor that I knew saw what was happening and recognized my symptoms. He gave me a few issues of *Fine Woodworking* magazine and said, "If you want to get into this stuff, this is all you need," and sure enough I got a subscription and was just swept away down a river of knowledge upon which I am still paddling madly. I had guzzled all of the Kool-Aid, reading voraciously of woodworking, and then beyond to boatbuilding.

If one is bewitched by woodworking (as I am) and one begins a program of study (as I have), then one must first assay the classic joinery—the mortise-and-tenon, the dovetail, the sliding dovetail, the mitre joint, the box joint, the finger joint. Eventually everything breaks down into simple techniques. The entire discipline of working with wood really only comes down to a handful of tools and methods with which you can do damn near anything with wood in three-dimensional space, to the extent of the limitations of your material. Once you master those simple tools and techniques, you can then craft toward whatever item your predilections steer you to. You might want to build bread boxes or bicycles or chess pieces or sailboats, and you can!

I was immediately and powerfully drawn to the work of George Nakashima, a Japanese American woodworker who popularized his table style consisting of a single slab of a walnut tree with the natural edges retained, resting upon different sculptural varieties of a trestle base. These tables look equally at home in an ancient temple or a modern-architectural house, because the slab of wood itself is the work of art. My first attempt was an homage to his Frenchman's Cove table, which his daughter, Mira, has been producing since she took over the Nakashima operation after her dad passed away. She maintains a very charismatic company in Pennsylvania, if you want to see some superb American work.

The more I learn about woodworking, the more I am convinced that I don't ever want to decorate my pieces with a lot of man-made gingerbread. Many virtuoso craftspersons work in many styles, and they do some mind-blowing things with solid wood, in the Federal style, Art Nouveau, Victorian, and others. Not so much for me. I think it's all about creating a piece of furniture that allows the wood itself to draw the focus. What Ma Nature has wrought in the grain and color and figure of a given piece of tree is generally much more magical to me than any dentil edge I might adhere to it. Finally finishing the wood, especially with a hand-rubbed oil finish, after careful scraping and sanding, simply reveals the story that particular tree has been getting ready to tell us for decades or sometimes centuries. Usually the story is full of twists and surprises and breathtaking beauty, but hopefully the story does not include a chapter about a lag bolt that someone screwed into the tree eighty years ago, only to be rediscovered by your expensive table-saw blade.

I knew I needed a shop space but could not find anything remotely appropriate and/or affordable, until one day I was helping my friend Daniel Wheeler, a high-end sculptor and maker of things, to cast Pat Roberts's supine form in plaster so that Daniel could sculpt a Formica-faceted mountain range in the rough shape of Pat's carcass (an amazing piece of loving work—the sculpture, not Pat's bod, although that's not too shabby either). My motorcycle needed a jump, so I went to the neighboring warehouse spaces looking for some jumper cables (I've never driven without cables since—and neither should you), and I found them at a large photography studio. The forty-by-eighty-foot white room was very barren, and the photographer told me he knew right where the jumper cables were because he was moving!

"Oh, really?" I replied, and immediately took down the landlord's information.

"Yeah," he said, "I used to do a killer business shooting the cover photos for VHS porn movies."

"You don't say?" I replied, looking at the expanse in a new light indeed. Were my boots lightly sticking to the concrete floor?

"Oh, yeah, the money was great," he said, "because the photo on the box is what gets your rental at the video store. Think about it. But the video store is dying. I can't afford to stay." He then toured me around the huge room, upon the walls of which were still poster-size versions of some of the photos he had accomplished there in this empty, dusty warehouse. There was a sandy beach scene, complete with water, and a snowy ski-bunny hillside, with pine trees and a cabin, and on and on, every photo with a scantily clad sexpot in a coy pose of one sort or another.

"Well, I'm sure things will work out," I said, licking my chops— no, not at the Chesty Morgans, but at the potential shop space!

I got the place and, with Marty's help, turned it into a woodworker's dream shop, where I still ply my troth to this day. Mr. McClendon and I both owe an undeniable debt of gratitude to *Fine Woodworking* magazine for the expert tutelage it has given us over the years. We have read that magazine cover to cover every month, completely infatuated even with the classified ads in back. I could tell you where to get tiger maple in Virginia or what gentleman in Ohio will tune up your antique molding planes for you. I'm the same way with *WoodenBoat* magazine, which is about as delicious as a periodical can get.

When Marty and his winning bride, Jennifer, were blessed with a bun in the oven, I was able to realize a dream that had been percolating for a while thanks to the *WoodenBoat* classifieds. A fellow named Warren Jordan had plans available to purchase for the "Baby Tender," which is a lapstrake-planked rowboat built to the scale of a cradle. It even hangs on custom davits! You can bet your sweet caboose I built that little boat for Marty and Jen with a hull of Alaskan yellow cedar and black walnut trim. Witnessing the hull of a boat take shape upon your bench is like spinning a Corvette from wool. Thar be witchcraft afoot in the boatshop, sure, now!

We continued to leapfrog off of each other, attempting projects ever increasing in difficulty. Ours was a beautiful partnership, fueled by the sounds of Kool and the Gang, the Gap Band, Parliament, and Funkadelic. Sadly for me, Marty was called back to Wisconsin to merely run an entire college theater department, the Lord's work, but we both still love to send each other pictures of our most recent sweet joinery. I could never have learned all that I have so far without his collaboration. In the last year, our circle of life has gone full-on "Hakuna Matata," *as we have both realized the crazy sex dream of writing articles for* Fine Woodworking! Who shot who in the what, now?! Check out *FW* number 231 to see McClendon's Greene and Greene–style bed in American cherry, but don't look at it unless you're prepared to BLOW YOUR LOAD.

Hooked on boats but good, I then had the chance to build my first canoe, *Huckleberry*, and shoot a how-to video of the process for Ted Moores and Joan Barrett of Bear Mountain Boats in Peterborough, Ontario, the premier company for all of your canoe-building needs. Ted literally wrote the book (*Canoecraft*) on building cedar-strip canoes and kayaks, a manual from which I learned to find my ass with both hands and many more techniques even more efficacious. Jimmy Diresta shot the video and earned himself my second canoe, *Lucky Boy*, as part of his recompense. These canoes are designed by Ted and Steve Killing, and I will reiterate that when the hull begins to reveal its voluptuous curves to the builder, boners there be, and that goes for the ladies as well. Experiencing a problem with depression? Ennui got you down? Build a goddamn canoe, and trust me, you will be happy as a clam at high tide. Most of the work is done with hand tools, which means you get to crank your tunes for hours of pleasure. Check out any Tom

Waits or *Petra Haden Sings: The Who Sell Out.* Iron and Wine is amazing on the spokeshave. I also played a lot of Supreme Music Program, a band fronted by Megan Mullally, whose three albums are like fully formed novels. Lady got pipes, y'all.

Even the paddle of the canoe can prove to be an immensely satisfying undertaking and a place I often suggest that beginners choose as their starting point. It's great training in the block plane and the spokeshave, and there is nothing so gratifying as crafting a handled tool from wood. To date I have carved a spoon and fork, several canoe paddles, a life-size replica mahogany axe, and a baseball bat. The moment of enchantment occurs when the item is nearing completion and you are sanding the shaft or handle. You can begin to feel the work that this tool will perform, whether it be rapping out a triple or paddling against a brisk current. I can tell you from many hours of experience that propelling a wooden canoe that you have built with a paddle also made by your hand carries so much more than a sense of pride. One begins to tap into the primal ingenuity that strings us together with countless generations of our clever forebears who collectively did all of the long division for us when it came to sailing and aerodynamics and, well, every sort of simple machine, really.

When I paddle across the big water, I feel a direct kinship with my ancestors, in that we have both cheated the river. With the chair and the table, we outsmart gravity. With the boat, we outsmart water and wind and distance. Lest we get too cocky, though, as soon as we (I) start to think this way, Ma Nature slaps us (me) with a squall and dumps my canoe over a submerged tree trunk, reminding me that behind that spokeshave there still stands a jackass.

14

Romantic Love

Engage in romantic love. It truly makes life worth living. Romance affords you the opportunity to do a lot of "giving," which I believe I have read is said to be better than "receiving." Trust me, once you give of your time and care to your loved one, you'll be doing a-plenty of receiving, if you follow me. If you don't follow me, I'm saying you'll be having a bunch of oral sex performed upon you.

One might examine the example of a triumphant marriage set for me by my mom and dad and determine that I was hopelessly lost to a life of romance from the outset. I'm not talking the saccharine stuff of Disney films. I'm referring to down-to-earth everyday give-and-take. A bouquet of sweet Williams gathered along the fencerow on the way home to Mom. Making sure Dad got the bone with the marrow at dinner (which he shared with me—good man). Little, commonplace gestures that say, "I'm thinking of you." The reason some may see my sappy side as a liability is that when faced with a decision, I will damn near always choose the more romantic (foolish) choice.

To wit: A mere couple of months into our courtship, my wife, Megan, took a major plunge by coming to my family's annual fishing week in remote northwest Minnesota. I was pretty nervous, as the accommodations are pleasant but spartan, and Megan would be meeting most of my family for the first time. These cabins are for fisherfolk and hunters, not vacationing legends of the entertainment world, so I wanted to go the extra mile or three to make it nice for my new lady. We arrived to a beautiful afternoon, light on the mosquitoes, and were happy to see the gang. I suggested we take the pontoon boat out across the lake to get a romantic view of the sunset. Megan agreed, so we snagged a bottle of wine and puttered away. For those who don't know, a pontoon (aka "party barge") is a good-size rectangular floor, say ten feet by eighteen feet, floating upon two pontoon floats, like two long cylindrical skis, with seating for twelve or so, and a nice-size but not overly macho motor (thirty-five to fifty horsepower). It's the minivan of the lake.

There is a retractable awning on the pontoon for shade, rendering the vessel a very comfortable place from which to catch one's limit, or just enjoy a cold can of suds while taking in some of the cheese curds one collected on one's way through Wisconsin and admire the majestic scenery. Or, say, shut down the motor, drift, and soak up the sunset with your new crazily foxy bombshell. Traditionally, and in order to comply with the law, a boater will turn on small lights at dusk so that other watercraft can see him/her and thereby prevent collisions from occurring. I understand the prudence in this rule, so I flipped on the "parking lights" and we had a glass of wine and discussed our burgeoning feelings, as well as my brother-in-law's penchant for the black Russian cocktail, while the sun set beautifully over the pine forest in which the cabin resort sat. If I do say so myself, this was a pretty devastating atmosphere of amour in which I had festooned our evening. Romeo-wise, I was looking pretty savvy.

By the time the breeze picked up and blew us directly into the far shore opposite our dock, it was fully dark and time to head in for

WOO A LADY

some late-night snacks and euchre. When I turned the key to fire up
the motor, the silence that greeted me was one of the most violent
sounds I'd ever not heard. I knew immediately what had befallen us,
thanks to a storied history of misunderstanding motor vehicles
throughout my youth. I'd left the maritime equivalent of the parking
lights turned on without the motor running (silence is romantic), and
the battery had been drained past the capability of answering our ig-
nition needs.

This was very bad. The lake was completely dark. A brisk breeze
was blowing us against the shore directly across the lake from our
destination. There was nary a light as far as the eye could see, as this
whole side of the lake was a preserve used by the Boy Scouts, who
were fully absent at this time. In short, I had no choice but to attempt
to compel the pontoon the mile and a half back across the water. But
how? I screamed a few times at the top of my lungs for my brother,
who was no doubt five beers into a euchre game back at the cabin.
Christ almighty.

I searched clumsily through the storage areas beneath the bench
seats and burst into (inward) tears of thanks when I came upon a pathetic, warped canoe paddle. It was incredibly lightweight and curved
so severely that if I had a pair of them I could have made a kick-ass
rocking chair with some exciting action. But given the circumstances,
I had never seen a more beautiful wooden implement in all of my life.
I proceeded to sit on the front center of the pontoon and set to paddling for all I was worth (not much at that moment) for about three
hours, directly into the wind, while Megan poured swigs of wine into
my mouth and sang a progression of songs into my ear, songs of love
like Randy Newman's "Real Emotional Girl" and "Marie"; Tom
Waits's "Johnsburg, Illinois" and "Ruby's Arms"; and her showstop-

ping version of "Danny Boy." The bees of love came swirling around me in a swarm of passion, coalescing in the air before me like a large cartoon fist before soundly bludgeoning me into servitude.

I couldn't stop and rest because of the severe headwind, so I set my jaw and paddled like a Phoenician, literally guiding myself by the Big Dipper until we floated safely into the dock. Standing on the dock, spent, under the stars, my then-girlfriend told me she loved me. Using my gifts of stubbornness and mulish stamina, I had achieved a romantic triumph that I might hope to repeat in our years of bliss, but preferably by less taxing means. When we arose the next morning, my family was disappointingly nonplussed at the recounting of my Homeric episode, refusing to believe that I hadn't killed the battery on purpose to provide myself a juicy opportunity to impress my lady. That hurt, but not nearly as much as what happened next. My dad took me out to the pontoon and showed me where the top pops off the motor and one could use a pull rope to start it up, in case the battery should die. The Offermans, ladies and gentlemen.

I nexplicably, but thankfully, Megan stuck with me. It wasn't long before Cupid sat me down and said, "You know what's up, right?" and I said, "Yes. Your work here is replete and seamless, and I will answer it." Megan and I had openly discussed the plan to one day marry, so I didn't feel terribly sweaty about making a proposal happen at first. After some water had passed under the bridge, however, it became clear that I should get the ball rolling, maybe after a year together. One day we were walking down Beverly Boulevard in LA, and I was pulling my Swiss army knife out of my pocket, as is my habit, and I also accidentally pulled out a quarter, which went tinkling onto the sidewalk. As I abruptly took a knee to retrieve the coin and replace it in my pocket, inadvertently striking the exact posture and gesture of a man traditionally proposing marriage, even down to the hand in my pocket, Megan facetiously said, "Oh my, god, honey!" and I, ever game, played along as though I had awkwardly lost the ring. "Oh, uh . . . ," I stammered. "I was just—I think I lost. A nickel."

Hilarious! We laughed long and hard and pressed on to our destination, while in the back of my mind a switch had been thrown. The placard beneath that switch read, "Many a true word is spoken in jest." (I don't know who writes the copy for these switches of mine, but they need to update their vernacular, bro.) The story of my "muffed proposal" made the rounds, and everyone agreed that it was a terrific chuckle. The foundation of the humor was to be found in our confidently solid romance. Acquaintances would sometimes exhibit alarm that I might "play so fast and loose" with a lady's expectations, but I would never risk hurting Megan's feelings, and she knew that, so the subject remained ripe for further ribaldry.

About this time, I was getting incredibly excited about a trip to Paris that we had coming up. Around the set of Will & Grace, I mentioned that it might be even funnier to extend my run of proposal comedy in the City of Lights. Without missing a beat, the costume designer (the sublime Lori Eskowitz) handed me a selection of gorgeous engagement rings of the costume jewelry variety, which I gratefully and surreptitiously pocketed.

Cut to: Gay Paree! Holy shit, you guys, there is a city in France called Paris, directly south of Amiens; it's on the Seine, and you should totally go check it out. We were absolutely swept away by the romance and beauty and history of that magnificent burg. Paris is indeed for lovers. We thrilled at buying crepes with butter and sugar

from a street vendor and then just sojourning about the arrondisse-
ments (neighborhoods arranged in a spiral pattern by number), soak-
ing in the architecture, the people, the museums, the food, the
flowers, and I was especially freaked out by the Art Deco designs of
the Paris Metro stops done by Hector Guimard at the turn of the
twentieth century. So much so that I did some homework and sought
out a couple of apartment buildings he had also assembled. Such
beautiful and highly crafted work!

We were high on the hill of Montmartre visiting the Basilica of
Sacré-Coeur, then just swooning at the majestic views of the city
from this, the highest point. At the base of the ancient stone steps
leading to the church, I suddenly dropped to my knees again and this
time pulled out a pretty bitchin' diamond ring. I launched into "Megan, you know I love you"—but my words were cut short when I
bobbled the ring and it flipped a few times in the air before neatly
dropping into the ancient iron gutter grate over which I was kneeling. Ever willing, Megan did not bat an eyelash, saying, "Oh my god,
Nick, what was that?"

"Um, nothing, I—I mean, I just dropped a twenty-centime
piece. . . ."

Terrific. We had a nice laugh and then continued touring that his-
toric hilltop, which once housed the studios of artists like Picasso,
Dali, Modigliani, Monet, van Gogh, Mondrian . . . not a bad lineup.
I'm telling you, Paris is totally worth it; I don't know why nobody
ever talks about it. It's in France, everybody.

Some of the finest gustatory experiences in the world can also be
found in this foxy bitch of a European capital. We got some good tips
from friends on some places to dine, including an incredibly romantic
café on the left bank of the Seine. So romantic that it felt like we were

sucking on one string of spaghetti together in *Lady and the Tramp*, and our postdinner stroll along the Seine was a dream. We crossed the river on the resplendent Pont Neuf bridge (so pretty—why has no one used it in a movie?! Woody Allen, please check it out!), which, thinking back on it now, was like an unrealizable fantasy of what I'd always thought a love trip should be. In the middle of our crossing, I took Megan by her two arms and placed her just so. Then I backed up about five steps to take a gallant, rolling start into my kneeling, but as I began to step to her, I unfortunately tripped and barreled straight into the bridge's side wall, catching the rail soundly in my gut, which folded me over the wall, sending the impressive diamond ring in my hand catapulting into the night air. Flipping cinematically end-over-end, catching the lights of the night city in its several expertly cut facets, the ring plummeted, as if in slow-motion, disappearing into the murky waters of the Seine. Can you even imagine how embarrassing this was for me?! Two incredibly expensive diamonds lost, not to mention I'd twice made a complete botch job of proposing to my devastatingly beautiful girlfriend. Megan and I laughed again, sincerely enjoying the now-running gag, but not so much as to take away from the sheer bliss of our romantic evening.

Near the end of our trip, after we had visited the Louvre Museum extensively and I had successfully photographed myself shirtless amongst the centaurs in the sculpture garden (those Louvre security guards are no joke—hey, somebody should totally set a movie there! It would be cool!), we figured that no trip to Paris would be complete without ascending la Tour Eiffel. It was later in the evening, which turned out to be a good move, as the daytime tourist crowds can be a bit much around the Tower. We rode to the top in an elevator, and it's really about as breathtaking as you might imagine, both for its sweeping views and (for me anyway, probably more than milady) the engi-neering and scale of this one-thousand-foot tower. I do love to see how we humans put things together. As you might have guessed, since comedy does tend to come in threes, I was feeling so swept away by this romantic pinnacle that I dropped to one knee and casu-ally dropped the third and largest ring through the grated floor of the Eiffel Tower, where it plummeted some 900 feet to the park below (never fear, I had carefully scouted the area to ensure I wouldn't acci-dentally plant it in someone's cranium when it fell).

Megan was gratifyingly entertained by my buffoonery, some-thing I continue to appreciate to this day. This brought to a close my famous hat trick of bungled proposals in the most passion-inducing city I've laid eyes on. I can't believe nobody knows about Paris. You should Google it!

These japes were good, clean fun, but the onus was rather on me now. If I was willing to joke so freely about the subject, then it was only appropriate that I man up and deliver the real goods at some point. Make my leavings or get out of the water closet, as it were. Some months later I managed to pull off the real thing in London, on another lovely vacation. I had secured a custom ring (with my pay-check from acting in a Fox pilot), made with a modest but beautiful stone in a "gypsy setting," a favored detail, which I had previously ferreted out of my beloved. We were walking through Regent's Park and we came upon Queen Anne's Rose Garden (which I had secretly selected from several proposed locations by our local guide). As we strolled along hand in hand, I shit you not, all of the insects were buzzing and courting in the air all around us. The birds and chip-munks were giggling and fluttering about, and the ducks in the stream were coupled off, engaged in some heavy petting. As I slowed to a stop upon a little wooden bridge and pulled "my insurance" from my pocket (a heart-shaped box carved in walnut, which hinged open to reveal the ring perfectly inset) and dropped to one knee, all of nature seemed to begin copulating around us, beating the very air into a syrup of carnal ecstasy. Pairs of pretty sparrows furiously sixtynining pinwheeled through the air like feathery fellating fireworks. The calla lilies were nodding approval at me as they began to gently butt-fuck one another. In hindsight, I may not have been completely right, as my heart was beating out of my chest. Something magical was certainly in the air. Spoiler alert: SHE SAID YES. The best part of my blissful life was now promised to continue, by mutual agreement between myself and the cause of said bliss.

Naturally, it wasn't long before we began a series of discussions about throwing ourselves a wedding. One of the first events we'd attended as a couple was Debra Messing's beautiful wedding on the coast above Santa Barbara, which was an absolute fairy tale. The breathtaking scenery was complemented by the large gathering of family and friends, a group in which I was flattered to be newly initiated. The one brief moment of displeasure occurred when a paparazzi helicopter suddenly appeared to snatch photos and video of the resplendent fete. Enormous efforts had been expended toward maintaining the secrecy of the particular details surrounding the nuptials, but, alas, there always seems to be some asshole willing to sell out one's privacy and comfort for a buck. The rest of the evening went off without a hitch, and I was powerfully excited to meet the cast and producers of *Will & Grace* for the first time.

Of course, the topic of the evil helicopter later came up in our own summit for the planning of our own wedding, and so we began to devise methods by which we might successfully avoid such an interruption from the parasites that pathetically invade people's privacy for a paycheck. I am still enamored of my first pitch, but I understand why it would have been a bad idea. The notion was this: Megan was nominated for an Emmy for the fourth year in a row (of an eventual seven), and I suggested that we ditch the Emmys and hold our wedding in secret during the awards ceremony. You have to admit that no one would have seen it coming, plus all the scumbags would have been otherwise detained, carnivorously trying to nab a shot of a Doris Roberts's nip slip on the red carpet.

Megan liked the idea but ultimately decided it would have been disrespectful to play such a trick on the academy and the *Will & Grace* family, so we came up with the next-best ruse. Inviting our immediate families to town to attend the Emmys was easy, and we had recently purchased our first house together in the Hollywood Hills, so we simply invited twenty of our family and friends over for a casual "dinner" the night *before* the Emmys.

Our guests arrived and had a lot of ooh-ing and ah-ing to do at our new digs. (I call it "the house that *Will & Grace* built," because at the time, Megan was in charge of things like the mortgage, and I was in charge of expenses like supplying the household with toilet paper. I also believe the purchase of beer fell into my bailiwick. So, we were both contributing.) Nobody designs an interior like milady, so our guests were well preoccupied with cocktails and visual splendor when we announced, "Now, friends and loved ones, will you please step into the yard, because this is our wedding."

Mothers wept. There was joy and also jubilation and some tears from the coterie in general. The evening was quite magical, with the entire ceremony taking place in front of our spectacular, sweeping view of Los Angeles as our guests looked on. There was more crying, which I hope and believe were tears of happiness and not "What the hell is she thinking?" My favorite part of the evening was how gorgeous my wife looked, as well as her willingness to make such a promise to me, to stick together as long as we were both still hanging around this big blue marble. A vow of this ilk is literally once in a lifetime, if you're lucky, and I think a person's odds of being lucky in that department increase drastically if the person means that simple vow when he or she makes it. Life is unpredictable. We have no way of knowing what might befall us in the next five minutes, let alone thirty years down the road, but the weight a marriage vow carries is that in the face of that very uncertainty, two people are willing to promise to stick it out together. That's my favorite part.

As I mentioned previously, my sensei, Shozo Sato, came to town and performed a wedding tea ceremony as part of the proceedings, which was also exceptionally special to both Megan and myself. He mixed a special bowl of green tea from which Megan and I sipped, as well as our parents. If you ever have the opportunity to experience a Japanese tea ceremony, I can't recommend it highly enough. Sato-sensei is a master of the form, and it was a great privilege to have our hearts joined by his ministrations. The simple grace with which I had seen him excel through art and life for the fourteen years I had known him was one of the most touching ingredients in the bouillabaisse of our evening. A beautiful and rousing mariachi band finished off the perfect recipe for our tiny secret wedding, and I reckon it looks like it worked, since we're about as sappy for each other today as we were on that night ten years ago, if not more so.

*   *   *

People often remark to us that they're pleasantly surprised to see a marriage last as long as ours in Hollywood, which is a very sad thing to say about Hollywood. One of the main reasons I think we are succeeding has to do with our propensity to stay home and be boring. We don't get caught up in the "business" here in town, meaning going out all the time to parties and bars and so forth. We are unencumbered by the need to "be seen." When we see a red carpet, we head the other way if at all possible. Of course, some of this silliness is necessary, as part of our work is to promote projects in which we appear, but we do try to keep even that to a minimum.

We prefer instead to stay home and read books. We do jigsaw puzzles or play cards. We watch movies. We make our relationship a priority so that it will survive all of the tumult (usually good tumult) that our jobs throw into our paths. A marriage bond needs a healthy elasticity so that when one of us is suddenly touring Australia for ten days the bond will stretch between here and Down Under without breaking. We have a strict rule: We never accept employment that will keep us apart for more than two weeks. In thirteen years together (and counting), we've only been apart for two weeks a couple of times, and even that sucked balls.

Megan and I have both experienced the benefit of some powerfully good fortune in our lives, which I believe means that at some point we'll see some low points to balance things out, as life tends to do. I am grateful beyond description to know that when we find ourselves in those doldrums, I will have a partner as smart and funny and supportive and strong and creative and loving as my wife. Her killer set of jugs also does not hurt my feelings.

Love Your Woman
(A Paean to Megan)

Megan Mullally.

Love-time? She is the reason for the season.

My best friend. My legal property. My wife.

I could honestly write a book solely devoted to my wife, and maybe I will, by gum, because there is at least a volume's worth of amazing magic glistening about her person that will thrill you to pieces and render you extremely envious of the fact that she is, in fact, my legal possession in the state of California. Read the paperwork.

Many know, adore, and rightly lust after her as Karen Walker, the gut-bustingly hilarious stack of curves on *Will & Grace*, one of the finest thirty-minute comedy programs ever to bless our airwaves and our living rooms, but I know her by some different names, particularly around the house. Names like Gettin' Juggy with It, Queen of My Pants and the Known Universe, Pandora's Box, Venus-and-then-some, Ark of the Covenant, the Bush, and, of course, Stacy BeaverHouse.

I met her when I was twenty-eight, working on a production of *The Berlin Circle* at Los Angeles' Evidence Room theater, a company we promptly joined, and one to which we continue to offer our fealty. Artistic director Bart DeLorenzo, a dear friend and genius of the stage, was one of the main influences that allowed Megan the opportunity to absolutely save my life (from myself), and we quickly fell into the grip of an ardor that only continues to grow, thank the pagan gods and their dogs.

This chapter, then, is a song of joy, hollered directly at her beautiful face area. (You check out those cheekbones? Fuck me silly. Also, if you don't already have it bookmarked, do a Google image search for "Megan Mullally Boobs," and check out that first picture that comes up. Right?) I have oft enjoyed the word *paean* in my reading, to describe just such a song of worship, and so I thought to discover the proper pronunciation, as I had never actually heard it uttered aloud. A few different friends gave me a few different opinions, so imagine my chagrin when I learned from the Internet that it is pronounced "pee-in." Perhaps I'll just stick with *hymn of praise*.

I suppose I'll start off the jamboree with a salute to another of her characters, the sexually insatiable Elizabeth in Mel Brooks's absolutely top-drawer Broadway musical *Young Frankenstein*. By the way, if you ever get the chance to see Miz Mullally tread the boards, especially if she's warbling a tune, run, don't walk. She makes a noise of pulchritude that would have made Ethel Merman hurl her boa to the stage in defeat and trudge off glumly to the pub. The never-ending cavalcade of chuckles that was *Young Frankenstein* included Megan's showstopping number, "Deep Love," a roaring, throaty, filthy tribute to the rigid trunklike love-member of the Frankenstein monster. By the end of the song, she was downstage in a single spotlight, barefoot in a torn dress, "singing her tits off," as she likes to say of others, to such effect that the subsequent blackout regularly brought the audience to their feet like they were at a rock concert. Have I made it clear that I am a fan?

For opening night, I put together this little ditty in the hopes that Mr. Brooks would bring me on as a writing partner, or at least a backstage broom. Still hoping for a call, Melvin. I give you "Elizabeth":

Chaste in all her speech
But a terror in the sack
Like a full-force Irish gale
On her feet or on her back

The voice of sweetest songbird
With the gaiety of a faun
Fellows brawl to rise and fall
In labor on her lawn

When she shops for diamonds
Or simply cuts a rug
They say that she's a handful
Aye (a handful of jugg)

She's god's gift to men
Oh she's keen to unwrap it
When the moon is in its wane
It's held that she can snap it

So if you wear the tackle
Nature gave man for love
Then "Huzzah" for Elizabeth
She is heaven from above.
And below.

My wife was born with a very unfair portion of talent. She seems to excel at whatever task on which she lays her hand. She decided to cut our poodles' hair, and an hour later they came out of the bathroom looking like they had just been drawn by someone who draws the very cutest of cartoon animals. Not content to rest on her god-given skills, however, Megan has inspired me again and again throughout our years together with her steady work ethic. For some reason I grew up with the misconception, or fantasy, really, that when a person "made it" in showbiz, they would no longer need to work very hard. I figured that once you hit the big time, you got to just chill in your trailer, smoking a ton of the finest weed, then head in and kill a few scenes on camera, then go meet David Lee Roth at the beach to hang out with some bikini-clad models.

Ah, puberty. It sells the shit out of some Bieber records, right? Or whatever dross from the Disney factory is passing for popular music today. Anyway, it turns out that these people at the top of their respective games in the entertainment industry don't, in actuality, smoke much weed at all while working twelve- to sixteen-hour days. Because weed is a sedative. Sedatives, whilst mighty pleasing, well, they slow you down. Turns out, the time to party is AFTER work.

I saw my wife rehearse every *Will & Grace* scene to the point of perfection and every song to within an inch of its life, driven by a desire to give the audience the most profound enjoyment possible. As I may have mentioned earlier, I quite enjoy hard work, but I had never seen anyone work, without being flogged by a coach, nearly as hard as my wife. This was a revelation. I realized that success on her level was only achievable through a gift of talent, consistent hard work to back up the talent, and a healthy portion of good luck on top of it. This is but one of the many, many lessons I have been gifted by "the lady with the heavenly poonts" who calls me husband.

Early in our relationship, we were in New York City, where Megan was engaged in some press for *Will & Grace*. In a Lincoln Town Car, the vehicle of note for NYC press work, we were running maybe ten minutes late for an appearance she was to make on *Letterman*, a show of which I was and still am a very big fan. My late grandpa Ray and I used to watch Dave, and the fact that all the fancy East Coast types appreciate his dry, Midwestern sense of humor has always made me feel all the more comfortable when rubbing elbows with the cognoscenti myself. That makes it quite simple to comprehend why I would be completely panicked that we were going to be late to *Late Night*, even though I was merely the husband along for the ride!

Our driver pulled up to the stage door, where there were eight or ten people on the sidewalk waiting for Megan, hoping for an autograph. Of course I barreled through them and opened the door for Megan, only to turn around and find that she was signing away. WHAT WAS THIS?!?! Once she had finished giving them some of her time, which amounted to all of two minutes, maybe three, she came inside and we got into the elevator to ascend to her dressing room. Once alone, I unleashed my righteous indignation: "What are you thinking? You're already late for Dave!" She replied, "Darling, if it wasn't for the fans on the sidewalk, and the fans in general, I wouldn't be on *Letterman* in the first place." Properly admonished, I stared at the round, lit button that read *5B* in shame. The elegance with which she has always handled herself in such public situations continues to be a master class that I attend daily.

On a more personal note, another of Megan's sublime talents resides in her acumen for interior design. It's an art that obsesses her to approximately the same degree which I am enthralled by woodworking, only she can decorate an entire room in the time it takes me to build half of a table. She has turned our home into such a work of surprising beauty that I am often caused to giggle when I trudge in from a day at the shop, covered in sawdust, at the idea that I should reside in a house as inventively appointed as this. Her color palette is intensely modern, using accents and shades that I could never have fathomed working in concert. What's more, she is an amazing collector of art, which is an attribute I appreciate very powerfully, as I am much inspired by the paintings and drawings that festoon our walls, even the ones with no naked ladies.

Let's see, we've discussed beauty, talent, artistry, elegance . . . ah. I see I've buried the lead. Megan's finest trait, even more apparent than the glorious volcanoes of flesh gracing her upper abdomen, is her sense of humor. She has, without question, the filthiest, most hilarious predilection for phrases and gestures that would make a sailor's cockring blush. When we became friends in rehearsals for *The Berlin Circle*, I would race home from rehearsal every night to report the day's delicious blasphemy via her lips. She couldn't make a crack without mentioning somebody taking a shit on somebody's balls, or, when no one but me was looking, pretending to masturbate furiously, with the fervor of a cleaning lady scrubbing at a stubborn stain on a rug, only to play it completely cool when the attention of the other actors turned back upon us. She just makes me laugh like nobody else can and has done so day in and day out for thirteen years now. That's one of the many reasons they call me the Lucky Bastard.

As a student of music myself, I have long dreamed of the opportunity to perform alongside Megan as she regales the audience with her brand of melodiousness. Recognizing this desire in me, she has coached me over the years to strengthen my singing voice with practice and hard work, until just in the last couple of years, to my great satisfaction, I've begun singing in front of audiences, mainly in my first humorist show, *American Ham*. Among the songs in my repertoire is "The Rainbow Song," which I wrote in 2008 for Megan's fiftieth birthday. I had asked, it being her fiftieth, if she didn't crave something fancy in the way of a gift for this milestone age, some sort of bauble or gewgaw.

(An aside—Megan has had zero "work" done. By "work," I refer of course to plastic surgery and Botox and all the other horrors that famous beautiful people traditionally inflict upon themselves. Let me just urge you, if you are contemplating anything in this realm, to please reconsider. There is nothing that a man or woman can do to improve upon nature. Your true self, no matter how much you dislike that self's lack of cheekbones, is the most beautiful version of you that can be presented to the world, and no amount of any doctor brutally butchering your flesh is going to buy you more adoration than simply your own personality, created by nature. And, admitting that in some shitty arenas having "corrective" surgeries actually does show dividends, do you really want the fruits of your life's labors to increase in bounty because you have bigger tits? Mightn't you be happier in another situation wherein you were valued for the person inhabiting the body you showed up in? [Implied answer: yes.])

For her fiftieth-birthday gift, Megan said, "No, nothing special, just make me one of your cards or do one of your funny dances. Or, you know what? I would actually love a rainbow for my birthday." I narrowed my eyes and scrutinized her face for a time, determining that no, she was not kidding. "Okay, honey," I said. "Cool. Sounds good. Let me make a few calls."

Shitcakes. A motherfucking rainbow? I was stymied for a long time, racking my brain for some way to provide Megan with a birthday rainbow (her favorite color, BTW), and coming up short. When it looked as though all would be lost and I would fail miserably, I was saved by the late, great Nina Simone and her charming song "Beautiful Land," which lists the colors of the rainbow, one for each verse! Ha-HA!! I would live to fight another day! I wrote the following lyrics and my dear friend, the wizardly mountebank Corn Mo, helped me set them to some old Irish chords, creating my first song. Thanks again, CornMo(.com)!

The Rainbow Song

(A rousing ⁶⁄₈ time)

You RED me my rights when you arrested me,
You put me on trial and gave me life.
But ORANGE you glad I didn't say banana,
When you made me your bitch and I made you my wife?

You YELLOW you yell when I ball a melon,
But you don't complain when I tickle your back.
We are both a'GREEN that we'll serve our time.
If I drop the soap I know you'll watch my crack.

Please enjoy this Rainbow Song,
And this gift of leprechaun romance.
Please enjoy as part of this well-balanced breakfast,
The Lucky Charms you will find in my pants.

You BLUE me away when you sang "Shock the Monkey,"
Your fingers inside me let the games begin.
INDIGO . . . Is a tough one to pun with,
But when we're apart, it's the mood that I'm in.

We get along so well, we could never be compared

To Jesus of Nazareth and Pontius Pilate,

But if you'll endure the slight of calling me sir

I'll be Peppermint Patty to your VIOLET!

Please let this song be your rainbow,

I've got my Cialis so I shall not fail.

Please don't deny my advances,

For tonight you're going to take it in the pail.

Please let my song be your rainbow,

I made it for you, this shit cuts like a knife.

Forever I'll follow this rainbow,

To that fifty-year-old sweet pot of gold,

That seems to grow foxy instead of old,

From which I hope to never be paroled,

My angel in a centerfold,

She plays more than Sousa upon my fife,

My jaw-droppingly beautiful wife . . .

15

Finding Swanson

The secret to getting cast? Don't give a shit about the audition. The secret to that? Being happy at home, being happy in love. Being happy in the rest of your life. Auditions are so depressing. There's a hallway full of dudes, and sometimes you see three dudes you know are fucking great, and it's horrible to see them, because you think, "Oh, perfect, these three great guys. They would all be ideal for this part." And then six other jerks, two of whom are your good friends. Or else, there are a couple of those guys who like to try to "psych you out."

I had this one guy—I wish I could remember his name so I could call him out in chapter 15 of my book. He's been breathing easy through the whole thing, thinking I didn't remember him, but now, here in this late chapter, I'm calling you out, BRO. You know who you are, all macho and shadowboxing. Actually going outside the building and then staring me down through the window. We're actors, man. We're just actors. I'm not interested in fighting you or anyone. I didn't become a boxer or a soldier or a paramedic or a badass in any other way; I became an artist, and I'm afraid the same is true of you (using a loose interpretation of the term).

It's so demoralizing—in this business that scores your abs so much higher than your enunciation—that the troglodytes can make it all the way through the filters to a callback for a fireman pilot. Half the time the people in the room for whom you're reading are barely even TV people. Sometimes they come from music videos. Or funny Internet shorts. Or business school; that's the worst. They might be great people, even really creative ones, no question, but their main interest is just not in telling stories.

It's easy to let yourself get down in the mouth when you're going to these auditions, because half the time what you have to offer they can't even see. They don't have the right goggles. You're applying all of your powers of storytelling to a scene, with humor or tragic pathos, but they're viewing you through Coca-Cola glasses, musing over whether your role might do better demographically if you were more buff, or blond, or Kardashian. It's important that you can set aside the idea that you wield an artistic agenda, as can the writer, hopefully, because the suits have an entirely different agenda, and that is to sell diapers. And pickup trucks and breakfast cereal. You're working with an entirely different box of logic than they. Know that going in, and you're ahead of the game. These are just a tiny sampling of the delights of the audition process, but never fear: Once you have the right someone to come home to, be it even a pet or a poster of Billy Jack, you can then think, "I don't fucking care. I can't make this corporation more artistic, so I'll just have fun here and do my best."

As soon as you can flip that switch—as soon as you don't care as much—your work becomes so much better, because you appear so much more confident. People think, "Hey, looks like you've got something going on, buddy!" After Megan and I got together, I started to religiously attend *Will & Grace* tapings, and I really hit it off with everybody in the cast and crew. I loved the show passionately. Being there while they were making the show was such a treat, especially watching all of these top-of-the-line professional artists doing their jobs so well. It couldn't have been more of a Disneyland for me, and there was also beer.

They took a shine to me as well, which was awfully flattering. They had written the role of a new boyfriend for Grace, Debra Messing's character, and they held a bit of a cattle call, which included me auditioning with maybe twenty other guys. The next day they had maybe six or eight of us back to read more. I was pretty excited just to get a callback. The next day, Wednesday, they had two or three of us back. It was to read even more new material, and I realized this was all getting pretty crazy and real. They were really looking at me. On the Thursday they had just me back by myself, actually reading the scenes with Debra for the producers and the director, television institution James Burrows.

They said, "Okay, we've written some new stuff. We really love you for this character. That funny little dance you do in the elevator is really working. But we can't give you the part yet—we're still working out some business. But it may go to you. In any case, we really love the stuff you're doing." Holy shit!

The next day, Friday, they called and told me that Jim Burrows had put in a call to Woody Harrelson back on Monday—they'd worked together on *Cheers*—and Woody had just now returned the call and said yes at the last minute. "So you were great, but sorry, you know how it goes." And Woody went on and did this great part for the whole season and was, of course, awesome. There are some very good reasons that he's the big shot that he is, not the least of which are that he's incredibly lovely and charismatic and funny, so unfortunately there wasn't much to goddamn about. But I have to say, even just going through that experience was so thrilling and really did my confidence an immense deal of good. Just the fact that they considered me in that legitimate way was a dream come true.

Later that fall they were doing their Thanksgiving episode, and as a bit of a consolation they gave me a small part as a plumber. I had these great scenes with Megan and it was super fun, but I'd never done a multicamera show before, so it was also kind of scary and stressful. Everything moves really quickly, especially with Jim Burrows, who could do it with his eyes closed, and often does (he directs by ear more than eye; it's mighty impressive). There's not a lot of rehearsal, so I was nervous and had the live audience there to boot. I was about to make my first entrance of the night and Sean Hayes is standing by the door, saying, "Okay, here it comes, get ready. Getting close. Don't fuck this up. You ready?" and making me giggle and freak out. I chased him away with as much composure (not much) as I could muster.

Getting to do that role on *Will & Grace* was very fortifying for me. It made me feel like I could play with the professionals at the breakneck pace of a multicamera sitcom, and getting to work with my lady, who had also quite quickly become my hero, was incredibly exhilarating. Shortly thereafter I got cast in a Fox pilot called *Secret Service.* As a young actor, or really an actor of any age starting out from scratch in LA, you have to take whatever you can get. You have to build up your union points, first to earn your union cards, and then, with cards in hand, continue to qualify for your medical and dental insurance. Eventually, when you start getting jobs and doing a little better, should you be so lucky, it's hard to break the habit and begin saying no to any jobs. I remember auditioning for and getting a guest-star job on this terrible Tom Sizemore show called *Robbery Homicide Division*. He was some sort of heroic homicide cop? I'm not sure. Never saw it. The part was some sort of psycho beating in a small child's head with a hammer. I had gone to the audition on autopilot and booked the job—I feel like I must not have known exactly what the whole script was about when I took the audition. In any case, when it all came to light, I decided to pass on it, which was a first, but even for pretend, I didn't want to beat a kid's face in. Let somebody else spend his day doing that.

It was really hard to learn that I didn't have to accept every job offered. A lot of early hopes were placed in the TV pilot basket. To roll the dice on a pilot and hope you might land on a *Will & Grace*. Or a *Friends*. Or an *ER* or an *NYPD Blue*. A great show that would pay you really well for eight years. So I was tickled when I got this pilot, *Secret Service*, until they suddenly said to me, "Oh, if this series goes, it's shooting in Toronto." And Megan was like, "Excuse me? Yo, buddy, what the fuck just happened?" We were just starting to set up house with each other, and a move to Toronto was not in the cards. Thankfully, everything pointed to the show not going. I really liked the people involved, but it was honestly pretty embarrassing. It was peopled by Fox's flavor of actors circa 2001, which basically meant models playing Secret Service agents. I was the only one who could have remotely passed as a Secret Service agent, and I would have been a tiny Secret Service agent. I'm five foot ten and a half and maybe two hundred pounds, which, on this Fox show, made me "the fat guy." This was a great example of how real life can unexpectedly supersede casting dreams. I finally won the actor lottery and booked a pilot, and because of the love in my life, I didn't want it to go to series.

I continued to describe myself as a slowly rolling snowball. I was still getting TV jobs. As I had become good friends with a lot of the *Will & Grace* writers, who were some of the best comedy writers working, a couple of them ended up gratifyingly writing me parts in new pilots they were working on.

One of them wrote a new pilot and wrote me a very specific and hilarious series regular role on his show. I went through the audition process, which was kind of a cakewalk for once, because it was written specifically for my particular sense of humor. The part was a weird navy intelligence guy in DC. I don't usually have my moustache—I know people now know me with my moustache—but, clean-shaven at the time, I thought, "This guy should have a kick-ass moustache." So I was sporting some fresh new whiskers, as I am wont to do, and I cruised all the way to the final network test to get the job, which was for CBS. I arrived at the test, and there were some other great actors there whom I knew, but I thought, "I got this. There's nobody here like me and it was written for me." I did the audition and, reportedly, Les Moonves, the head of CBS, said after I left the room, "This guy's good, okay. But you know, I'm not really feeling the moustache this year." And my friend the writer said, "Okay, he could shave it." Les replied, "Well, we've got a couple of weeks left before we need to cast this part, so let's just see if we can get someone with a little more juice." That is an exact quote. Network executives like to throw around terms like *juice* and *heat*. Eight days later they

gave the part to an actor apparently dripping with the stuff, Mr. James
Van Der Beek. That's right, gentle reader, it was Dawson from *Dawson's Creek*. So we've come full circle once again.

I was getting these nice shots at success with some frequency, but I
was consistently losing to douchebag corporate decision making
like that. I have nothing bad to say about Mr. Van Der Beek, who does
fine work, but when a comedy role written *for me* is handed to a heart-
throb from a young-adult soap opera on the WB—a very different
type than myself is what I'm driving at—I'm going to find that upsetting. I don't care if it's James Van Der Beek or Ryan Gosling or Anthony Hopkins. But that's the business. (For the record, I have lost no
jobs to Gosling or Hopkins. Yet.) Eventually one learns that many of
the jobs for which one is "rejected" turn out to be incredibly bad experiences in one way or another anyway, which allows one to be more
unaffected by the guys who don't "feel like a moustache" this year. So.
I continued to plug away. I was getting good movie parts in delicious
Sundance movies, also known as really intelligent independent films.
I was becoming slightly more known around town as a dependable
character actor, and that went a long way toward supporting my artistic morale. I was able to maintain my confidence, thanks to little signals here and there from the universe. One evening Megan and were
strolling along the beach in Malibu, enjoying the tickling of our toes
in the surf, when we unexpectedly happened upon none other than
Garry Shandling. He and Megan exchanged greetings, having been
previously acquainted, before she introduced me to him. I was (and
am) a very big fan of his, so I was hanging back a bit. When I stepped
forward to shake hands, ankle-deep in the gentle Pacific swell, Garry

looked piercingly into my face and asked if I was in the business. I replied that I aspired to be so, and he said, "Stick around. You've got something." Such random moments of generous magick would feed me through months and years of artistic starvation. Whenever I would even begin to think about changing paths, Shandling would appear in my mind's eye, reassuring me to stay the course.

I went to an audition for *Deadwood* and met David Milch. After reading the delectable script, I literally said to him, "Where the fuck have you been? I've been looking for this show for my whole life." We got along, and I got this really great part in the second episode of the series. Unfortunately, I got killed by Wild Bill. Spoiler alert: He shot me in the belly at the end of the episode. Still, to this day it's one of the best dramatic items I have on my actor's reel. That moment in Milch's embrace fed me for five years. Receiving the approbation of an artist of his ilk went a long way toward bolstering my persistence.

Around this point something started to seem weird to me. I was reading for a lot of dramatic stuff but not much comedy. As a theater actor, one generally engages in whatever's in the season that year. You'll do a Shakespeare, you'll do a Sam Shepard, then you do a Feydeau farce, then some August Wilson. Or Martin McDonagh. You're facile. I love doing comedy as much as I love drama and everything in between, but it began to dawn on me more and more that people really want to compartmentalize you in Los Angeles. They want you to be a specialist. They want you to do comedy, or play tennis, or speak French, but they don't want you to do all three.

I started griping to my agents—I should mention that right around the time I met Megan I moved to a slightly bigger agency, the redoubtable Silver, Massetti & Szatmary, and I started griping to them, "Ben Stiller just did this movie with all these weird, funny male models. I never even heard about an audition. This other movie was all firemen. There wasn't one guy out of thirty-seven firemen that I could audition for?" Just as I was starting to grouse in earnest, I ended up landing a part on the George Lopez sitcom. A great director named John Pasquin cast me on *George Lopez* as Randy, which was a little bit of a leap of faith, since I didn't really have the character nailed down. He and I played around with it on set and he even had me try it with an Irish dialect for fun, with a touch of the leprechaun. We finally dialed it in with this silly, sort of bombastic dumb-guy voice. On the show, I was dating and then got engaged to Belita Moreno, who was playing George's mom, Benny. Randy was this much younger, weird trucker type who was really silly and great fun. I ended up recurring for a couple of seasons and had an absolute blast with the good people over there.

Coincidentally, Sandra Bullock was one of the executive producers on that show, and I'd known her for a couple of years because she's old friends with Courtenay Valenti, Pat Roberts's wife. She was in their wedding party, as was I, and we had run into each other over the years socially. I had done a small role in her movie *Murder by Numbers*, in a small cop scene that got cut down to an even hilariously smaller appearance.

Up close, it's easy to see why she's such a success, because she's always having fun. She did an episode of *Lopez* as my obsessive ex-girlfriend who was also blind. We ended up doing this really hilarious episode together that had a bunch of clowning and physical comedy in it, which was really a blast and felt like another few rotations of the snowball. A short while later, she and John Pasquin were doing a movie called *Miss Congeniality 2: Armed and Fabulous*, and they were trying to find an unknown (i.e., cheap) actor to play the main bad guy. In other words, it wasn't a great enough part to spend their budget on any "juice." So, I had to jump through some hoops and do some auditions for the studio, but I ended up getting this part, which was incredible for me. It was the first big studio movie I ever did, and quite an education. This great guy and superior actor, Abraham Benrubi, was my brother, and we were your classic simple and scary thugs. We had such a gas in a bunch of scenes with William Shatner and Sandra, shooting all around Vegas, in and out of the casinos. At the end of the film (spoiler alert), Sandy ends up beating the shit out of me across the casino floor at Treasure Island. Everything about that job was a dream, but the best part was that I had won the role from my work, further solidifying my snowball.

Shortly thereafter I got a nice part in this movie *Sin City* that Robert Rodriguez and Frank Miller made, based on Frank's graphic novel series of the same name. This came about from a really random audition recorded on video in a room at the Four Seasons, so I never met the directors until I went to shoot it, but I think it went well because things were kind of starting to roll now. I was making a nice living as an actor, still working in TV, guest-star stuff, and more small film jobs. My woodworking was going great. My work and home life made me happy, which then helped me land more and better work, which made me even more happy and confident, and so on.

In 2005, I did this movie called *The Go-Getter*, written and directed by Martin Hynes. It's such a sweet, beautiful movie and I'm going to plug the shit out of it right here. It's one of several films I've done that went to Sundance, but apparently the timing wasn't just right, because it should have been a total hit. Premiering a film at Sundance is a huge victory in itself, by the way, especially considering that just shooting a feature film to completion and affording and surviving post-production until you have a ninety-minute work of art that you are proud of . . . well, let's just say that a film must surmount a row of hurdles immeasurably long and high in order to even reach a movie screen in the first place. This film has Zooey Deschanel and Lou Taylor Pucci and Jena Malone, all doing exquisite work as the beautiful young people that they are, not to mention Maura Tierney and Bill Duke in great supporting turns.

I went in to read for this little part in the movie, and this is something I did a lot—if I was reading for one or two smaller scenes, like the guy at the bus stop, or the guy at the hardware store, or what have you, I'd go through the script and see if there was something else I could reasonably do. I'd go in and say, "I've prepared the bus driver as requested and also the thug at the end with the baseball bat, if you'd care to also see me assay that role as well." At *The Go-Getter* I was reading to play the shitty night manager of a shitty hotel. It was a really fun scene, and it went really well and they were happy. I then said, "I don't mean to be an asshole, but I also prepared the role of the potter. Can I try that?" And Hynes, the director, a bit befuddled, said, "Uh, yeah. Sure." In his mind he was thinking, "This audition for the night manager was the best one we've seen. I love this guy already." So when I asked about the other thing he was a bit confused. I then fortunately did an audition for the potter that he also really loved. I left and, as he told me later, he thought, "Oh, boy. What do I do? I love him for both parts." He went back and forth between the two, and finally the producers said, "Well, give him both parts, then."

I was working in my shop when he phoned to tell me that he wanted me to do both parts. According to him, I then said, "Excellent. What else you got?" And he laughed and said, "Everything's cast except I need an accordion player and a trumpet player, but it's a small part. Kind of nonspeaking." And I said, according to Martin, "I've got your accordion player and I play a little trumpet," to which he laughingly agreed. The accordion player was Corn Mo, and Martin ended up using both him and his kick-ass song "Angel" in the film. So I ended up with three parts in the movie and we have remained great friends on top of it. It's a beautiful movie. You should see it tonight, preferably with a date, and I guarantee you won't be sorry. *The Go-Getter.*

I had found my stride. I could go in to casting sessions with confidence knowing that my weirdness was appealing to the right people in the right way. I had cottoned that it was only going to be every thirtieth director or so who was going to get me, because the other twenty-nine were looking for tits or blond hair or fast talking. Or I don't know what. Juice? You just have to find the people who are on the same page as you are.

To my great delight, Megan then got cast in Mel Brooks's *Young Frankenstein* on Broadway, so we went to live in New York at the drop of a hat. I'd always wanted to live there, anyway, at least for a spell. I was frankly tickled pink. I took a bag of tools, as I knew I was going to find a shop and build my first canoe. While there, I ended up doing this movie with Ryan Gosling and Kirsten Dunst called *All Good Things.* It was a really interesting, cool project, directed by smarty extraordinaire Andrew Jarecki, who, once again, cast me off of a videotaped audition. I am still awfully grateful for the continued votes of confidence like that which kept me in the game.

A whip-smart friend of mine from the Chicago days named David Cromer, who has since become a very successful Broadway director, had a musical called *Adding Machine* at the Minetta Lane Theatre downtown. It was a great show, and I ended up replacing a guy (the handsome Jeff Still) for a couple of months. It was such a savory musical, easily the best thing I saw during my time in New York besides *Young Frankenstein*. It boasted incredibly original music by Joshua Schmidt as well as a succinctly scripted book, adapted by Schmidt and Jason Loewith from the 1923 play by Elmer Rice. Once again, my Chicago theater community was paying dividends, this time in the form of an exceptional musical in New York City! (Especially exciting because I had been given to understand that if one can make it there, then one can make it anywhere.)

Right before New York, I had been cast in another indie movie called *Patriotville*, a fine title later changed to the terrifically generic *Taking Chances*. Rob Corddry was the main bad guy—he played the mayor of this town, and I was his sheriff. I was a HUGE fan of Rob's from *The Daily Show* and I was really quite starstruck to meet him and subsequently work with him. We had so much fun together, we two white jackasses. It was really the first time I learned that I could substantially improvise, as it was the first project I had worked on where they wanted us to make up funny stuff to augment the script. Rob and I did, along with the rest of the cast, including the resplendent Justin Long and Missi Pyle, and oh my god, he made me break (crack up) so hard. That guy is so wickedly smart and funny (which is now even more common knowledge since he's brought *Childrens Hospital* into our lives). I really hit it off with Rob and we became good friends.

Later on, when I was in New York, he sent me the first scripts for *Childrens Hospital* and was hinting pretty heavily that he wanted to see if Megan would be interested in playing the role of Chief, which of course she did. She read it—at the time it was a web series, like five or ten episodes. She said, "I don't care what it is, this is the funniest thing I've read in years. I want to do this next." So, thank providence, we both got involved with *Childrens Hospital*.

C asting directors, after *George Lopez*, had begun to say to me, "I saw you on *George Lopez*. I didn't know that you do comedy." Again, it's as though they were saying, "I didn't know you specialized in identifying precious gemstones." I said, "Yeah, I perform entertainment. That's what I do. Comedy is included in that." Even Megan wasn't always considered a person who "does comedy," even after *Will & Grace*, because she was from the theater and not a sketch or improv background. It was unbelievable.

I had known Amy Poehler way back in the early nineties in Chicago, and we had remained friends across the years. Through Amy and Rob Corddry I knew of the Upright Citizens Brigade, or "UCB," Theatre in New York. I called up Amy and said, "Where do I start? What class do I take? What do I do?" and she said, "There's a couple of shows we do that are specially designed for actors to play in, and you don't need to know the ways of improv. Come on down."

The percentage of comedy talent that comes to light today through the pipeline of the UCB is staggering. My first performance of a show they call *ASSSSCAT* included an improv cast that will blow the mind of any comedy nerd reading this today. The show was hosted by Amy, Seth Meyers, and Horatio Sanz, who then played in the scenes with Jessica St. Clair, Jason Mantzoukas, Rob Huebel, Lennon Parham, Scott Adsit, John Lutz, Tami Sagher, Brian Stack, Miriam Tolan, Paul Scheer, Christina Gausas, Tim Meadows, Chris Gethard, Bobby Moynihan, and Jack McBrayer, for cryin' out loud, and I'm sure I'm forgetting a couple!

So, during my time in New York in 2007, I started doing these shows with this insane bunch of talents and that was it. Megan came around as well, and suddenly—poof!—we both "did" comedy! Between the UCB and Corddry and *Childrens Hospital*, both Megan and I were suddenly welcomed into this community of "comedy" people. They hailed from the UCB Theatre and also from a show from the nineties called *The State*, as well as tried and true institutions like Second City, ImprovOlympic, and the Groundlings. All of these people with whom I had done comedy shows in New York moved out to LA at the same time that Megan and I moved back home, so suddenly everything funny was being cast from this pool of chuckle-smiths that we had sort of stumbled into. Fortunately, they welcomed us with open arms. It's a very nurturing community, unlike other artistic cliques (lookin' at you, Oscar winners). There's not a lot of competition happening so much as people stating, "I'm going to do a show and I'm going to need eight of you. I'm thankful I know this circle of the best, funniest, filthiest people, because I always have the best quality to choose from."

In 2008, I'd just gotten back from New York and my first audition was for a one-line part in some movie George Clooney was producing. I'd worked with him on that live *ER* and he was super friendly to me. He had wanted to cast me in a small role in his movie *Leatherheads* but I had had a conflict. He's known for, among other obvious things, this crazily heroic talent for remembering everybody—I saw him at a party seven or eight years after *ER*, and he remembered that we had stood around a big pot of soup backstage singing "The Wreck of the Edmund Fitzgerald" together. It had been chilly and breezy in the soundstage, because they had the enormous "elephant doors" open, and a bunch of actors and crew standing around a steaming kettle of chowder had just felt very maritime to us. When I saw him at the party years later, he pointed at me and said, " 'Wreck of the Edmund Fitzgerald.' " And I said, "Well, do I blow you now, or should we step into a more private chamber?"

Although George denied me the opportunity to provide him with an oral pleasuring upon that particular occasion, I decided I'd go read for this new film anyway, as I'd found out Grant Heslov was directing, and I knew he was an ace. I went in to read for this one-line part, and it was just the fucking casting hallway from hell. The role was small and not great, so the assembled talent was not the finest crop of produce one might have hoped to assemble. I had prepared a "bit" with a pair of glasses that I was planning to impishly remove before pronouncing my one line. It was just on tape for the casting lady, and it wasn't even the lady, actually, it was the lady's assistant. Unimpressed by my terrific "bit," she said, "Are you going to do that with your glasses? Don't do that." To which I said, "You know what, I've got this one line. This is the bit I prepared. I'm just going to do my bit." So I did my bit. I stood my meager ground and pulled my glasses off to say the line, and I went away and I never heard anything further from them.

A couple of months later, Megan and I were vacationing up in Calistoga in the Napa Valley wine country. Out of the blue, I got a call from my agent: "Hey, you got that Clooney job, and your first scene is in Puerto Rico night after tomorrow." I said, "Oh, the one-line thing? Jesus, okay." They said, "But the good thing is that George Clooney is playing the lead. He'll be in your scene with your one line." That was sounding better.

The film business can be hilarious in that one day you're totally unemployed, on vacation in a remote California town, and the next, a production can send a car for you to scoot you over to San Francisco so you can fly to Puerto Rico at the drop of a hat. So I flew to Puerto Rico and I got hustled right into a trailer to be dolled up. There was kind of a buzz around the base camp, like something extra exciting was going on. I finished hair and makeup and put on my eighties army fatigues, and I went into the room in a school where we were shooting, and would you looky here. My scene was with George Clooney, and also these two other guys, Kevin Spacey and Jeff Bridges. And me. Just the four of us. I thought, "Well, shit. I'm glad I went to that stupid one-line audition. If I ever write 'a book,' this'll make a good story."

The film was *The Men Who Stare at Goats*, and I ended up in a good portion of the movie as a private in a platoon of psychic soldiers. Mainly, I got to stand there at attention while Jeff Bridges talked to us a whole bunch, then we improvised a session of exploratory dance with him. If you enjoy the man's voice and demeanor half as much as I do, then you can understand how I was about as jubilant as a pig in effluvia to find myself in this freak-out of a job. I felt like a valued scout in a troop being led by George, Jeff, and director Grant Heslov. Clearly, the moral in this story was to always remember, before turning my nose up at a one-liner, that it *could* result in the unsurpassable delight of dancing with Jeff Bridges.

*   *   *

Right about then, in the fall of 2008, the word was going around town that they were making a spin-off of *The Office* and Amy Poehler was set to play the lead. Megan and I were major fans of *The Office* and watched it religiously. I would often remark, "If I'm going to make it, if I'm ever going to get my shot, it's going to be on a show like this, in a part like Rainn's." I had known Rainn Wilson for several years. We met in the late nineties, reading against each other for "weird guy in the basement" parts. I had always liked him, as he's such a smart, funny, sweet guy, not to mention he also comes from the theater. We had become buddies just from seeing each other at auditions so much, when he got a great part on *Six Feet Under* for a string of episodes. I believe this was when the world in general really noticed him and I thought, as we all do when such a thing occurs, "Excellent. Well thrown, Wilson. Score one for the good guys." Then, not long after that, he won his role on *The Office*. The mighty, transcendent role of Dwight Schrute, a portrayal which I am certain nudged the earth at least a quarter degree farther off her axis. My adoration blossomed even more when Rainn commissioned an oak trestle table from me in the style of Gustav Stickley and then insisted on paying me 50 percent more on top of my suggested price, a number which had been, admittedly, too "friendly." A scholar, a sweetheart, a gentleman, and a clown of the highest order.

Hence, when the word came down about Amy's new show starting up, I thought, "You've got to be fucking kidding me. I've got to get on this show." Allison Jones, one of LA's most top-drawer casting directors—her IMDb page is gob-smacking, especially for comedy— had originally called me in years earlier to audition for the role of Michael Scott, the lead of *The Office*, among many other things over the years. She brought me in for *Parks and Rec*.

The creators of the show, Greg Daniels and Mike Schur, were initially reading me for a different role, named Josh, and the material was just so funny and so right on the money for my sense of humor. Megan was coaching me in our kitchen, as was our habit, and we were saying, "This is it. This writing. Oh my god, this is it. Don't fuck this up, fat boy."(We don't pull any punches in the kitchen.) I had been in to read with the producers and some writers, and we were getting along great, when we arrived at a hilarious day, in hindsight—they had two guys come in to shoot scenes with Rashida Jones (a "chemistry read" to determine how well two actors play together). The two guys were me and Adam Scott. I had known Adam for about eight years and was a big fan, and I thought, "Oh great. Me and Adam Scott up for the guy who gets to kiss Rashida. He's devilishly handsome and charming and funny. I'm . . . dry? Husky? Even I—even *my mom*—would cast him over me."

I knew the producers liked me—I could tell they somehow thought I was special, and the feeling was powerfully mutual. A couple of weeks went by before I got the inevitable call. Sure enough, NBC had literally said to Mike and Greg, "We asked you for someone in the neighborhood of Aaron Eckhart [a very attractive neighborhood], we asked you for handsome, and you hand us Nick Offerman? Um, no." And Greg and Mike said, "Okay. You're right, you're right, he's really unattractive. But we really want Nick on the show. We have this other part we wrote, the part of Amy's boss, so we'd like to put Nick in that part. His name is Ron Swanson."

Greg and Mike had called my agent and told us about the Aaron Eckhart news, which was not unexpected but still crushing. I tried not to let it get to me. I had gone to Big 5 Sports to buy a jockstrap, as I have been known to do of a Tuesday, and I was in their parking lot when I got the call that it was over with Josh. I went inside and glumly bought a pack of athletic supporters. When I returned to the parking lot twenty minutes later, I got the next call: "But we're trying to put you in this other part of Amy's boss." Okay. Crisis averted for the moment. Now, let's get these jockstraps home to Megan.

NBC said to Mike and Greg, "Look, we love Nick. Historically, we love to test him for pilots and then not cast him; I mean, let's be real, he's not handsome—but anyway, that boss guy should be older."

They then ended up putting me through four more months of spo-radic auditions along with every other guy in town. They looked at old guys, fat guys, skinny guys, even handsome guys. You name it. Everybody and their dad read for that part. NBC expanded the search as wide as they possibly could and then slowly narrowed it again until it was finally back down to just me and Mike O'Malley—a splendor-ous actor, hilarious comedian, and fantastic guy.

I didn't know he was going to be there, as I had only received a call from my agent saying, "Okay, Amy has moved here from New York. They want you to come in tomorrow and go on tape for the network one last time, improvising with Amy, and this will be the last time." As you may have surmised . . . I went. I stepped out of the elevator and there sat O'Malley. My heart sank, to see a hilarious and charm-ing proven comedy veteran sitting there. They put both of us on tape with Amy, improvising a couple of Ron and Leslie scenarios, and we went home to wait. After all that, five months total, I found out the next day that I had gotten the job, and not only had I gotten the job, but they hadn't even turned in O'Malley's tape to NBC. At the end of all that network hand-wringing, Mike and Greg had obstinately only turned in my tape, which is what I believe the kids today would call a "baller move."

It was Mike Schur who called me with the news, and I'm not ashamed to admit that I cried. I cried like a little baby boy who has just dropped his bacon slice in a pile of cow shit. I said, "Listen, Mike. Please keep talking to me, and I am so happy, but I'm just going to cry while we're talking." And I just openly sobbed for, like, twenty minutes while he told me this story.

Three years earlier I had auditioned for a small guest-star part on *The Office*. He was one of the five people in the room that day and I didn't even know it. I didn't even know that I'd met him. He had wanted me for that role, but I'd had a scheduling conflict and couldn't do it. Well, he liked something about me, so he went home and wrote my name on a yellow Post-it note and adhered it to the bottom of his computer monitor, where it remained for three years until they were creating *Parks and Rec*, and he said, among other things, "I want this guy on the show." I mean, come on, after reading this fucking interminable chapter about casting in Hollywood, all of the bullshit, to then have that happen to me after twelve years in town? Megan immediately hit the nail on the head when she said, "If you'd gotten any of that other less perfect stuff, you never would have gotten this. Everything happened for the reason that you were meant to get this job."

All I can say is that I'm glad I stuck it out without getting sour, and I am so grateful for the opportunity to work with a collection of the nicest and smartest and funniest people I have come across. And also Jim O'Heir, who plays Jerry Gergich on the program. Having borne the pain of so many ugly casting stories firsthand, and having heard secondhand of so many more traumatic, soul-crumbling rejections, I am left with no choice now but to turn squarely into the bright sun, take a deep breath, and mind my manners as hard as I can.

Let Your Freak Flag Fly

When a director, producer, or casting director reads a script, he or she then imagines their ideal actor for each role, just like anybody does when reading a book. You imagine Aragorn for yourself, and maybe yours looks like Viggo Mortensen, or maybe yours looks like your dad, or Screamin' Jay Hawkins, or Gregory Peck. When anyone reads any paginated material containing characters, then that person is required to envision the characters in some way. In casting, then, one is invariably going to develop an idea of what's "right," as in "What are the right attributes?" or "What is the right look?" or "Mark Wahlberg is so not right for this," or "You know who's right for the role of 'Susan'? Molly Shannon!" When you are auditioning for a role, you're essentially presenting your own opinion of the character's attributes, your "choices," as rendered through the presentation of your own body and voice, through performance, to some people who will almost certainly have differing opinions from your own, and that's before you can even begin to address the matter of your skill level and your ability to communicate your opinion effectively.

When I first got to Chicago I was immediately confronted with the harsher side of "the business." I got hooked up with a sweet but tough agent named Marla Garlin, who undertook the gentle guidance of my fledgling efforts. I started out auditioning for plays, commercials, and the very occasional TV show or film, and almost immediately, casting people started pigeonholing me: "You're a farmer. You're a plumber. You're going to play a lot of blue-collar stuff." I was fresh out of college, all bright eyed, bushy tailed, and full of piss and vinegar, so I thought, "A plumber? Go fuck yourself. I am amazing, I am going to play an old lady, then an opium-addicted elf, then I am going to play a stick and shove it up your ass, bitch." (Apparently I used to engage in some pretty tough thinking.)

Marla tried to calm my ire and explain that these things take time and that eventually people would see that I was more than a plumber, but I was not to be mollycoddled by Marla. I was so bent on vindication that I had a headshot taken with a huge foam-latex cock (from the Defiant production *Big Mother*) in my hands and sent it to everybody in town. An audacious statement of defiance the meaning of which no one had any fucking idea. A lot of them thought I was trying to be funny, which I suppose was also what I was trying to do, to an extent.

I did much better in the theater than anywhere else. After a couple of years I became better at acting, reaching the level of "intermediate," and I started getting film roles, which was exciting because there weren't that many films coming through Chicago, maybe four or five a year. I quickly learned that any kind of pandering was the wrong idea, but that it was important to simply be myself through the whole casting process. If I just presented myself as sincerely as possible, that was the best way to have a chance of getting hired. And, by god, it seemed to work.

Nineteen times out of twenty they're just not looking for you, and you have to learn to not take it personally. If the people are nice and you're prepared, then you can tell when they think you're good and you can also tell when they think you're not good. There's a certain level of trial and error to auditioning, and you must simply try to continue to learn to behave in the way you did when they made you feel that they thought you were good. You also learn what mannerisms turn off a room and then try to subsequently avoid those behaviors. Insincerity, especially "chipper" insincerity, will close down a room faster than ripping a crisp fart, the discharge of which will also, I can assure you, take some of the air out of your credibility. Save it for church.

By the time I left Chicago I was depending upon a few casting directors who were putting more and more faith in me, and having me come in for increasingly great stuff, swinging for the fences. Sure, I struck out most of the time, but that's how it goes. They were hoping, along with me, that I would get lucky and connect with one of the pitches thrown at me, and I am very grateful that they saw something unique enough in me to keep sending me up to bat. You really cannot begin to do even remotely well as an actor without casting directors who put their faith in you, and once they do, so long as you continue to do a good job, they will keep bringing you back time and time again. The few ladies in Chicago who championed me really got me off on the right foot, and after four years of their benevolence in that magnificent town, I had amassed a very healthy résumé.

That is precisely why, when I tried to transition my song and dance to LA, I had such a shitty pill to swallow, because nobody was really interested in theater work. Some few were, and I think that's why they are the best, or the least lazy, casting professionals, because they have the wherewithal to examine and utilize the great pool of talent that exists in the small quality theater productions that LA can offer. Other than those exceptional casting pros, nobody really cared that I had done these plays. I was still able to do a good job in my auditions, but I had lost my Chicago advantage, where people more often than not would have seen my work onstage. With or without a leg up, casting is just a brutal process for the initiate. They might be looking at two hundred people, or only twenty people, but either way there will almost always be a few good people competing with you. Even if you do a great job, it might not matter, because maybe they want a taller guy or a more muscular guy or a handsomer guy and you just have to learn to bear that simple hardship.

The better things began to go, the better the auditions I got, until I began occasionally testing for "series regular" parts on TV pilots. A pilot test is the most exciting lottery ticket one can lay hands on, because a TV pilot will generally look at "unknown" talent more seriously than a film will. Therefore, a person can suddenly find him- or herself with a legitimate shot at a show like *Friends* or *Girls* or *Mad Men* or *Parks and Recreation*, shows that value their performers' relative obscurity, upon which fresh characters can be painted.

So, imagine you're living in LA in some version of squalor, chasing your dream of working on great material as an actor, whether you hope to make people laugh or cry or shit, or all three at once (my dream), and I'll walk you through the emotionally vacillating steps of a pilot audition process.

First of all, these are coveted auditions, so you're a lucky son of a bitch if you are getting maybe twelve to sixteen new pilot scripts to peruse. Your agent has managed to get you auditions for the casting directors of three shows, let's say as an alcoholic cop in one, a chubby stoner working in a Milwaukee donut shop in another, and in a third, you run a low-rent law firm representing

primarily soft-core porn stars. That third script is clearly exploit-
ative and terrible, so you reluctantly pass. There goes 33 percent
of your hopes. The alcoholic-cop part will string you along, strok-
ing your imagination for three or four auditions, but ultimately
break your heart when it's offered outright to Jeremy Piven, who
was the guy who played that asshole agent on *Entourage*, which
was a show that was on cable. I told you, it's a tough business.
So, a few weeks into pilot season, you are left with one basket
into which you must gingerly place your hopeful eggs. All of your
eggs. In the one basket of the chubby Milwaukee stoner, who is
named Blowfish.

   You have been in for the casting director, and she had liked
you already, so you come back in again for her as well as the
writer and maybe a producer or two. They really like you. You
get the jokes, and they let you know that they are really enjoying
your comprehension of their humor. You are elated; holy shit, this
seems to really be happening! You come back a third time, to
read for all of them as well as the director this time. After the
reading, which is once again full of enthusiastic laughter, they tell
you in a conspiratorial tone that they really, really want you to be
their Blowfish. The show's creator confides, "Nobody is even
coming close to 'getting' the writing the way you are, and your
voice is exactly like what I was hearing when I wrote it." Simpa-
tico. Splendid! Seems like it's in the bag!

   Now it's time for your "network test." This means the network
executives need to scrutinize you for themselves, so that they may
hold your performance and your résumé and appearance and
demeanor and personality up against the statistical charts in their
minds, a schematic of the current fashions in the zeitgeist. "Sure,

he's a good actor, but will the *Maxim* readers dig him?" They have already chosen to spend a lot of money on the writing and the premise of the show, their "fishhook," and now they are hoping to choose actors who, one way or another, will be as irresistible to the national audience as juicy night crawlers upon said hook. This makes these execs simply the *worst* audience for whom you will ever perform. They are bankers and accountants, and they are not in the room to be entertained by you, they are there to judge your worth as bait, without sentiment. They are Upper East Side ladies shopping at Barneys, and you are but one of several pairs of fancy shoes being paraded in front of them for possible purchase. It's the most exciting step in the sequence that can lead to booking a job on a television show and easily the most unpleasant.

Before you can even get into the room, however, there are a few hurdles over which you must handily spring. Firstly, the night before the test, you hear from your "people" that there will be three other guys auditioning against you. Two of them you have become very familiar with from seeing them at the recent string of Blowfish readings, but the third remains a mystery. Your agent tells you that the network is probably bringing in a "ringer." A ringer is an actor who boasts some sort of impressive television résumé, indicating proven and dependable chops. A person of whom the network can say, "Well, we didn't like any of the new guys, but the kid from *Freaks and Geeks* is hilarious if we're in a pinch."

For the last week, your agent has been hungrily discussing your "quote" with the network's "business affairs" office. This means that the network is trying to leverage the cheapest possible price for your services, whilst your agent fulminates with whatever ammunition he/she can brandish to win you (and him/her, to the tune of 10 percent) the fattest possible episodic salary.

Your "deal" is made before you arrive on the day of the test, so before you can take your turn to stand in judgment before the bankers, you must sign all of your contractual paperwork. The pragmatic reason for this preemptive bargaining is so that, once the network wants you, once *they* are on the hook—"I must have Van Der Beek! Bring me the juice!"—James cannot then counter with, "Okay, swell. I would like thirty-seven million dollars."

The problem with this deal-signing step lies in the weakness of the human will (certainly mine, anyway). Let's say this is your first time, and it's one of the big networks, say ABC. Perhaps by now you have greeted the other two guys in competition, and also discovered that the mystery third man is in fact the second-funniest geek from *Freaks and Geeks*. You arrive at the equivalent of the network's Death Star and are led sedately into a room, just short of being bound and blindfolded. Alone, you are seated at an intimidatingly vast conference table, where a lawyer from business affairs quickly walks you through the signing of a thick sheaf of papers, which is when you begin to see the numbers that make you weak.

You multiply the episodic salary (say $17,500) by the number of episodes (twenty-two), then you multiply that by the number of years named in the terms of the contract (seven). Your vision immediately begins to swim with dreams of acreage in Illinois's idyllic Sangamon River Valley and a brand-new pickup truck and some of those "fancy" jeans like McConaughey wears. It could not be made any more plain to you that your shitty life will be 100 percent salvaged if this 137-page lottery ticket to which you are applying your several signatures hits, and it doesn't help matters that you are staring ravenously at one-in-four odds.

Your head has completely flown out the window, and it is *now* that you are invited into the room to perform your rendering of Blowfish for the network comptrollers. Sure, there are a few friendly faces, like the casting director and the show's writer/creator, who are also busy shitting little green apples of their own. (Especially the writer, as he/she watches helplessly while the corporation tries to thread disparate baits onto the hook that he/she has so lovingly and painstakingly crafted. "Let's try this leech. Hm. Okay. Now the worm. Okay. Nice. Now bring in the wood grub. Oh, wow. I like this grub. I like it a lot. Do we have any other grubs? Can we look at some stink bait?") Mainly this audience is hilariously unfriendly.

One guy is just typing into his laptop the whole time, never even looking up at you. One lady is holding up a centerfold of Will Smith, looking at it with one eye and you with the other. Three be-suited versions of Hugo Weaving as Agent Smith in *The Matrix* fix their steely gazes upon you, without apparently comprehending you as a human being who is attempting to weave a clownlike diversion for their enjoyment. The casting director gamely tries to laugh at the right moments, generously sprinkling what I call the "courtesy laugh," as does the writer, when he/she is not vomiting into his/her stainless steel water bottle. Needless to say, it's a tough room.

You are dismissed. You suddenly come to, finding yourself behind the wheel of your vehicle, blindly driving while replaying the audition over and over in your mind's eye, coming up with *way* better versions than the one you just laid, slick and steaming, on the floor of the judgment room. Speeding toward the comforts of home or the coffee shop or the pub, you manage to keep your compulsive examinations of your cell phone to only every twenty-four to twenty-eight seconds. Finally, after a couple of excruciating hours, your agent calls. This is it!

"Okay. You did great. But I'm sorry. It's not going your way. They didn't hire anybody, and they're not sure what they're going to do. They're talking about retooling the character a little bit, and unfortunately for you I also think now they're going to go after 'a person of color' for Blowfish. . . . I heard Esai Morales."

Again, I aver: Do not get into this business if you can help it. The scenario I have just described is not only quite par for the course, but one is considered incredibly lucky just to have the *opportunity* to have one's guts ripped out so. Remember that, on every level in this business, you are an artist trying to get a job at which you will be paid (sometimes incredibly) well to perform or display your respective art to as large an audience as possible. If you are a purist who would simply like to create artwork, then you can do that wherever you are, beholden to no one, without ever going through bullshit of this brand. If you dive into the pool of sharks that is commercial entertainment, then you will forever be butting heads with the corporate interests that are trying to use your art to sell sandwich condiments, and that is invariably going to be an uphill battle.

When I first moved to LA, John Cusack was coming by our house to pick up a mutual friend so they could go play basketball.

When he arrived, we literally heard him coming down the block because he was screaming at someone on his phone. He blew in; shook hands, apologizing with, "Sorry, guys . . . my agent"; collected our friend; and they were gone. Pat Roberts and I looked at each other and said, "Always remember this. You can even be John Cusack, and you're *still* just trying to get what you want, while the business is trying to get what they want *from you*." Something I continue to learn about folks—really people in every business, but this one specifically—is that we're all just people, people whose wants are often incredibly disparate. Knowing this and remembering this helps to keep the bitterness from encroaching on any territory in my soul.

If you are as big a fool as I, and you can't help but take a crack at a potential dream life of whiskers, scotch whisky, and steak, at a job where you are *paid to eat bacon on a regular basis*, then here are some tips on auditioning, which you can choose to heed as you wish or ignore completely.

1. Perform wherever and whenever you can. Theater, improv, sketch, stand-up, whatever floats your boat. Practice will keep you sharp, and you never know when you'll happen upon the "right place and time" for opportunity to strike. Sure, maybe everybody tells you you're cute anyway, or you're hilarious, but if you also continue to hone your skills in performing, it's only going to up your confidence level "in the room."

2. Do more than perform. Work backstage at the theater, or get work on a film set, or even a music video. Watch the masters at work, studying all of their disparate techniques for effective storytelling. Think about different ways in which you might play a scene if you were thrown onstage or in front of the camera. If you can help out at any auditions "behind the camera," jump at the chance. Run the video camera or help out by reading the scene material aloud with the actors. You will be guaranteed an inordinate amount of invaluable lessons from the parade of hopefuls on what to do and what not to do, I promise.

3. BE YOURSELF. Megan talks about this a lot as well. When you read the audition scene, don't ever think, what do I think these people want to see? Because that just weakens your strength, what makes you special. The only thing you have going for you is you and your unique take. What makes you and your friends laugh? That is the right way to approach any material. Megan spent years trying out different weird and funny voices at auditions, and the majority of the productions thought she was a crazy lady, until someone saw the vein of golden talent running through her hills and gave her the opportunity to create Karen Walker on *Will & Grace*. She never would have achieved that triumph had she lacked the guts to persevere in delivering her brand of strangeness.

4. Be prepared. Don't be a lazy fuck. Know your lines. Do your homework.

5. Eat red meat. Producers like a pelt with a healthy glow.

6. Don't dress like a cop when you're auditioning for a cop part. You don't need a cowboy hat when you audition for *Bo-*

nanza. You're never going to score points that way. Think about it. "Well, he was only okay. I mean, he didn't really know his lines. But y'know, that was a pretty sweet fucking stethoscope and set of scrubs he had on. Let's give him another look-see." The best outfit you can wear is confidence.

7. (This is the most important, and it goes for life as well as auditions): Make your life happy. Sounds pretty simple, right? As you already know, it can be anything but simple, but check out this sweet-ass John Lennon quote:

"When I was 5 years old, my mother always told me that happiness was the key to life. When I went to school, they asked me what I wanted to be when I grew up. I wrote down 'happy.' They told me I didn't understand the assignment, and I told them they didn't understand life."

When I first started auditioning in Los Angeles, I was depending upon the results of those auditions to make me happy. I quickly and efficaciously learned just how much that was a losing proposition. Even when things were going well, there just wasn't enough love involved to feed a body, which was understandable, because it's simply an arena of commerce when you get right down to it. It's easy to become distracted by the beautiful people, the good times, and the swag, but ultimately, it's just a business. What it is most certainly *not* is a life. Another John Lennon jewel: "Life is what happens while you are busy making other plans."

This one really hit me in the bread box. Recognizing the relative dissatisfaction that my "other plans" were bringing me, I immediately shifted my focus to filling in the rest of my life with whatever goodness I could muster so that my momentary involvements in show business held much less sway. It took me a few years, but I managed to create a deliciously satisfying life full of woodworking, theater, friends, and family, but most importantly the love of a good woman named Megan.

I cannot stress enough what a positive effect this practice can have upon your auditions, and here's the greatest part: Even if the people at the auditions are assholes and you are totally rejected, the joke's on them, because you no longer give a shit! This security lends an undeniable swagger to your auditions. Gone are the days of sweating bullets through your reading because the one-week guest-star paycheck hanging in the balance would hand you the lifesaving two months of back rent you owe. The best part of step 7 is that even if, for some reason, you *never* get an acting job, you have tricked yourself, *despite yourself*, into enjoying an enduring happiness anyway. Pretty good trick.

Now let's wrap it up with a few thoughts for the people on the other side of the table: the suits at the networks. I don't know if I can get through to you. I'm not even certain that you read books. Some of you are totally decent, sure. You tend to succeed and you also tend to get along with your artists. A percentage of you have your heads in the right place. My beef is not with you. My umbrage is with the suits who feel the need to "help" the artists in the actual creation of the art.

Here is my trip with you guys and gals: You and your company run a broadcasting business that is funded primarily by advertising dollars. The method by which you increase the amount of dollars coming in is to program content that engenders popularity, increasing the amount of viewership. The advertisers writing the checks to you naturally want as many people as possible watching their commercials, so if your television shows garner the most viewers, you will thereby reap the greatest amount of dollars.

To that end, you try your darnedest to hire writers, also known as "creatives," who will bring you original, gripping material so as to ensnare as many of those aforementioned viewers as possible. The brilliant men and women of which I speak, these creatives, then fabricate entire worlds for you from whole cloth, peopled with characters of every flavor, for the embroidering of stories which will hopefully engage an audience for years to come. These writers are just about my favorite people in town, from the point of view of both a fan who is grateful for the heartwarming times they have provided me and my family and friends over the years and an actor who directly benefits from the opportunities they perpetually create for those of my ilk to make a dollar doing work we can actually stomach.

The creators envision the shows, they write the shows, they're going to shoot the shows—THEY MAKE THE SHOWS. You, the suits, are, in effect, hiring a painter. You've seen their earlier paintings and greatly enjoyed them. You think that perhaps your company can sell their new paintings to America and the world beyond on your company's art channel. You run this art channel; you were a business major or a broadcasting major. You look at popular-culture magazines and read newspapers and the Internet tastemakers, and you evaluate charts of trends that are "popping" and "hot." You then get in your BMW to drive over to the art studio to tell the painter that football, pulled pork, and small children

in cute, miniature vehicles are really happening right now—
they're "trending." "Can the painter put some of those in his/her
painting?"

And the painter will maybe try, because maybe the painter is
contractually obligated to try, even though the painter was presumably competent enough to choose his/her own subject matter
in the paintings that got him/her the job in the first place. But you
don't leave it at that. You then tell the painter what kind of canvas
to use, and you stand with the painter as the painting begins, and
you hand her/him brushes as you suggest changes to the picture's
composition. The painter commences daubing on a cadmium orange mixed with a little primary magenta, and you say, "Hey,
can we try blue, actually?" You have the temerity to tell this artist
how to create his/her art, wholly forgetting an incredibly salient
fact: YOU DON'T PAINT.

I don't have to tell you, network suits, how many millions of
dollars are thrown away every year on failed pilots that are often
embarrassingly terrible. All I am asking you to do, here in chapter
15B of my book, is reduce your penchant for gambling by trusting
your storytellers. The funny thing about the brilliant minds you
have enlisted to create your "paintings" is that THEY HAVE BRIL-
LIANT MINDS. If left to their own devices, they have the potential
to paint your pictures in colors you'd never even have remotely
imagined before they showed up. When you replace an actor
who has been chosen by your show's creator with a different *type*
of actor who has been chosen by a poll in *Tiger Beat* magazine,
or wherever teenage girls and boys now register their collective
opinion, you are not thinking like a storyteller; you are thinking,
instead, like a toothpaste company. You will not sell more tooth-

paste by adding flavor crystals or the phrase "Now more minty!" to your show. You will sell more toothpaste by allowing your show to be its own original animal, giving it its best chance to rise above the fray of mediocre dental-hygiene programming, attracting hordes of toothpaste-consuming viewers. Then we might all have something to smile about.

16

Nowadays

Mom, I can't imagine anyone else has stuck with me this far, so I'll launch this final set of musings in your direction, and yes, I'll try to keep it light on the fudgin' sailor talk. My strangely fortunate life as I now know it really commenced with the advent of *Parks and Recreation*, but before I dive into that multicolored dream-pool of magic pudding (not a euphemism, Mom), I want to describe an earlier event that has proved to be rather poignant for me.

Megan and I had been living together in her West Hollywood duplex for a couple of years when we made a loose compact that we would get married at some point. We knew that we would be joined at the hip in any case going forward, but we thought it would be nice to do the official secret handshake and whatnot, and also get our people together for a love party. We had also been talking about buying a house, "movin' on up," as it were, in the parlance of *The Jeffersons*. After some shopping around, we found an incredible house in the hills above West Hollywood, right next to Blue Jay Way, a street made legendary in a song by this cool band the Beatles. (Mom, I told you 'bout 'em, 'member? You like their cover of "Till There Was You" from *The Music Man*.)

We moved in, and it would never fail to amuse me that I was coming home to this house, a home that Megan had created and designed so that it felt like a welcoming and cozy work of art. I'd pull into the garage, covered in sawdust more often than not, and just have to giggle as I stepped into the front hallway to be greeted by three enthusiastic poodles, into this new life as a guy who lives in the finest abode.

Soon after we got settled in the new house in 2003, which included a lovely little pool in the yard, I was dumbstruck one day to realize that I had "made it"! Thanks to Megan, I was a well-off dude living in the Hollywood Hills like a king! My whole life, since high school anyway, I'd had a fantasy image of what life would be like if I ever was successful enough to have a house with a pool. The dream was simple: I would smoke some weed and listen to Neil Young and float in the pool. It had snuck up on me so sweetly that I was completely flabbergasted to realize that I had all of the necessary ingredients to make that noble dream a reality! Without dawdling, I smoked some fine California herb and put Neil Young's *Rust Never Sleeps* on in the house and then casually flipped the switch to pipe it through our OUTDOOR SPEAKERS. Living the fucking dream, people (sorry, Mom). I made a cool drink and took my leisure like a gol-danged king, reclining on a floatie raft in the pool under the brilliant Southern California sun. It was rich. I mean to tell you, it was delicious. It lasted all of two songs.

Apparently I was an old dog by then—a robust thirty-three years old—because I was not about to learn any new tricks. As I floated in the pool, blissfully reclining to Neil's admonition that "it's better to burn out than to fade away," I grew restless rather quickly. I took a step back and examined my prone form bobbing upon the sparkling blue water.

"What am I, an asshole? What am I gonna do, buy a yacht and just be a rich asshole floating on my yacht? Jesus, man, look at yourself. The sun is up. You should be getting something done!"

* * *

What I had learned was that I don't achieve my happiness by taking it easy, but instead by using my time and abilities to be productive. I mainly focus my productivity in the arenas of performance and woodworking, but I also prefer to be spending time with Megan and our dogs, my friends and their kids, and my family whenever I can get to them. I am thankful that I had the opportunity to learn this for myself firsthand, or otherwise I might have spent my life wishing foolishly for that stoned pool time. That day in the pool taught me that I still just want to make things with my time, but being more financially successful simply meant that I might make things whilst sporting a nicer pair of socks. Whether they're from Sears or L.L.Bean, I still want to get 'em dirty. Or else, what am I? A goddamn layabout? A man of leisure? Fuck that (sorry again, Mom). Until these hands give out, I believe there's work to do.

When *Parks and Recreation* looked like it might stick around for a little while, I was faced with a choice: Close up my woodshop and lock the doors, letting it sit dark and silent until my time freed up again, or find some help to keep that beautifully shitty old warehouse cranking out sawdust and shavings. My whole life had been spent actively participating in the healthy lives of productive communities, starting with my huge family in Minooka, followed by my theater families in college and Chicago, as well as the Evidence Room family and my circle of fellow artists in Los Angeles. It only made sense that I would now create my own sphere of support at Offerman Woodshop.

With my usual bounty of dumb luck, my friend Sam Moyer (an excellent fellow woodworker) introduced me to a small lady from Berkeley who had helped him install a kitchen. According to Sam, she had outworked the three strong men she accompanied. This was hard to believe when I met Lee, since she is about as tiny as my bride. Welp. I've been wrong before, and the smart money's on my being wrong again. Lee regularly out-hoists me, and I'm not a weakling by any stretch. Beyond her brute strength, far beyond, she comes ready-made to administrate a shop with an almost eerie specificity. A life-long woodworker, she has worked for years at San Francisco's Exploratorium, an extremely progressive think-tank laboratory of a museum that has been scientifically challenging and educating its visitors for more than forty years. As if museum-level meticulousness wasn't enough, she then took some further learning from the venerable College of the Redwoods in Fort Bragg, California, in a woodworking program created by famed furniture master James Krenov. And she's strong as a mule, aka two Offerman boys. Lee has become so valuable to me that I would gladly exchange my right hand before losing her, and bear in mind, that's my burger-flipping hand.

I immediately made her my new shop manager, and together we have collected a charming fellowship of elves that is ever shifting and always learning. A wonderful aspect of having a few heads in the shop at any given time is the different perspectives we all can bring to problem-solving. I look forward to all of my fellow OWS craftspeople surpassing me in experience so that I may begin to dodder in my age and lean upon their superior know-how. Any minute now. I greatly admire these peers of mine for the courageous choice of devoting their lives to making exceptional pieces in wood, even though it's terribly difficult to eke out a living as a craftsperson. This is a shameful state of affairs, but it is all too real in our modern consumerist economy. At Offerman Woodshop we are doing our best to help foster the rebirth of handcrafted goods into the mainstream of middle-class furnishings, but there is a long way to go. We make everything by hand, meaning we will never employ computer-driven fabricating tools, such as a CNC router or a 3-D printer. Furniture by robot is the opposite of what we're after. Factory furniture is only better in that it makes the manufacturer more profit for cheaper prices, but you get what you pay for. In every other way, our products are vastly superior, made one at a time with love and skill. I'm proud to be a part of this movement of noble handcrafting, which I believe will strengthen our society immeasurably, or at least to the point where we're not dependent upon foreign manufacturing to make our furniture and clothing and many other items, all of a quality that renders them disposable. When we make you a table at Offerman Woodshop, we intend for your family to enjoy it for a couple of hundred years at least. Now compare the prices again with that in mind.

While the elves are having all the fun with the shed full of tools over at Offerman Woodshop, I'm toiling away at my pesky dream job at *Parks and Recreation*, a job that feels like toil about as much as a muskrat feels like a jellyfish. What can I say about this playground which Mike Schur and Greg Daniels have built where I can be rewarded with money and food for the hardship of watching Amy Poehler and Aubrey Plaza stare each other down like two beautiful gladiators in a battle of mighty comedy wills? Each and every cast member makes me laugh with an unadulterated delight. Amy, Adam, Rashida, Aziz, Aubrey, Rob Lowe, Retta, and Chris Pratt. Every single one. There is no one else associated with the cast who merits my admiration, I could never leave any of them out. Jim O'Heir, who plays Jerry, is also a member of the cast. Pratt is my special favorite, which I believe is also the case for most of, well, the human population. His hijinks more than any other's leave me peeing in my britches with consistency.

It's all completely stupid, by the way. The beauty of our jobs is that we are allowed to behave in a juvenile manner of an ilk that the rest of polite society has been forced to eschew because of a development called "maturity." To wit: One day we were shooting the episode "Two Parties," and all the boys were at the freaky aroma bar called Essence, where every cocktail comes in some crazy form, like a mist or a lotion or a flash of light.

Pratt's character, Andy Dwyer, received a "beer" that he ordered, which was inexplicably in the form of a sphere of cotton candy. Pratt proceeded to sculpt a vagina (very masterfully; he's a talented visual artist with an apparently intimate knowledge of the female genitalia) in his cotton candy, which, it must be noted, is not the easiest medium for sculpture. He then proceeded to subtly display his cotton-candy vagina to us, nibbling and licking it for our edification, as we all tried to maintain a straight face because we were *on camera performing our scenes.* By the end of the take, he had eaten the entire sphere, maybe a ball with an eight-inch diameter. That's a fair amount of sugar to put in a lad, even a large boy like Christopher. Well, you get along to the sixth or seventh take, and you realize that there have been six or seven more balls of cotton candy with subsequent vaginas, all dutifully consumed by Mr. Pratt.

Now it's go time. When he gets sugared up, he completely becomes a five-year-old in terms of hyperactivity and volume and hilarity, which has not escaped the notice of our producers. I have not had this confirmed, but I believe every third or fourth script finds Andy Dwyer in close proximity with some form of candy or cake or other sugar-based item. Pancakes with syrup, a bowl of Skittles, several racks of pork ribs slathered in sweet BBQ sauce, you name it. Seems like something more than coincidence to this investigator. Whatever the provenance, nobody is complaining, because "candy Pratt" is better than any cartoon, and I've seen *The Ren & Stimpy Show* and *The Big Snit.*

So the day was really fun and long (which just translates as more hours of fun), until we finally finished up the shooting at an ice cream parlor, again with all the boys, bachelor party–style. Everyone got to order his ice cream of choice, which didn't really suck as far as "things you have to do at work," but here is a bonus tip for aspiring actors: Whenever you get to enjoy an indulgence in a filmed medium, just remember that you might have to "enjoy" that treat as many as twenty times in a row, once per take. I can't tell you how many times I've made myself green in the face by deciding to smoke heavily throughout a scene, only to be ready to go gills-up by the fourth take. You want to take it easy.

With that in mind, I asked for one little scoop of butter pecan in a sugar cone. My plan was to eat just the small scoop of ice cream and none of the cone, so I'd end up with a nice dessert of maybe six small scoops of ice cream. Rob Lowe and Adam Scott, sagacious veterans, chose to just barely nibble at theirs so they wouldn't be forced to overeat if the scene ran long.

They chose wisely, it turned out, as we ended up moving the cameras a couple of times, with six or so takes per camera position, so your author ended up eating twenty-one small scoops of ice cream. I was pretty happy, honestly, with about the first fourteen scoops or so, but then they began to hurt. The price of showbiz. If I was feeling beyond bloated, I can't imagine what discomfort Pratt was enduring, having chosen a large scoop of strawberry in a waffle cone, one per take. His seventh or eighth sugar buzz of the day kicked into high gear, which made the literally creamy vaginas he was now sculpting into his strawberry treat even more hilarious. Bear in mind that an ice-cream cone involves tongue work rather than sculpting by hand, which was the case with the cotton candy. I thought I was going to need hospitalization, he was making me giggle-cry so deep and long. And it is for performing activities like this that I receive a healthy salary. How could I ever lose sight of what a lucky son of a bitch I am?

This acting job has literally put more bacon in my belly than any butcher shop. It has caused more Lagavulin whisky to course through my veins than any well-stocked public house. I miss my time at the shop, but my role of Ron Swanson only requires my presence on an average of three days a week, which leaves me two days at the shop. We even shot an episode at my goddamn shop! ("The Possum," in case you're curious.)

At the time of this writing, we have completed ninety glorious episodes and are gearing up to produce another twenty-two this coming season, which will be called season 6. I have met a lot of great writers in my day, but I could never have dreamed that I would run into writers like Mike Schur and his gang of smarty-pantses. If you like Ron Swanson, then imagine how I must feel when I open a new script and see lines of dialogue like "When I eat, it is the food that is scared." It's like Christmas every week, if your folks got you a present every week that was better than your fondest wish.

How an ignorant kid from Minooka who likes to crack wise could end up with such an unbelievable bounty of good luck is certainly beyond me. I do my best to keep my karma in check by working hard and minding my manners. It's easy to do when I see so many (about 130, give or take) people on our crew busting their humps around me every day, without the pleasurable benefits of delivering delectable jokes like mine, nor being fed bacon and steak at every turn.

By now I am well-satisfied with the experiences I have been afforded as an actor. If folks continue to let me befoul the air of their theaters/film sets from here on out, I will be quite grateful, but at some point I imagine they'll have had their fill of my particular brand of wolf bait. When that happens, I'll simply be afforded more time in my woodshop, a situation that I believe is referred to as "win-win."

On top of that, I recently discovered a new sideline in which I might be allowed to continue cutting my cheese: that of "humorist." Never in a googol years did I dream that I would perform for audiences as "myself," not to mention playing the guitar and singing without irony, but when a couple of American universities invited me to come entertain their students, I decided to take a crack at it. They let me finish all of my material, which I take as a high compliment, and by now I have performed at dozens of colleges and also beautiful theaters and even some crappy theaters all over the country. It's a great deal of fun, and I don't have to memorize any lines, plus I don't have to build any scenery! In truth, this book only came about because of my first humorist show, *American Ham*, which, when witnessed by some people in my corner, caused them to tell me, "That sounds like your book," so I thought . . . alrighty, then.

One of the greatest aspects of touring as a humorist has been the opportunity to experience fans in a way I never had before. For example, at Iowa State University, there was a healthy contingent of tailgating in the parking lot before my show. Several grills were busily engaged in the creation of Ron Swanson–themed meat items. What was this?!

Despite my need to prepare for the show, Mom, I couldn't help but follow my nose in a meandering search that led to the clutches of students happily shoving bacon and turkey legs and steaks and burgers, not to mention noble beers and estimable scotch whiskies, into their beautiful pieholes. It was a privilege to shake their hands, and an even greater honor to be handed a jalapeño-cheddar-bacon cheeseburger with which I handily stuffed my own gob. I told them that this must be the most charismatic fan interaction ever, in which they were providing me with the fuel which I would then shortly burn in the entertaining of them.

Mother, as you know, when I first met Megan working on *The Berlin Circle* at the Evidence Room, one of her numerous top-drawer selling points quickly came to light: her singing voice. "Bitch got pipes," as I believe the kids are saying these days, in their "hipster parlance." Early in our acquaintance I asked her what her singing was like, and she quietly sang "In the Gloaming" into my ear with a bit of whispered tremolo that delivered but the first of Cupid's many darts to my ursine heart. I came to understand that she sang in many different flavors and styles and mediums, from rock clubs to Broadway, and I fell head over heels for her voice just as I was becoming soundly smitten with the rest of her. She has a few records available with her band Supreme Music Program, which make for truly beautiful listens, upon which she favors "story songs," or ditties with a bit of narrative, in other words. Tom Waits, Bobbie Gentry, Patty Griffin, Randy Newman, John Prine, Brecht/Weill, Dolly Parton, George Jones, and Jack White are just a sampling of the artists whose songs she covers with her re-imagined dramatic renderings of each number. It is, simply put, damn good shit. (Mom. Sorry. I give up.)

In 2011 Megan and I were in Austin, Texas, shooting a film called *Somebody Up There Likes Me* with our friend writer-director Bob By-ington. Bob had cast a local Austin actor who had garnered some notoriety for her work in the SUPERLATIVE television series *Friday Night Lights* (as Devin, the bass player for Crucifictorious) by the name of Stephanie Hunt as one of the alluring young ladies in the film. In-advertently, Megan and Stephanie found themselves in a car one af-ternoon, and Megan asked her to sing one of her ukulele songs that we had heard about. Stephanie replied that she would oblige, but only if Megan joined her in the chorus. So they sang a song in close har-mony, and they immediately sounded so good together that the PT Cruiser in which they sat turned itself into a GMC Yukon. These la-dies could sing. Thus was a new legendary force of female entertain-ment born, the duo that calls themselves Nancy and Beth. These two ladies sing close harmony and perform choreography by Megan with such élan and goddamn pizzazz that it's all the audience can do to keep their seats, so "toe-tapping" and "finger-popping" is the nature of the noise they make. (You've seen 'em, Mom, you know.)

At some point, our two forces combined, à la so much chocolate and peanut butter, so that we began to perform tour dates together. I crack wise and play my silly songs, then they floor the audience with talent and an overabundance of feminine ka-pow!, and then we do some songs together. Between these joint shows and our work to-gether onstage, on TV, and in film, Megan and I have come to feel like an old-fashioned showbiz couple, an almost vaudevillian comedy team, which really knocks me flat. Singing in her vicinity feels like showing off my backhand to Venus and Serena Williams, but I give it the old college try nonetheless. Our mutual affection is surely on display, and that brings some production value with it, upon which I can lean when necessary. Performing in this way has been one of the most unexpected pleasures of my recent years, and it's a gig I hope I can hang on to for a long time to come.

As you can see, my dear mother, all things considered, my only gripe these days is wishing for more hours in the day. I've figured out (and lucked into) how to have so much fun at "work" that it has become my main vice. After spending years trying to find opportunities to perform for more and more people in my own style, I have now stumbled upon a moment where I can fill up a calendar year with such employ. Knowing all too well the fleeting nature of my business, my inclination is to strike whilst this here iron is a-heated, but too much of that will cause me to neglect the balance in my life. Therefore, while continuing to entertain folks when I can, I also do my best to see my family and friends and also to just spend some time doing nothing, lounging about with my wife and dogs, making sure we don't burn the candle too virulently at both ends. It's a challenge sometimes, being faced with too many tempting opportunities, which is what we call in our house a "champagne problem." More often than not, I have found beer to be an effective solution. But I guess Dad already let you know about that, didn't he, Mom?

Go Outside

I'm assuming my mom thought the last chapter was the end, so now that she's gone to bed, let's fire up the real final chapter, motherfuckers! Pack that shit up full and gimme a match (cool weed talk). In case I haven't gotten it across to you fine folks by this point, here's my trip: I'm opposed to a lot of the time that we as a civilization have come to spend looking at screens. For my money, life is much more delicious damn near everyplace but inside that screen.

Take film—I go see films that I think I'll like, starring and shot and written by women and men toward whose work I am favorably inclined. I don't see a lot of films. Taking in a film with Megan on a date is a delectable treat, and then I don't care as much what's on the screen, but still.

Take TV—I don't regularly watch TV as an activity. I find a show I like, be it *Deadwood*, *The Wire*, *Bob's Burgers*, or *Breaking Bad*, and I watch THE SHIT out of it, on my own schedule, which is a luxury afforded us by modern technology and broadcast systems. My favorite method by which to consume a series is by acquiring said program in its entirety and watching it on a vacation binge with Megan. Hole up in a hotel someplace with a view of the ocean or the forest or the desert and indulge. Drink deep and long and then have done with it.

Take the Internet—is it an insanely amazing information system? Duh. It's the insanely amazingest. Easily. The world in which we now exist, especially within our minds, has been so irrevocably altered by our collective ability to access virtually any information in existence with a few well-chosen keystrokes. The World Wide Web is a resource that I use with some regularity to answer questions.

When working on a canoe, for example, I regularly visit the builders' forum that Glen Smith runs at the Bear Mountain Boats website, wherein all of my questions tend to find an answer or three. The various conversations in that "chat shed" are fascinating to me, and if I'm not careful I'll catch myself reading correspondence well beyond the information I sought in the first place, so, believe me, I understand how fiendishly the Internet can tempt a body to indulge in diversion from one's responsibilities, more commonly known as iniquity. Idle hands are never the devil's workshop more than when those recumbent mitts are resting upon a computer keyboard.

And that's just the Internet. I do reluctantly use Twitter to communicate information to the folks who seem interested, about humorist tour dates and film screenings and new releases from Offerman Woodshop, because it's an incredibly effective way to reach an audience directly. That doesn't seem particularly foolish to me. I even add some occasional ribaldry and eye candy to my dispatches, to keep the flypaper a little sticky, if you will. Yes, I am comparing my fans to flies, but only in the most poetic of fashions. In truth, I imagine they are for the most part jackasses (as are we all) to a similar or slightly lesser extent than myself. I digress.

What I am driving toward with all due haste is the simple, comforting message that spending time outside in nature, to my way of thinking, is a much more gratifying diversion than anything one can engage in upon a screen.

"Hang on, guy," you interrupt, "don't you make your living through people looking at screens?" Yes, adroit reader, indeed I do. Nicely observed. And I sincerely hope that each and every one of you watches and enjoys *Parks and Recreation* and *Childrens Hospital* and my films as well. I know that not all of you will see it all, and if you do, not all of you will enjoy all of the content, because people simply have differing tastes. How else do you explain feta cheese? In any case, I only work on material that I think is well worth people's time and that I would be proud to display upon my résumé. So I'm not suggesting that you never watch filmed entertainment—no, far from it in fact. I'm suggesting that you only watch programs containing my wife or myself. Have a good laugh on us, perhaps rewind a few of your favorite moments, and *then* get your ass outside.

When I am at my family home in Illinois, we love to visit the old towpath along the Illinois and Michigan Canal. It's as picturesque there as any postcard, brimming with wildlife and all of the local flora that we find so charismatic. There are other gorgeously appointed state parks we love to frequent, champing through the woods, exclaiming our pleasure at nature's grottos with all the gusto of Theodore Roosevelt. We also love to vacation in Minnesota, as I have mentioned, where our main activity is to float ourselves out upon a lake in a boat or pontoon, fishing, sure, but really the fishing is just an excuse to sit on blue water in the middle of verdant green forest, packed with both deciduous trees and conifers, beneath Mother Nature's gorgeous and vast sky, often quilted with cumulonimbus confections. My folks and my siblings and I have always loved to ramble about any part of the planet on foot, but we seem especially drawn to scenery that juxtaposes water with the woods. I believe that makes us "Mid-westerners." It seems worth mentioning that we are a pretty mellow bunch who don't seem too affected by stress, and I can't help but see at least a slight cause-and-effect happening here.

Many people react adversely when I suggest a venturing into nature of any sort, sometimes stating without shame that they don't want to "get dirty." I tend to stare silently for a moment in response, containing my disappointment, before calmly explaining to them that getting dirty is the whole point. If you're getting dirty, that means that you have traveled to where there is no pavement. When you sojourn into such terrain, you greatly up your chances of experiencing some full-on wild nature. I reckon it's not for everybody, but "everybody" is not penning this tome about fundamentally delicious living. I am.

I am personally opposed to the recent development that positions young parents so violently apposite to germs and dirt in general. I have enjoyed a life of terrific health, knock wood, while remaining generally filthy most of the time. Every time I have the opportunity to eat some food that has fallen on the ground, especially in an airport bathroom, I jump to it, in the firm knowledge that I am solidly fortifying my immune system. The "cleaner" we keep our children, the weaker they will become. One man's opinion. Also, most bugs are pretty tasty.

Finding yourself a spot by a creek or under a tree or atop a butte or along the shore where you can sit and look and *not* think brings a peace that not even the most mellow of Enya tunes can achieve (Enya made some records in the eighties and nineties that were super cool and mellow, you guys, and she's still at it). Seeing sunlight dapple the leaves of a tree whilst a breeze plays across those same leaves, weaving endless permutations of imagery and soothing sound, is going to do you some good, is all I'm saying. When I spent some beautiful days in the mountains of Japan, I was quite taken with the philosophy of the Shinto discipline. In short, it is a form of spirituality that links the indigenous people to their past generations as well as nature. Hiking in those mountains, we came upon exceptional examples of nature's beauty, such as an ancient oak tree or a waterfall, which would have been distinguished by the Shinto priest with a white ribbon to communicate the exceptional power of the spirit in this special object or place. I felt much more akin to that expression of "sacred" than I have ever felt to the trappings of a Western church.

If you incorporate hiking or cycling into your robust chill-trip, so much the better. "Clockin' yo cardio and peepin' dopiaries" is how some of the modern skateboard-enthusiast kids might describe this practice. "Dopiaries" are, of course, dope-ass topiary bushes. Obviously, topiary work requires landscaping, which indicates civilization, so we would tell those "def street" sprouts to head a little deeper into the wild.

Now, let's kick that shit up a notch. Get yourself a kayak or canoe. I don't even care if you don't craft it by hand out of wood. I don't. You should at least make your own paddle, though; that's not asking too much. Now get out on the water, and view all of the same exquisite scenery from a silently gliding watercraft. One mighty advantage to the small boat is your stealth factor. Whilst cruising downstream in small California rivers or cutting a swath across a Minnesota lake, I have happened upon critters quietly drinking at the banks with great frequency. If you think that a doe and a couple of fauns standing a few yards away watching you float by, or a beaver swimming along with a willow branch for its front porch, won't chill you out and heal the hole that getting too many e-mails is eating in your brain's ozone layer, then your thinking parts might be in need of repair.

Can't lay hands on a boat? Get an inner tube. Use your noggin. String together some shipping pallets and float them on four five-gallon water-cooler bottles. Set a couple of lawn chairs on top (I might screw them down) and take a leisurely and restorative voyage upon the king's barge! Besides the enjoyment in getting one's britches both wet *and* dirty, such marine trips are incredibly inexpensive to produce. If you're dealing with moving water and you're not a complete ignoramus, you can have a rather perfect afternoon for the price of those Guinnesses in the cooler.

Finally, the most delicious combination I have found in life is created by bringing your romantic love into your rustic constitutionals. Experiencing all of the naturally exquisite features described above hand in hand with your beloved cannot be topped. Except *maybe* by encountering the same setting whilst sixty-nining each other. That might just be the most truly delicious living. Megan and I love to hike in all different terrains, sometimes with the dogs, sometimes with a bottle of wine, and yes, sometimes mouthing each other's genitalia. We have a regular excursion in Northern California that culminates in a breathtaking stretch of coastline, where we powerfully savor the view, the elements, and the company. At the end of the tale, I can't imagine you'd ever wonder why they call me the Lucky Bastard.

WATCH ME BURN

Photography by Matthew Micucci, original art by Rob Kimmel, airbrush replication and lettering by Martin McClendon

Paddle Your Own Canoe

Siddhartha said life is like a river,
The thought of watching it pass me by causes me to shiver.
So I grab life by the balls, I got some advice to deliver.
Get off your caboose. Paddle your own canoe.

Young Teddy Roosevelt was a weak little puss,
But he exercised and became quite an ornery cuss,
'Til he could whip two bears and also Cuba without a fuss.
By god, number 26 paddled his own canoe.

You like to smoke some reefer, and you like to dance.
The preacher tells you to keep yer pecker in your pants,
But the preacher'd be kissin' your nephew given half the chance.
(He can go to hell.)
Then you can spend your Sundays paddlin' your own canoe.

I mighta mentioned Jesus Christ himself got high in my van.
I told him I wouldn't go to church, and he shook my hand.
He said, "My son, just lemme run inside and use the can
(number two)
Now let's get some Doritos and paddle your sweet canoe."
What would Jesus do? Paddle my goddamn canoe.

Take the road less traveled says Robert Frost,

Keep your stone rollin' so it don't accumulate no moss.

Leave the faint of heart suckin' on your exhaust.

Live a little life and paddle your own canoe.

Don't while it away masturbatin' in the ditches.

Put yer tackle away and hitch up your britches.

Then provision your boat with several pulled-pork sandwiches.

Indulge in savory meatstuffs, paddle your own canoe.

PADDLE YOUR
OWN CANOE

ACKNOWLEDGMENTS

To my editor, Jill Something, for gently navigating me through these heretofore unpaddled currents without ever once hurting my feelings. To Dana Borowitz, Monika Verma, and Daniel Greenberg for providing the map with which I was able to find my way to Jill Something and the fine folks at Dutton, particularly Jamie McDonald and LeeAnn Pemberton. To Catherine and Frederic Offerman, who made me. To Megan, my wife, who continues to tolerate me at an astonishing rate. To my teachers, without whom I would be exponentially more unfit for public consumption. To Mike Mitchell, and all those who delight us with their pencils. To Lee and the other elves of industry at Offerman Woodshop for cleaning up their areas. Finally, to all of the family and friends in my life who shared remembered details, sometimes in hilariously disparate versions from my own, for reminding me that I'm simple. You tend to keep me around anyway, and for that I am grateful.